Social Capital and Armed Conflict in Somalia

Disclaimer

"The thesis and book is not related to Kiyoshi Matsukawa's assignment as a United Nations staff member in/on Somalia, and does not in any way or form convey views of the United Nations."

Note from the Publisher

This book is developed out of a PhD dissertation. Our editors noticed that converting its dissertation format to a format readable for the general public requires complete rewriting that will bring major change to its structure and approach. Instead of doing such conversion which may take the author years of work, we decided to publish it with only minor modification and copy editing as the work contains valuable information on the conflict in Somalia.

SOCIAL CAPITAL AND ARMED CONFLICT IN SOMALIA

KIYOSHI MATSUKAWA

THE RED SEA PRESS

TRENTON | LONDON | NEW DELHI | CAPE TOWN | NAIROBI | ADDIS ABABA | ASMARA | IBADAN

THE RED SEA PRESS

541 West Ingham Avenue | Suite B
Trenton, New Jersey 08638

Book and cover design: Lemlem Tadesse

Library of Congress Cataloging-in-Publication Data

Names: Matsukawa, Kiyoshi, 1972- author.
Title: Social capital and armed conflict in Somalia / Kiyoshi Matsukawa.
Description: Trenton : Africa World Press, [2020] | Includes
  bibliographical references and index. | Summary: "This book examines the
  variances of violence and social capital between five cities in Somalia.
  The research inquiry applies social capital theory to analyze inter-clan
  and intra-clan associations, trust, quotidian and associational
  networks, and social cohesion with armed conflict. Variances in violence
  and social capital between five cities in Somalia are analyzed
  quantitatively and detailed case studies are presented for three cities
  qualitatively. The research looks at the paradoxical power of social
  capital in creating and resolving armed conflict. It investigates
  several questions pertaining to issues surrounding social capital and
  armed conflict: Does social capital contribute to armed conflict or does
  it help resolve it? What kinds of social capital-bonding, bridging, and
  linking-contribute to armed conflict and what kinds mitigate it? In
  addressing the above issues, different proxies are used to
  quantitatively and qualitatively distinguish the concepts of bonding,
  bridging, and linking social capital"-- Provided by publisher.
Identifiers: LCCN 2020004549 | ISBN 9781569026045 (paperback) | ISBN
  9781569026038 (hardback)
Subjects: LCSH: Violence--Somalia. | Social conflict--Somalia. | Ethnic
  conflict--Somalia. | Social capital (Sociology)--Somalia. |
  Insurgency--Somalia. | Civil society--Somalia.
Classification: LCC HN790.Z9 V563 2020 | DDC 303.6096773--dc23
LC record available at https://lccn.loc.gov/2020004549

TABLE OF CONTENTS

LIST OF ILLUSTRATIONS

List of Figures

List of Maps

List of Tables

ACKNOWLEDGEMENTS

This book developed out of my PhD. dissertation. At first glance, the journey of a PhD. student seems one of solitude and personal hardship. However, in reality, it is a journey taken with many different people providing continuous support while also causing hardship to those closest by.

This thesis would not have been possible without the help, guidance, advice, support, and patience of numerous people. My advisor, Professor Mitsugi Endo, patiently guided me through this long journey no matter where I was living or what I was doing. The Thesis Committee Members—Professor Nakanishi, Professor Nakamura—and the expanded Committee Members, Professor Ishida and Professor Shimizu, also guided me for eight years. Professor Ohno, of Aoyama Gakuin University, introduced me to the concept of social capital and statistical analysis in the social sciences.

I am indebted to all the Somalis who shared their wisdom, insight, knowledge, and time with me. Their kindness and enthusiasm overcame the logistical and security challenges I faced, including the solitude of conducting fieldwork. Many of the Somalis I met supported me as though they were undertaking the research themselves and went out of their way to ensure I was able to collect the information I needed.

My appreciation goes out to my colleagues at the United Nations working on Somalia who provided support on this endeavor and "made things happen" for me to conduct research under some very difficult situations. Gratitude goes out to the United Nations Office of Human Resources Management who provided me time and funding to pull this thesis together, including my immediate supervisor, Rania

Dagash, and the United Nations Political Office for Somalia Chief of Staff, Hasmik Egian, for supporting my research.

I thank my fellow (ex) PhD. candidate colleagues at the University of Tokyo who helped me with theory building and statistical analysis and overcoming (and avoiding) epistemological and phenomenological issues, while all along providing philosophical justifications for the existential hardships PhD. candidates encounter. The University of Tokyo—especially the Human Security Program faculty, staff, and students—provided me with a "home" to always come back to while the "Professor Endo Seminar students" always gave me encouragement and hope.

I am indebted to Professor Takeshi Thornton, ex-classmate from Yokohama International School, Class of 1990, who was the main catalyst that made me consider graduate school (following endless philosophical discussions) and always provided me ad hoc accommodation in Tokyo whenever the need arose.

Most of all I am indebted to my wife Risa, who stuck by my side during this long journey while also giving birth to our son, Kei, and daughters, Reika Noumena and Noema Lisa. This thesis is dedicated to them and all the people of Somalia. Finally, I hope this thesis will inspire others, especially my son and daughters, that studying is a lifelong endeavor that nurtures the mind and soul and contributes to humanity.

July 2020

"Y'know what I think? Don't really matter what I think. Once that first bullet goes past your head, politics and all that shit just goes right out the window."

—Hoot, in the movie "Black Hawk Down" (2001)

An all too familiar scene, have I become numb to chaos and anarchy? Surrounded by men and boys with guns dressed wearing shorts and flip-flops. I find myself in the only real failed state in the world. Cameras in hand, perspiration soaking my flak jacket, African equatorial sunrays penetrating my skin, I felt the tense atmosphere amongst the gunmen. Voices rose above the sound of secondhand Toyota mini vans passing by on the potholed streets of Mogadishu, as I tried explaining to the gunman I had not taken his photo. Agitated and seemingly trigger happy, the gunman pointed his gun at me. I obediently gave him the roll of film in my camera. Moral of the story: never argue with someone holding a gun, even if he is hired to protect you as your bodyguard. Welcome to Mogadishu.

—Matsukawa 2004: Master's Thesis (based on my first trip to Mogadishu)

"You know why Xamar (Mogadishu) is such a mess? It's because all the good and educated people have left. The ones who are left are the bad people; the warlords, criminals, drug dealers, and uneducated people. Those are the people that you, the UN, end up dealing with and talking to. They are all criminals."

—(Civil society leader, Mogadishu 2011)

PREFACE

My "relationship" with Somalia started in 2004 when I decided to compare the philosophical aspects of the state of nature and social contract theories with the alleged "anarchy" and "statelessness" of Somalia, specifically Mogadishu, for my Master's dissertation. In September 2004, just prior to the formation of the Transitional Federal Government (TFG), I ventured into "stateless" Mogadishu to conduct fieldwork, driving around the city with my privately hired "security". Thereafter I was privileged to engage with Somalia from a professional perspective. From September 2008 to February 2010 I worked as a political affairs officer on Somalia for the United Nations Department of Political Affairs in New York. In March 2010 I joined the United Nations Political Office for Somalia (UNPOS) as a Programme Planning Officer focusing on coordination and strategic planning of United Nations activities in Somalia with a focus on economic development and security sector reform. As Mogadishu continued to be under siege by anti-government elements throughout this period, it was only in April 2011 that I was able to return to Mogadishu. During the next two years I was fortunate to travel extensively in Somalia. In April 2013, two months prior to UNPOS ending its mandate, I went on sabbatical leave to complete this dissertation. Overall, this dissertation consists of research, experiences, and information on Somalia accumulated over nine years. It attempts to collate my thoughts, experiences, and fieldwork findings for the purpose of furthering the academic discussions related to Somalia.

The research paradigm used to analyze armed conflict in Somalia is social capital theory. The issue of trust and social relations in the area of peace and conflict studies has been under-researched. The objective of this research is to look at the significant relationships that exist between social capital and armed conflict in Somalia. Variances in violence and social capital between five cities in Somalia are analyzed quantitatively and detailed case studies are presented for three cities qualitatively. The research inquiry asks the following questions: Does social capital contribute to armed conflict or mitigate it? Alternatively, does armed conflict affect social capital, if so, how? What kinds of social capital—bonding, bridging, and linking—contribute to armed conflict and what types mitigate it? In short, "to what extent is social capital related to peace and conflict? (Cox 2009:2)" Furthermore the research inquiry attempts to provide new insights into the armed conflict in Somalia and analyze the relationship between state and non-state actors in (mis)managing conflict.

The proposed analytical framework is used for both the qualitative and quantitative approach with social capital as the independent variable and armed conflict as the dependent variable. Qualitatively, the research uses secondary and primary data based on fieldwork conducted from 2004 to 2013. Despite the security and logistical challenges, fieldwork was conducted for Mogadishu, Burao, and Galkayo and includes key informant interviews, focus group discussions, and a small-n survey for each city. Quantitatively it descriptively and inferentially analyzes secondary large-n data to identify trends and relationships between variables related to violence, trust, social networks, social cohesion, community leadership, and identity. Proxies are identified to quantitatively and qualitatively distinguish the concepts of bonding, bridging, and linking social capital. Specifically, social capital theory analyzes inter-clan and intra-clan associations, trust, quotidian and associational networks, and social cohesion in relationship to armed conflict and violence within the five regions.

The research inquiry is organized into five chapters. Chapter one provides an overview of the research inquiry. It introduces the problem statement, that of armed conflict and social capital in Somalia. A literature review of social capital and armed conflict, including peacebuilding, is presented followed by an introduction of the methodology. The research design concludes chapter one. Chapter two describes the analytical framework and hypotheses by first providing a short history of Somalia and an overview of the "root causes" of the armed conflict. This is followed by a description of the independent and dependent variables. The analytical framework, hypotheses, and related theoretical predictions are presented. The chapter concludes with the limitations and challenges to the research design. Chapter three quantitatively analyzes the large-n secondary data sets using descriptive and inferential statistics – readers not familiar with basic statistical analysis may want to skip over this chapter. Applying the analytical framework, logistic regression and discriminant analysis look at the relationships between social capital and armed conflict at both the national (aggregate) and city level. The chapter also identifies three cities (Burao, Mogadishu, and Galkayo) for further qualitative analysis. It concludes with a comparison of the quantitative results against the hypothesis and theoretical predictions. Chapter four qualitatively analyzes these three cities using the analytical framework. Analysis is based on secondary data and primary data collected through fieldwork conducted in Burao, Mogadishu, and Galkayo. A contextual background and conflict setting are also presented for the three cities. The chapter compares the qualitative results against the theoretical predictions. Chapter five provides a summary of the qualitative and quantitative results. It then reviews the hypotheses against the qualitative and quantitative results. It also reviews the theoretical predictions for the three cities both qualitatively and quantitatively. Scholarly and policy implications are presented and areas for further research regarding social capital and armed conflict conclude the chapter.

It is my wish that this research inquiry will contribute to the academic discourse related to Somalia and other protracted and complex armed conflicts and provide fellow researchers, policy makers, and students with new ideas regarding armed conflict.

CHAPTER 1. INTRODUCTION

1.1 Objective

The objective of this research is to look at what kinds of relationships exist between social capital and armed conflict by analyzing the variances of violence and social capital between five cities in Somalia. The research looks at the paradoxical power of social capital in creating and resolving armed conflict. It investigates several questions pertaining to issues surrounding social capital and armed conflict: Does social capital contribute to armed conflict or does it help resolve it? What kinds of social capital—bonding, bridging, and linking—contribute to armed conflict and what kinds mitigate it? In addressing the above issues, different proxies are used to quantitatively and qualitatively distinguish the concepts of bonding, bridging, and linking social capital. This research inquiry applies social capital theory to analyze inter-clan and intra-clan associations, trust, quotidian and associational networks, and social cohesion with armed conflict.

In a protracted complex conflict such as Somalia, various epistemologies have been used to analyze the different dynamics related to armed conflict. Although use of social capital theory has been limited in the areas of conflict studies, its application has slowly increased to provide new insights on how trust and social networks can mitigate or promote violence. While exploring the roles of trust, norms of reciprocity, and networks in armed conflict, social capital theory provides an alternative approach to conflict resolution and peacebuilding. By investigating how social capital is related to armed conflict, the relationships between peace and social capital will also be highlighted. This in turn will provide options for policy makers to focus on initiatives that promote local peacebuilding.

A point of importance for the research inquiry is that I focus only on an approach using social capital theory and acknowledge that there are many factors and variables outside of the social capital arena that may mitigate and trigger armed conflict. I also acknowledge that there are multiple dynamics at play that may have an effect on the building or erosion of social capital, such as developmental aid, technology, and media. I therefore intentionally focus on social capital and exclude other approaches with my main contribution focusing on the complex relationship between armed conflict and the various types of social capital. Although social capital is treated as the independent variable (the causal factor) and armed conflict as the dependent variable (the outcome), this relationship is analyzed considering that the direction of causality may go in both directions.

Although numerous articles, policy papers, reports, and books have been written about the Somali conflict, only a minority have used a scholarly approach (Barnes 2006, Besteman 1999, Besteman and Cassanelli 2004, Brons 2001, Gundel 2006, Hoehne 2009, Le Sage 2005, Lewis 1999, Little 2003, Luling 2002, Renders 2012, Webersik 2005, 2006, 2008). Since 2010 numerous reports, too many to mention here, have been written using anecdotal evidence and second hand information. These reports have usually been published based on the need of institutional clients based in Nairobi or Western capitals who are able and willing to pay for this type of "analysis". The ever-changing political developments and dynamics on the ground requires donors and the international community, usually based in Nairobi, to outsource this type of work to consultants with extremely short deadlines in order to remain on top of events. As donors and the international community are usually concerned with policy related issues, security and political developments, good governance and humanitarian issues, these reports are written targeting such an audience (with the obvious caveat that this readership usually funds the reports).

With overall demand lacking for lengthy academic research, which would most likely be outdated following the usual peer review mechanisms, quotidian literature related to Somalia understandably focuses on "quick and dirty" reports and "analytical" papers related to political and security developments. In addition, the security and logistical challenges in Somalia unfortunately do not attract academics, graduate students, and researchers compared to neighbouring countries, such as Kenya and Ethiopia, where the environment for conducting research is safer and most likely much more comfortable.

Another deficit is that field research in Somalia, where conducted, tends to focus on the more stable and peaceful areas of northern Somalia, especially Somaliland, with very few non-Somali academics venturing into south central Somalia (with the exception of a few researchers such as Roland Marchal, Joakim Gundel, and Magnus Bellander over the past few years). My intention here is not to criticize these mainstream reports or researchers who have focused their fieldwork in Somaliland or Puntland but to highlight that the academic literature related to the Somali armed conflict based on actual fieldwork has been limited (for a variety of reasons). My hope is that this research inquiry, which uses primary data collected on the ground and also newly acquired statistical data, will contribute to the academic discourse on the armed conflict in Somalia and allow other researchers to challenge or build on the findings from my analysis. Importantly, it also looks at providing further insight into the relationship between social capital and armed conflict. Specifically, the following issues are looked at in detail: What kind of relationships exists between social capital and armed conflict? Does social capital contribute to armed conflict or does it help resolve it? What kinds of social capital—bonding, bridging, and linking—contribute to armed conflict and what kinds mitigate it? Do the levels of bonding, bridging, and linking social capital differ between cities in Somalia?

1.2 Armed Conflict and Social Capital

In this book, the word "armed" is purposely used to highlight violent and destructive forms of individual and group conflict, including quotidian crime[1]. In the literature of conflict and violence studies, there are a variety of different definitions for armed conflict (ACLED 2013, Arendt 1969, Kalyvas 2006). The research here concentrates on violence being used outside of the immediate family for any variety of reasons, therefore excluding domestic violence.[2] Violence refers to acts of any force using small arms and light weapons (SALW), including knives and machetes, with the end purpose to inflict bodily harm. While the reasons for using violence are numerous, conflict using SALW is seen as dichotomous: it is either violent or non-violent.[3]

For the study, five different cities in five regions of Somalia with various degrees of violence experienced are used.[4] I argue that these five cities also have different levels of "stateness" in terms of state legitimacy and capacity of government institutions in delivering or coordinating services. The benefits of studying five cities allows us to create boundaries not only for time but also for space and establish control of the time-space framework for analysis and highlight the relevance and implications of the results. This approach is further justified by the large physical distances between the five cities with the two closest cities being at least a six-hour drive by car.

Conventionally Somalia is seen as having experienced over twenty years of civil war and state collapse. "Mainstream" qualitative studies—conducted by practitioners, such as the United Nations, thinks tanks, and consultants—have repeatedly analyzed the reasons and causes for the armed conflict in Somalia and have arrived at a variety of conclusions.[5] However, according to available research, the conflict in south central Somalia has yet to be analyzed quantitatively.[6] This is not because the qualitative research approach outweighs quantitative methods but instead because Somalia provides serious difficulties for any kind of quantitative analysis to be undertaken due to a lack of reliable and consistent data to produce statistically meaningful results. Simply conducting any type of fieldwork in Somalia, especially Mogadishu, creates personnel risk. Any serious quantitative or qualitative approach to analyze the conflict in Somalia requires the researcher to constantly consider security issues.

In addition to the difficulties of collecting reliable data, the researcher must decide on the type of data, such as national or regional, to analyze armed conflict. Numerous approaches looking at inter-state conflict globally have been implemented by researchers to quantitatively analyze the causes and solutions for armed conflict (Collier et al 2003). However single country specific based analysis that takes domestic variances of armed conflict into consideration on the other hand have been few and limited (Kalyvas 2006, Posner 2005, Varshney 2002).

Following the end of the Cold War, armed conflicts have mainly been intrastate affairs with ethnic, religious, land, natural resources, and economic issues being seen as possible causes. As such, there has been a tendency to portray armed conflicts as being conducted on a national scale without taking into consideration the *variances* of violent conflict within a country. The reality on the ground, such as in Somalia, is that violence is not always widespread and instead it is commonly localized, albeit the level of "localization" of the conflict may vary widely. In a country where ethnic violence is rampant, parts of the country where two different ethnic groups live in relative peace rarely make the news headlines. Researchers and practitioners tend to concentrate their efforts on studying parts of the country where things are burning up in flames and tend to pay less attention to areas where ethnic groups and communities have been able to mitigate violence from erupting. Pockets of peace may in actual fact be more of the norm than the exception and full-blown armed conflict across the country may actually be rare. In agreement with Varsheny, *ethnic armed conflict needs to be analyzed at a local and regional level* to gain a better understanding of the dynamics regarding the variances of conflict (2002:52). Simply looking only at the nation level limits, the reach of the analysis to understand the essence of armed conflict. To achieve a deeper understanding of social capital and armed conflict at the local level in Somalia, analysis is therefore conducted across five regions in five cities.

The research uses a relatively unused analytical approach in the area of conflict studies, that of social capital theory. It also incorporates newly collected fieldwork data to study armed conflict in Somalia. By applying social capital theory and using quantitative and qualitative analysis for the data collected, the research attempts to provide new insights into the armed conflict of Somalia on a regional level, therefore pushing below the national level of analysis and beyond the dichotomous dynamics between state and non-state actors. Furthermore, it attempts to analyze the relevant local dynamics and variables that contribute to armed conflict.

Research specifically focusing on trust and social networks— including social capital—has been sparse in the field of armed violent conflict (Cox 2009, Bhavnani and Backer 2007&2010, Colletta and Cullen 2000a&b, Lederman et al 2002, Rosenfeld et al 2001). Here, social capital theory looks at issues of trust, social cohesion, and civic participation in detail as the explanatory variable.

In Somalia, a country where certain regions have lacked an effective government for over 20 years, social networks and relationships have provided the basic foundations for survival and social order. Even in areas with institutions of governance, such as northern Somalia, the line between formal and informal governance has been blurred due to clannism, lack of clear governance structures and outdated regulatory frameworks. Social networks and relationships are the foundations of security, family, clanship, patriarchy, nepotism, citizenship, and nationness. These relationships can be the first and last resort for survival, contribute or challenge the foundations of the state, and also be a cause and solution for armed conflict.

In Somalia, these relationships—outside of the immediate family—have played an important role in conflict creation and resolution. However previous research has tended to ignore the importance of quotidian and associational relationships and networks in regard to resolving and mitigating armed conflict. Scholars have instead highlighted how traditional social structures, especially those involving clan elders, have declined in relevancy in Somali society (Bradbury et al 2010, Renders 2007). Other examples include the weakening of traditional mechanisms to deal with conflict and the emergence of freelance militia (Menkhaus 1999&2004). Quotidian and associational relationships provide an alternative insight for analyzing variances of armed conflict on a local and regional level and social capital theory will be used to analyze these dynamics in the context of armed conflict.

In addition to associational relationships and networks, the importance of civil society—which is closely connected to the social capital literature—is vital to explain the variances of violent conflict within a country according to Varshney: "civil society is the missing variable in all available traditions of inquiry" for explaining ethnic conflict (2002:39). Paffenholz and Spurk argue that "there has been little systematic analysis of the specific role of civic engagement and civil society in the context of armed conflict and even less regarding its potentials, limitations and critical factors" (2006:1). As a first attempt Cox et al look at the paradoxical power of social capital in creating and resolving conflicts, and specifically to what extent social capital is related to peace and conflict (2009). Cox et al highlight the need for further research to address the issue of causality in this area and look at the possibility of endogeneity.

In researching armed conflict, the nexus between civil society and social capital cannot be ignored and is seen as vital when analyzing armed conflict. As history has shown, civil society has flourished in Somalia since the state collapsed in 1991 (Menkhaus et al 2010).[7] Menkhaus et al highlight the paradoxical role of civil society organizations (CSOs) operating in Somalia, where some organizations may intentionally or unintentionally reinforce and create social cleavages (2010:341). My own fieldwork and professional work experience with CSOs in and outside of Somalia reinforces this point. As discussed later on, civil society and social capital are analyzed in detail in the context of armed conflict and the case studies of Mogadishu and Burao provide interesting insights.

1.3 Why Somalia?

Somali officials and the international community have highlighted how Somalia has not only become a threat to itself, but also a threat regionally and globally. Somalia has been branded with producing pirates that create insecurity for the global shipping industry; a safe haven for terrorist groups who attack neighbouring countries; a battle ground between Jihadists and "Christian infidels"; a "prime example" of a failed stated; and the epicenter of the 2011 famine which caused a humanitarian crisis. In terms of corruption, Transparency International has ranked Somalia as the most corrupt country, and other statistics, where they exist, highlight deficits in a variety of areas from health to education.

From a political philosophy perspective, Somalia provides a precious "living example" of the state nature which may initially seem in Hobbes' famous words a situation where life is "nasty, brutish, and short". However, upon careful inspection, Somalia shows us that groups of individuals can perfectly function with no governing central or non-central state and challenge the central tenets of the social contract between the individual and the state (Matsukawa 2006). Frequently treated as an outlier in peace and conflict statistical models, or an exception in international policies and treaties, Somalia provides a sense of nostalgia to anarchists and libertarians and reminds us that the concept of the modern nation-state is a recently created phenomenon.

Furthermore, as Menkhaus has highlighted, the situation of Somalia is "in a class apart" from other collapsed or failed states: "Somalia is a failure among failed states" (2004:17). Somalia has lacked an effective central government for more than twenty years with the exception of some areas in Puntland, Galmudug, and Somaliland. With the state in south central Somalia relying on de jure existence, it has struggled to achieve nationwide de facto legitimacy while the northern region of Somaliland enjoys de facto legitimacy but lacks de jure recognition from the international community. In Somalia several different "states" exist in one nation, within the internationally recognized borders of

Somalia, providing interesting insight into the issues of de jure sovereignty and de facto states.

The cities and regions analyzed here also provide a wide spectrum of the different statenesses in Somalia. Here, the term stateness is loosely used intentionally as concepts related to the state are extremely fluid and ambiguous in the Somali context. For example, the role of the state from a de jure perspective varies between regions and ambiguity is compounded by the various decrees and bylaws issued by municipal governments in addition to outdated legal frameworks. Levels of stateness become even more unclear when de facto state authority is taken into consideration. Various local state and non-state actors exercise different levels of authority which for the populace can make the differentiation unclear between state and non-state entities and further complicate the "rules of the game" related to governance. Therefore, it is difficult to provide an accurate picture of what a state is in the current context and to describe its responsibilities from a de jure perspective. That said, however, the thesis differentiates the level of stateness for the five cities researched from a de facto perspective.

For the research inquiry I have chosen the following five cities that are the regional capitals based on the demarcations of the Somalia state during Siad Barre's government[8]: Burao, Las Anod, Bosaso, Galkayo, and Mogadishu. The city of Burao is considered to be part of Somaliland, a self-declared republic that is seeking independence and international recognition from the rest of Somalia. Las Anod is located in the disputed area between Somaliland and Puntland and is under control by the Somaliland state. Unlike Somaliland, the Puntland state is not seeking independence from the central Federal Government of Somalia (FGS). The port city of Bosaso is located in Puntland and Galkayo is a politically and administratively split city between the Puntland state and Galmudug state. Mogadishu is not only the regional capital of the Benadir region but also the capital of Somalia.[9]

In terms of stateness at the regional level, Somaliland can be viewed as a "post-conflict state", Puntland and Galmudug as a "fragile state", and south-central Somalia as "failed state" in protracted and complex armed conflict.[10] At the city level, Burao and Bosaso portray characteristics of increased stateness relative to the other three cities in terms of local governance. This is followed by Galkayo and Las Anod which also have local governance state structures but suffer from high levels of insecurity, thereby putting a strain on the local administrations in delivering basic services compared to Burao and Bosaso. Mogadishu has decreased levels of stateness compared to all four cities. A lack of or complete absence of basic services delivery, unclear roles between the municipal administration and central government, lack of revenue generation and weak public financial management, and a recent history of a predatory state still clearly remaining in the minds of the population contribute to the decreased stateness in Mogadishu.

Finally, Somalia provides numerous challenges (and frustrations) for practitioners regarding spoiler management, arms proliferation, poor governance, economic development, environment and natural resources, land ownership, and (un)civil society. By studying Somalia, we may find interesting discoveries regarding the essence (and ontology) of the nation-state model and solutions to deal with armed conflict in other parts of the world.

1.4 Social Capital Analyzing Other Armed Conflicts – A Brief History

Social capital theory has been widely used in researching civil society, democracy, economic growth, poverty alleviation, good governance, informal sectors, social trust, business transactions, health, and education (Burt et al 2001, Burt 1992&2005&2010, Halpern 2005, Lin 2002). However, research on armed conflict using social capital theory is still sparse, with only a few researchers having looked at this specific relationship (Bhavnani and Backer 2007, Colletta and Cullen 2000a&2000b, Cox 2009, Paffenholz 2009). I am not aware of any research that has used bonding, bridging, *and* linking social capital simultaneously in the context of analyzing armed conflict or on Somalia for that matter.

Colletta and Cullen (2000a) use social capital theory to look at the violent conflicts in Cambodia, Rwanda, Guatemala, and Somalia using a qualitative approach. For the Somali case study, they compare the social capital in the two cities of Hargesia and Boroma, which are both located in the relatively peaceful area of Somaliland. Their findings are inconsistent with their hypotheses, where they predict social capital levels would be lower in Hargeisa which has experienced more trauma and violence than Boroma (2000a:52,64,68). Instead they find Hargeisa to exhibit higher levels of social capital, described as social responsibility and social initiative, versus Boroma which had exhibited lower levels of both social responsibility and social initiative (2000a:69).

Rosenfeld et al (2001) analyze the crime-reducing impact of social capital in the United States using structural equation models based on national statistics. Their results indicate that "depleted social capital contributes to high levels of homicide" and "where levels of generalized social trust are high and civic engagement is widespread, homicide rates are low, regardless of the level of deprivation, the density of the population, and other socio-demographic influences" (2001:283-300). The analysis shows a relationship between social capital and homicide rates however the issue of causality remains and the authors highlight the need for further research in this area.

Lederman et al (2002) look at the statistical relationship between social capital and violent crime rates and its crime-reducing effect using data from 39 countries, albeit with no cases from Africa or Asia. By using an ordinary least squares estimator approach and generalized method of moments, they "find that the sense of trust among community members has a significant negative effect on homicide rates" and that the effect of other social capital proxies, such as civic membership and church attendance, is not clear (2002:529). Although not referring to the terms of bonding and bridging social capital, the authors highlight the need for future research to discriminate "the effects of group-specific and society-wide social capital" (2002:529).

Varsheny (2001&2002) provides a useful insight into how *interethnic*, and not intraethnic, networks mitigate ethnic violence in India between Hindus and Muslims. In terms of networks, associational forms of civic engagement are seen as being sturdier than quotidian forms of engagement for maintaining peace in large urban settings (cities and metropolises). Varsheny argues, by using statistical analysis and process tracing, that "what matters for ethnic violence is not whether ethnic life or social capital exits but whether social and civic ties cut *across* ethnic groups" (2001:392).

On a multi-country comparison and aggregated level (based on 16 countries), Bhavnani and Backer (2007:5) use *Round Two of the Afrobarometer Survey* (2002) to conduct an analysis to see whether social capital reduces political violence and if it influences the nature and prevalence of political violence. The authors conclude that "the most consistent factor in lowering such violence appears to be social cohesion... equality also seems to have beneficial effects, as do select forms of associational membership, civic engagement and trust" (2007:4). Their results regarding social cohesion as being important are similar to the conclusions of Colletta and Cullen (2000a). However a surprising conclusion in their study is how "membership in religious groups is linked to a lower likelihood of engaging in political violence" and how memberships in professional and business associations are linked positively to political violence (2007:4). Interestingly, and importantly, this conclusion is contradictory with Varsheny's (2001) findings where he sees religious groups as being intraethnic and exclusionary (therefore contributing to ethnic violence), and business associations as being interethnic and inclusionary (which provide a mechanism for mitigating violence).

Other scholars, such as Widner and Mundt (1998), attempt to understand how social capital influences state-building in Africa and to also confirm Putnam's (1994) argument that social capital produces effective government. Based on survey data from Botswana and Uganda, they argue that participation in voluntary associations does not specifically increase social capital, as argued by Putnam, and instead higher levels of social capital simply lead to greater amounts of associational life (Widner and Mundt 1998:22). They also find that *no clear relationship exists* between social capital and governmental effectiveness (1998:2), therefore challenging Putnam's argument that higher performance of local institutions actually mitigates political violence. Conclusions presented in their research suffer, they admit, from endogeneity—as seen in the relationship between social capital and effective government—and clear causal relationships are difficult to establish in regard to statebuilding and social capital (1998:22).

The specific issue of endogeneity and causal ambiguity in the study of social capital is highlighted by Chapman (2008&2009) who notes the possibility "that civic organizations that preach tolerance and encourage peaceful participation are formed by individuals who already hold those attitudes, while insular groups are formed by and attract individuals who embrace violence" (2009:161). In his analysis Chapman uses an instrumental variables approach to correct for endogeneity and concludes that "civic membership *cannot be shown* to affect individual attitudes toward violence... and that the relationship between social capital and attitudes may be far more complex than often recognized" (2009:167). With the important argument that attitudes drive civic membership, Chapman goes one step further to suggest that "the presence of vibrant social capital may be a product, not the cause, of peace and prosperity" (2009:168).

11

In *Social Capital and Peace-building*, Cox et al illustrates the paradoxical power of social capital in creating and resolving conflict (2009). Through a series of case studies, statistical models, and theoretical essays, the edited collection brings together for the first-time essays that analyze the role of social capital in instigating and mitigating violence. The authors note how the dark side of (un)social capital—respective to the criteria established by Putnam regarding trust, norms of reciprocity, and networks—can be used to create conflict while on the other hand it can be used as a public good to mitigate violence and contribute to peacebuilding.

As past research shows, there is a need to further investigate the relationships between armed conflict and social capital. Can clear causal relationships be established or is endogeneity an essence of social capital and armed conflict? Is equifinality present in the relationship? These are just some of the challenging questions that further research is required to help better understand the relationship between armed conflict and social capital. The research here on Somalia hopes to look at some of these issues and further explore this complex relationship.

1.4.1 Bonding and Bridging Social Capital

The following definitions related to social capital have been selected and are based on terms widely used in the social capital discourse (Putnam 2000:22). In short, and for the purpose of this research inquiry, bonding social capital is related to *exclusive* social networks and norms of reciprocity that tightly hold groups and individuals together. Bridging social capital relates to social networks that connect various groups and are *inclusive* social networks.

Importantly, before bridging social capital can be created, bonding social capital needs to be present (Larsen et al 2004:65, Nan 2009:172, Warren et al 2001:9). Trust and social cohesion within groups are precedent to bridging social capital being developed and so when bonding social capital declines, bridging social capital is also expected to decline (Putnam 2000&2002). This decline in bridging social can lead to an increase in ethnic tensions as the avenues for information sharing and building trust erodes (Nan 2009:172).

Trust is a key issue in the social capital discourse. Putnam's theory on social capital focuses on trust, norms of reciprocity, and networks (2000&2002). Trust can be understood in two distinct ways: thick and thin trust (Putnam 2000:136). Thick trust is personal trust between individuals who know each other. Thin trust, or general trust, involves the confidence extended to unknown third parties. Extending these concepts, bonding social capital can be viewed as thick trust and bridging social capital as thin trust. Put another way, "bonding social capital constitutes a kind of sociological superglue, whereas bridging social capital provides a sociological WD-40" (Putnam 2000:23).

During armed conflict, or when the state is unable to protect the citizenry, bonding social capital will prevail over bridging social capital as "primary groupings such as kinship, tribal, religious, and traditional political structures, as well as communities... serve as coping strategies for people in response to state collapse" (Spurk 2010:19). In such a context, bonding social capital can also have a "dark or uncivil side" (Spurk 2010:23) and Putnam has elaborated in much detail the concepts of good and bad social capital, summarized succinctly by Spurk:

> Good social capital is built when associations develop strong bridging ties—such as including members from other ethnic or social groupings—whereas bad social capital is characterized only by bonding ties or strong inward social capital. Such social capital is usually evident when only members from the same ethnic or social grouping are included. They are more inclined to act violently against others in comparison to associations that have stronger bridging ties (2010:26).

As highlighted by Putnam, bonding and bridging social capital are not "either-or" categories but an issue of levels and degrees of social capital, such as "more or less" (2000:23). No single indicator or proxy can represent the different levels of social capital or its components and Putnam notes, "I have found no reliable, comprehensive, nationwide measures of social capital that neatly distinguish 'bridgingness' and 'bondingness'" (Putnam 2000:23).

1.4.2 Linking Social Capital: Hard and Soft

In addition to bonding and bridging social capital, a third category, linking social capital is also included (Halpern 2005, Woolcock 2004:4). Literature on linking social capital widely defines this as vertical relationships and networks with somebody who is in a position of higher authority—a person or organization that can assist with access to private or public goods that are restricted—or higher economic

13

status (Halpern 2005:22). Some scholars see linking social capital as simply being a form of bridging social capital (Colletta and Cullen 2000a&2000b). In my research, linking social capital is used to look at how leadership and people in authority—in the form of vertical networks and social relations—encourage or deter individuals into armed conflict participation. I see linking social capital as particularly important in the context of armed conflict and as having two forms with different characteristics.

The first is vertical relationships with people possessing sanctioning power, *hard power*, to mobilize and coerce individuals into armed conflict. Specifically, individuals with vertical relationships to people in leadership positions with hard power (e.g. warlords, political persons, and powerful businessmen) are more likely to be influenced or forced to take up arms by these people to maintain their vertical relations and the assistance provided to access private or public goods. This can be seen as the classical patron-client relationship where "strongmen" control access of goods towards a group of people.

Even though one may not want to participate in armed conflict individually, pressure exerted from people in authority with hard power can lead to personal discretion and choices being overruled. This can also stem from a fear of losing out on assistance from above to access private or public goods. Individuals may find themselves in situations where the interests of a select group of people with hard power, such as politicians and warlords, mobilize others vertically towards armed conflict, superseding individual preferences not to participate. Simply put, individuals lack the option to "opt out" of the decision taken by others in authority to participate in armed conflict. I term this type of vertical relationship with sanctioning power from above as *hard linking social capital*. In such relationships, individuals may find themselves dealing not only with peer pressure but with sanction mechanisms from above.

The second form, *soft linking social capital*, focuses on vertical relationships between individuals and leaders who lack enforcement and sanctioning power but have moral authority. This includes clan elders, religious leaders, and civil society leaders. In these types of vertical relationships, the individual has the option to go against the leader's decision to maneuver the group without fear of sanctions or reprisal. The individual may also see a lack of incentives to adhere to the leader's decisions. In short, the leaders lack the hard power and enforcement mechanisms to mobilize individuals into armed conflict. The theoretical concepts of hard and soft linking social capital are elaborated further in the next chapter (section 2.4.2).

Although entrepreneurial leadership has been looked at elsewhere—where "key individuals with authority, charisma, initiative, etc. can frame an agenda and thereby persuade individuals to act" (Bhavnani and Backer 2007:5)—no research has focused on the relationship between linking social capital and armed conflict as far as I am aware of[11]. Linking social capital can be used to analyze whether certain vertical relations within the community contribute to or mitigate armed conflict. Referring to the two types of linking social capital highlighted above, the issue of hard and soft power based civic associations will be looked at and their relationship to armed conflict.

By using the above mentioned three types of social capital (bonding, bridging, and linking) and the various theoretical frameworks on social capital and trust (Gambetta 1988, Halpern 2005, Putnam 1994&2000&2002), I propose a new framework to qualitatively analyze the relationships between social capital and armed conflict. This is achieved by establishing a clear distinction between the proxies for bonding, bridging, and linking social capital and looking at how hard and soft power based civic associations and relationships influence armed conflict.

1.5 The Clan System

One cannot go about studying the armed conflict in Somalia without making reference to clans—referred to by some Somalis as a curse and the root cause of the conflict. The clan system—based on patrilineality—is a confusing system for the outsider and consists of sub-clans and sub-divisions that have ad-hoc alliances and extremely fluid relationships with other clans (Gundel 2006, Jama 2007, Luling 2006, Menkhaus 2004&2010). There is no clear agreement on the lineage of the clan and sub-clan structure in Somalia and even the number of the "main" clans varies ranging from five to six clans: Darod, Dir, Isaaq, Hawiye, Digil and Mirifle/Rahanweyn (Brons 2001). The first four clans are perceived as nomadic pastoralists raising cattle and camels while the last two clans practice settled farming. The reality, though, is quite mixed with any clan practicing pastoralism or farming. In addition, the Gosha people make up a minority group consisting of the Bantu and other minorities who also practice settled farming (Besteman 1999, Menkhaus 2010).

Webersik notes that "Somalia is less homogenous in terms of ethnicity, religion and language, in particular in the South, than claimed by some Somali scholars (Latin and Samatar 1987...)" (Webersik 2004:525). With a variety of clans, Somalia provides an interesting environment to study the issue of identity, ethnicity, and political culture.

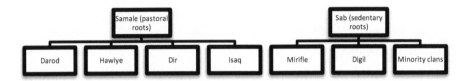

Figure 1. Main family clans in Somalia

1.6 Analytical Context

A two-pronged approach is used to analyze the relationships between social capital and armed conflict. The first, a quantitative approach, analyzes large-n data previously collected from several sources between 2009 and 2013. The data sets consist of opinion polls conducted for the United Nations Support Office for the African Union Mission to Somalia (UNSOA) in Mogadishu in 2011 and 2012 and a baseline study on violence conducted in 2009 and 2010 by the United Nations Development Programme (UNDP) from five cities in five different regions with over 4,600 samples.

The second, a qualitative approach, uses primary and secondary data. Primary data is based mainly on my fieldwork[12] conducted from 2004 to 2013 using focus group discussions and interviews[13] in the same five cities from the UNDP study. It includes interviews conducted in Djibouti, Uganda, Kenya, and the United Arab Emirates. The qualitative approach also consists of using original small-n survey data based on a questionnaire I designed and was answered by a small group of around thirty participants in each of the five cities.

In terms of secondary data, the research design uses several sources to address the research inquiry: publicly released written material and "gray literature"; focus group discussions and surveys; and individual interviews. A desk review of existing public literature related primarily to Somalia and social capital theory was conducted against over 600

16

articles, which included working papers, non-papers, refereed journal papers, "think tank" reports, and dissertations. This was in addition to published books and edited volumes on Somalia, social capital theory, conflict and peace theory, peacebuilding, civil society, and identity.

Importantly, over a five-year period from 2008 to 2012, there were major developments in Somalia in the areas of politics, humanitarian affairs, economics, and security. The details will not be elaborated here and will be touched upon as necessary in the discourse. The point emphasized here is that in a fast and dynamic (combat) environment, conducting research on the ground becomes extremely difficult not only from attempting to maintain a robust inquiry but from practical issues of safety and logistics. For example, the complexities and challenges of conducting research in Mogadishu are completely different from undertaking research in northern Somalia. During the time of research, Mogadishu was undergoing extensive military operations which included combat offensives by the African Union Mission in Somalia (AMISOM) and asymmetrical attacks by the anti-government group, Al Shabaab. In addition, several regions of south central Somalia were being declared as famine areas and Mogadishu was experiencing an influx of internally displaced persons (IDPs) due to the humanitarian crisis. Galkayo was experiencing a proliferation of kidnappings in early 2013 and Bosaso saw a tense political situation surrounding the Puntland president's term being extended with ongoing security operations against Al Shabaab south of Bosaso. Las Anod was strictly off limits to international United Nations staff members and Burao had a newly appointed mayor. It is in this mosaic of developments that an academic inquiry was conducted to unravel the essence of the issues.

Finally, the timeframe for analyses primarily focuses on the transition period of the Transitional Federal Government of Somalia (TFG) between 2004 and 2012. The TFG emerged in January 2005 and officially ended in August 2012. This specific timeframe is used for several reasons. First, the conflict in Somalia has been ongoing for over 20 years and there is an abundance of literature regarding the debacle of the intervention by the United States and United Nations prior to 1995. To contribute further to this discourse would mean conducting a labour-intensive historical review of events during that time. Second, the period from the emergence of the TFG has seen a variety of major paradigm shifts, as mentioned previously, in the context of the Somali conflict. From initially being a government in exile, the TFG established a firm presence in Mogadishu and had for the first time full "control" of the capital city after the withdrawal of anti-government elements, such as Al Shabaab.[14]. Third, my personal research started during this time when I first visited Mogadishu in 2004. This followed by working on Somalia as a practitioner with the United Nations Department of Political Affairs in 2008 followed by the United Nations Political Office for Somalia in 2010.

1.6.1 Data Sources

The primary data for the small-n survey was collected in a focus group discussion setting. First the small-n survey was issued to participants to fill out. Following the small-n survey, focus group discussions were conducted with the same participants to improve understanding of the regional and local context while also discussing issues related to conflict and social capital. The small-n survey is a questionnaire that was specifically designed for this research. Questionnaires were answered by two cohorts in Mogadishu: youth and local business people. In the remaining four cities the questionnaires were answered by youth, primarily university students. Many of these university students had never experienced a "functioning national state", while most of the student participants in Mogadishu would had been born after the state had collapsed in 1991, effectively being born and raised in "statelessness"!

The questionnaire was developed in English using the analytical framework to investigate the relationship between social capital and armed conflict and will be discussed in detail separately. It was translated into Somali by a diaspora living in the United States and underwent a translation check by a Somalia academic from the diaspora. It was finally reviewed by two Mogadishu-based secondary school teachers before being administered.

The focus group discussions for the small-n survey targeted 30 participants[15] in each city and were conducted in a variety of sizes from around five persons to a large group of 30 persons. The surveys were personally conducted in four cities[16] with the exception of Las Anod where the survey was outsourced to an enumerator and coordinator due to the political and security situation making it not possible for me to conduct a field visit.

In addition to the small n-survey and focus group discussions, numerous interviews with a variety of individuals were undertaken in the four cities using the "snowball sampling method"[17] for conducting research in conflict zones (Cohen and Arieli 2011). These included informal and formal discussions with business people, leaders of civil society and NGOs, Somali and non-Somalia academics, government officials, international aid and development workers, United Nations staff, and members of the diplomatic corps.

The quantitative analyses use newly collected data from two sources. Baseline surveys conducted by UNDP related to crime and victimization from October 2009 to July 2010 provide for the first time important data to analyze armed conflict and violence in Somalia. The baseline study covers five cities in five different regions: Bosaso, Burao, Las Anod, Galkayo, and Mogadishu. With a total sample size of over 4,600, the baseline study provides rare data to study social capital and armed conflict on a large-n scale. The other source of data used is from two opinion polls with a sample size of around 1,000 conducted in Mogadishu by UNSOA in 2011 and 2012. Both survey results were publicly released and the raw data was kindly provided by the two United Nations entities for this research inquiry[18].

1.7 Discourse Outline

For the remainder of this monograph, the discourse is structured as follows:

i. Introduction and explanation of the analytical framework to quantitatively and qualitatively analyze the relationship between social capital (the independent variable) and armed conflict (the dependent variable);

ii. Introduction of the hypotheses and related theoretical predictions;

iii. Undertaking quantitative analysis, based on logistic regression, of the armed conflict and social capital using data from the UNDP baseline study and UNSOA opinion polls to identify relevant and significant variables for the qualitative approach;

iv. Conducting discriminant analysis for the UNDP baseline study to identify three cities for the qualitative analysis;

v. Providing a background and context setting of the three cities (identified from the discriminant analysis) based on existing literature and personal fieldwork;

vi. Qualitatively analyzing armed conflict and social capital using *secondary* data collected from existing literature for the three cities;

vii. Qualitatively analyzing armed conflict and social capital using *primary* data collected from interviews, focus group discussions, and the small-n survey;

viii. Comparing the findings from the quantitative and qualitative analyses at both the city and aggregate level with the hypotheses and theoretical predictions;

ix. Consideration of other variables that may support or counter the findings;

x. Identifying areas for further research and policy implications.

Notes

1 At times where the word conflict is used as standalone, I still refer to conflict as being "armed", in a violent form. "Unarmed" conflict will refer to non-violent forms of conflict.

2 "There are different definitions of armed conflict in the literature. Their common determinants are that armed conflicts involve organized, armed groups, in most cases with the government as a party to the conflict" (Paffenholz and Spurk 2006:14).

3 I discount that a show of arms, inputting fear into the local populace by displaying SALW, is seen as a non-violent action based on the argument that *implementing fear* can also be a violent act. For analytical purposes I use the issue of inflicting "bodily harm" as the premise for an act to be categorized as violent in my field survey.

4 In addition to the levels of violence varying, the history of armed conflict for Somaliland, Puntland, and south central Somalia varies. I agree with Menkhaus that Puntland has "been almost entirely free of war" while Mogadishu has experienced heavy armed conflict and Somaliland has "experienced both periods of severe insecurity and impressive public order and rule of law" (2007:75).

5 Reasons for the causes and continuation of the armed conflict in Somalia are numerous and will be discussed later.

6 The study conducted by Colletta and Cullen (2000a) researches Somaliland and *does not* cover south central Somalia, such as Mogadishu. Mubarak (1996) uses statistics to analyze how the Somali economy collapsed during and after the period of Siad Barre's rule.

7 Fieldwork: 13 to 20 September 2004, Mogadishu; 16 to 25 May 2011, Mogadishu.

8 Mohamed Siad Barre was the military dictator and President of the Somali Democratic Republic from 1969 to 1991.

9 The legal status of Mogadishu is still not clearly defined. Based on the

Provisional Constitution, adopted in 2012, Mogadishu is the capital of Somalia however a City Law for Mogadishu has not been adopted (Interview: McAuslan 2012, email).

10 Personnel communication: Schumicky 10 April 2013, Garowe.

11 Samatar argues that "the central actors responsible for the destruction of the Somali 'world order' are the dominant elite (1997:688)… the Somali nightmare is not the result of genealogical divisions among the population but of the narrow accumulation strategies of the [Somali] elite (1997:706) ".

12 Due to security constraints and logistical challenges, the fieldwork was carried over numerous visits to Somalia ranging from several days to several weeks with the majority of field research being conducted in Mogadishu between 2011 and 2012. As a United Nations staff member working on Somalia from 2008 August to 2013 April, I was on one hand afforded the opportunity of being able to access various parts of Somalia and interact with a wide range of actors during duty and off duty hours. On the other hand, I had to follow United Nations rules and procedures (including movement restrictions related to security) at all times.

13 Formal interviews with United Nations staff members and international developmental partners have been conducted on the premise of contributing to this research and "informal" anonymous discussions have been intentionally omitted with a few exceptions. In certain cases, at the request of the interlocutors, some interviews have been kept anonymous and are simply referred to as the time and location the fieldwork was conducted. This has usually been the case for Somali interlocutors based in Somalia.

14 For a detailed history and background information on Al Shabaab, see Hansen (2013) who conducted extensive field research in Somalia.

15 Participants in Mogadishu and Las Anod were paid ten US dollars for transportation costs while participants in northern Galkayo were paid 30 US dollars each. Participants in Burao, Bosasso, and southern Galkayo were not paid. In each city where I conducted the survey, a translator and coordinator were utilized.

16 Throughout the focus discussion group surveys I usually had one translator and local research coordinator to help administer the survey and carry out the discussions in Somali. Individual interviews and discussions also included a local research coordinator or translator. The list of people who assisted me in arrangement, translation, and support in the four cities are mentioned in the Acknowledgements. I am indebted also to numerous Somalis, too many to be mentioned, who provided introductions to relevant actors and for simply "making things happen" on the ground.

17 The "snowball sampling method" is a method for conducting fieldwork in conflict zones where interlocutors provide introductions for further interviews. This approach obviously has its benefits and drawbacks as highlighted by Cohen and Arieli (2011).

18 I am grateful to Daniel Ladouceur of UNDP and Simon Davies of UNSOA for providing the data.

Chapter 2. RESEARCH FRAMEWORK FOR SOCIAL CAPITAL AND ARMED CONFLICT IN SOMALIA

2.1 Introduction

This chapter focuses on the analytical framework pertaining to social capital and armed conflict. It also provides a background setting of the armed conflict in Somalia through a short synopsis of the history from independence to state collapse and state emergence. The "root causes" of the conflict based on widely available literature are highlighted including the two schools of thought used in Somali conflict studies.

Definitions are proposed in the research framework and the limitations and challenges related to analyzing social capital and armed conflict are highlighted. Within the discourse, theoretical issues related to civil society, associational relationships and networks, and the important role of customary law, known as xeer in Somali, are addressed in the context of armed conflict. Following the theoretical discussions and definitions, the hypotheses and analytical framework are presented. As with any research framework, the parameters of the research design have been set to address the inquiry. One of the main objectives of this chapter is to provide the context and logic to how these parameters are set and utilized.

To recall, the genesis of this research is based on the inquiry to look at what kinds of relationships exist between social capital and armed conflict by analyzing the variances of violence and social capital between five cities-regions in Somalia. For the research inquiry, a distinction is made between different proxies to quantitatively and qualitatively distinguish the concepts of bonding, bridging, and linking social capital. Social capital theory analyzes inter-clan and intra-clan associations, trust, quotidian and associational networks, and social cohesion with armed conflict and violence within the five regions.

For the purpose of this discourse, I do not go into the extensive debates and criticisms related to social capital[1] (Durlauf and Fafchamps 2004, Fine 2010). Nor do I go into the various theories and approaches related to social capital in other areas (Burt et al 2001, Halpern 2005, Woolcock and Narayan 2000). This would be outside the scope of the discourse. Instead I selectively apply certain elements of social capital theory to the research inquiry to analyze the protracted conflict in Somalia.

2.2 A Brief History from Independence to State Collapse and State Emergence[2]

Menkhaus notes "Somalia is a failure among failed states" (2004:17). But how did Somalia become a "failure" as frequently mentioned in the mainstream literature? What were the so-called "root causes", if any, and is Somalia really a failure to the world order of nation-states?

A brief look at Somalia's pre-colonial history never provided comfort for foreign powers that had colonial ambitions in the Horn of Africa. Even before independence, Somalis were well known for their proud nomadic culture[3] that centered upon the clan system and self-reliance (Lewis 1999:29, Peterson 2001:9). Britain and Italy were the main Western powers who took upon colonizing modern day Somalia. In 1960, the British and Italian parts of Somalia become independent and merged to form the United Republic of Somalia. Seldom referred to, Somalia had democratic elections and Aden Abdullah Osman Daar was elected as its first president. In 1967 a peaceful transfer of power occurred with the election of Abdi Rashid Ali Shermarke. However turbulent times arrived in 1969 when Muhammad Siad Barre assumed power in a coup after Ali Shermarke was assassinated by one of his bodyguards.

From 1970 till 1991 Barre dictated Somalia as a socialist state and nationalized most of the economy, implementing "scientific socialism" which officially was aimed at destroying the ancient clan system. Political and administrative power focused in urban cities, with Mogadishu as the centre of political power. Barre initiated a nationwide literacy campaign, sending teachers to rural areas. Based on socialist ideals women were given an increased role in Somali society in terms of education and health, albeit in urban settings, and a trend of study abroad for bureaucrats, military and police officials increased.

During Barre's early rule, Somalia was at relative peace under a central dictatorial authority. But a turning point occurred in 1977 when Barre invaded the Somali-inhabited Ogaden region of Ethiopia, trying to pursue a vision of a "Greater Somalia" (Barre was related to the Somali clans who inhabited this region). This venture took an unexpected toll after Somali forces were pushed out of Ogaden, therefore losing the war with Ethiopia, and instead allowed the opposition towards Barre's regime to mobilize and take advantage of the situation. More importantly, the war with Ethiopia, and the ever increasing militarization of the country, led to the wide distribution and spread of arms in Somalia. With fear of Ethiopian troops conducting a counter-offensive, Barre distributed weapons across the country in order to have ordinary Somalis defend their homeland (Peterson 2001).

With the war against Ethiopia lost and a peace accord signed in 1988, opposition towards Barre's regime increased after he further excluded members of the Majeerteen and Isaaq clans from key government positions and instead favored members of his own clan (Marehan, Ogaden, and Dulbahante), contradicting his anti-clan policy. With power and resources being shared with selected clans, including summary executions and imprisonment of opposition clan elders, Somalia eventually fell into full blown civil war. With a proliferation of weapons, an abundance of clan grievances which included political and economical marginalization, and state coffers dried up after the Soviet Union ended its military and financial support to Barre's government, the opposition clans ousted Barre in January of 1991. Barre was forced to flee the country and with no transitional government or process in place after his departure, Somalia became, as commonly known, a "failed" or "collapsed" state.

With Barre's government gone, Somalis took advantage of the power vacuum left by the state and looted their country, including the arsenal from Barre's military. According to Peterson, the amount of military hardware in Somalia at that time was immense, with the Soviet Union having given a total of $270 million in military aid, the United States $200 million, and Italy $500 million (Peterson 2001:13). With the total amount of military weaponry in Somalia nearly at $1 billion, warlords in urban settings quickly jockeyed to increase control and build up their power bases, spreading the amount of weaponry amongst the different militia and civilian population.

In addition to looting the country's arsenal and state infrastructures, warlords sought to also fill the political and security power vacuum and control of the capital Mogadishu. Following the expulsion (or exodus[4]) of the Darod clan and their sub-clans, Mogadishu was divided between the Haber Gedir and Abgal clan (who both belong to the larger clan family of the Hawiye) which had both fought together to oust Barre under the United Somali Congress (USC) banner. General Mohamed Farah Aidid, from the Haber Gedir clan, waged war against the rival Abgal clan, which was led by Ali Mahdi Mohamed who had appointed himself president after Barre's regime collapsed. The armed conflict between these two sub-clans (of the Hawiye clan family) escalated and spread to other parts of south central Somalia and the main victims were as usual ordinary Somalis, mainly from the minority clans who did not have clan protection against the larger clan families.

Food shortages spread across the country and distributing aid became a high-risk venture as food convoys were targeted by local militia usually related to one of the main warlords. In January 1991, the United Nations humanitarian agencies pulled out of south central Somalia and the International Committee of the Red Cross (ICRC) became the main distributor of aid. However the scale and depth of starvation was on a massive scale and in September 1991 the ICRC noticed severe malnourishment amongst the population (Peterson 2001:41). In December 1991, according to Peterson, the first signs of famine were noticed. But it was not until August 1992 that the famine was "discovered" by the media, which was also considered to be the height of the famine. In this complex security and humanitarian setting, food became a source of currency for Somalis.

In August 1992 the first United Nations peacekeepers arrived in Somalia to help protect the distribution of food aid. The United Nations Operation in Somalia (UNOSOM I) consisted of only 500 Pakistani soldiers and had been approved by the Security Council back in April of 1992. In December of 1992, United States troops landed on the beaches of Mogadishu, sent by President Bush to stop food relief being looted by the militia. The five-month mission called Unified Task Force (UNITAF) consisted of 38,000 troops, of which 25,000 were from the United States, and was authorized under chapter seven of the United Nations Charter to use force to open food corridors and protect aid but not disarm the militia. UNITAF was eventually transformed into UNOSOM II which ended in March 1995.

Following the withdrawal of the last United Nations troops in March 1995, Somalia fell deeper into a void of "statelessness" with international efforts to reestablish a government focusing primarily on south central Somalia. Meanwhile different parts of Somalia established various administrations, with Puntland and Somaliland receiving the most attention from the media and academic community. Somaliland declared its independence from the rest of Somalia in May 1991 while Puntland declared itself as an autonomous regional state of Somalia in July 1998.

In south central Somalia, numerous peace conferences and mediation efforts were initiated by regional organizations and countries, with the 2000 "Arta conference" producing a transitional national government (TNG). With limited de facto authority, the TNG quickly lost any legitimacy it had and was eventually replaced by the Transitional Federal Government (TFG) in October 2004, following the two and half year long "Mbaghati process" led by the Intergovernmental Authority on Development (IGAD). Abdullahi Yusuf was chosen as the new president and the TFG was initially based in Nairobi for nearly six months as Mogadishu was considered too dangerous for the president and parliamentarians to be based. In February 2005 some parliamentarians returned to Mogadishu however the TFG and remaining parliamentarians relocated to Baidoa, a regional city located 260 kilometers from the capital.

In early 2006, the TFG found itself being challenged by the Islamic Courts Union (ICU), a group claiming to cut across clan lines and abolish the evils of warlordism and anarchy. The transitional federal parliament convened for the first time in February 2006 while warlords in Mogadishu battled the ICU. With a number of political deliverables expected from the TFG, such as developing a constitution and conducting a referendum and national elections, the TFG found itself unable to deliver basic services or public goods to the population. In contradiction, the TFG founded itself being accused of contributing to insecurity and anarchy and faced multiple antigovernment elements in addition to the ICU, ranging from die-hard extremists, warlords, Islamic movements, and separatists.

The ICU took full control of Mogadishu in June 2006, evicting warlords backed by the United States and other militias supporting the

TFG. However the ICU rule of Mogadishu, known to many Mogadishu residents as the "golden era of peace", was short-lived until December 2006 when the ICU retreated after Ethiopia mobilized its troops into Somalia to counter the Islamic forces which were seen as a regional risk. After the ICU was evicted from Mogadishu, the TFG president relocated to the capital city for the first time under the protection of Ethiopian troops and in March 2007 the first AMISOM troops arrived in Mogadishu to provide security to the TFG.

In mid-2008, a new peace initiative led by the United Nations, known as the "Djibouti peace process", brought members of the ICU and TFG together to establish peace talks to form a new government[5]. Following several peace agreements in January 2009 the expanded TFG, which now included members of the ICU, selected a new president, Sheik Sharif Sheik Ahmed who was part of the ICU leadership. However, it was not for another three and a half years until the TFG was able to produce a provisional federal constitution, under the auspices of the United Nations, and pass it for vote by a National Constituent Assembly. Following a vote of support by the Constituent Assembly, the TFG formally ended in August 2012 and was replaced by the Federal Government of Somalia (FGS) which was selected based on the provisions of the provisional federal constitution. The following four years was a busy period as Somalia undertook a rapid process in terms of regional state formation and consolidation in south central Somalia. With a new federal parliament and government in place, under the presidency of Hassan Sheikh Mohamud, Somalia saw four new regional states emerge: the Interim Jubba Administration, the Interim South-West Administration, the Galmudug Interim Administration, and the Hir Shabelle Interim Administration. Between January and February 2017, Somalia's new federal parliament, which now included a lower house (House of the People) and a new upper house, elected a new Speaker and President of the Federal Republic of Somalia.

Importantly, Al Shabaab continued to control large parts of south central Somalia following the expulsion of the ICU from Mogadishu in 2006. The United Nations Security Council's mandate for AMISOM's deployment in January 2007 to protect the TFG and combat Al Shabaab changed the security power dynamics on the ground, especially in Mogadishu where Al Shabaab controlled most of the capital. Some of the fiercest fighting occurred in mid-2009 between

AMISOM and Al Shabaab in Mogadishu during the failed "Ramadan offensive" by Al Shabaab. Despite the failed attack in Mogadishu, Al Shabaab was still able to control large areas of south central Somalia and gain important access to revenues to fund their operations. However, as AMISOM's presence and control slowly increased in Mogadishu and other parts of the country, with the Kenyan military also joining AMISOM, Al Shabaab found itself retracting from main urban areas and conducted a "tactic withdrawal" from Mogadishu in August 2011.[6]

From a Somali-wide perspective, and for the purpose of this study, it is important to note that the military operations and combat between Al Shabaab and AMISOM/FGS have focused entirely in south central Somalia with Mogadishu seeing the brunt of the military combat from 2007 to 2011. This has major implications and obvious bias on the research and field work, including the UNDP survey for the data related to Mogadishu which was conducted during this period. Secondly, since the Barre state collapsed in 1991 and the TFG emerged, numerous local and regional initiatives have emerged to fill in the void of statelessness. As mentioned earlier, Puntland and Somaliland are the most well-known regional entities to have emerged. There have been more than 20 other state formation initiatives by self-acclaimed "regional states" from 2010 to 2012, many that have received minimal Western media coverage, if any.

What is important from these regional initiatives is that the regions on the periphery of Mogadishu politics have taken the initiative to establish minimal state structures in order to recreate concepts of stateness and government structures. Whether these statebuilding initiatives were undertaken because of "greed" or "grievances" is unclear. But the point is that actors in the periphery were able to do this without any major interference from the core, such as the FGS, TFG, United Nations, and international community. The proactive dynamics and initiatives—from a political, security, and economical perspective—by these actors in the periphery, since the state collapsed in 1991, highlights issues that may have a direct influence on social capital and armed conflict and will be looked at in further detail.

2.3 "Root Causes" of the Armed Conflict in Somalia

In the discourse of Somali conflict studies, the issue of root causes and underlying conflict variables are frequently discussed and referred to. The following section highlights these variables from the mainstream literature. Second, Somali conflict studies can be distinguished into two primary schools of thought. The two schools of thought are introduced briefly including my contribution to this discourse.

2.3.1 Frequently Mentioned Conflict Variables

This section does not analyze or critique every possible conflict variable related to the armed conflict in Somalia. Neither is it meant to produce an exhaustive list. Its aim is to provide a short summary of the main causes of the conflict, also referred to as "root causes", as repeatedly highlighted in the mainstream literature related to the Somali conflict. I intentionally avoid counterarguments and my own opinions regarding the conflict variables. Readers familiar with the related literature may want to overlook this section.

There are many issues in Somalia that contribute to the root causes of armed conflict, such as abundance of idle youth, drug abuse from qat, poverty, environmental degradation, lack of health infrastructure, absence of public utilities, poor road infrastructure, economic disparity, etc. In certain aspects some of the root causes are intertwined. For example, due to the existence of militia there could be insecurity and a proliferation of weapons; the proliferation of weapons and existence of militia could also create an abundance of spoilers. Furthermore, the list does not take into consideration the variances of the root causes across the country. Each individual root cause is explained briefly below (Matsukawa 2006).

> ➢ Resource scarcity—Reference to resource scarcity is abundant in the literature related to Somalia. This reference is made usually in the context of the harsh Somali climate. However the climate in Somalia varies with desert, semi-arid terrain where only livestock rearing is economically feasible, to fertile areas in southern Somalia where agricultural opportunities are abundant. What might be more relevant instead is a lack of resource management related to land usage in the areas of farming and grassing of livestock[7].

➢ Land—Linked to resource scarcity, land has been referred to as one of the main root causes for armed conflict all across Somalia. Draconian land nationalization polices during the time of Barre's government, conflict over grassing rights, illegal land enclosures, land grabbing in urban centers, and controversial land entitlements to urban elite are repeatedly highlighted as causes of conflict (Besteman and Cassanelli 2004).

➢ Lack of security—The state monopoly of violence by the state has continuously been challenged following state collapse. Regional administrations have arranged security arrangements based on formal and informal mechanisms that have limited civilian oversight, predictability, and reliability (Menkhaus 2007).

➢ Proliferation of weaponry—As mentioned earlier, the collapse of the state and spread of arms to fight Ethiopia led to a proliferation of weapons in the country. A study commissioned by the European Commission in 2003 estimated that 64 percent of Somalis possessed one or more firearms (CRD 2004:25). In another study specifically for Somaliland conducted in 2008 to 2009, 74 percent of households owned small arms, with an average of 1.27 arms per household (DDG 2009: iiv).

➢ Freelance and clan militia—With no particular loyalty towards any specific clan, freelance militia perform activities such as assassination, kidnapping, car-jacking, roadblocks, rape, drug abuse and burglary. Clan militia on the other hand have "command and control" through their communities, such as clan elders and the business community. Both types of militias challenge the government's security apparatus and its monopoly to control violence (Bryden and Brickhill 2010).

➢ Numerous spoilers—Due to the abundance of weaponry and ever-changing clan loyalties, it is fairly easy for different players to disrupt peace talks and negotiations creating numerous external actors who possess power to spoil and effectively have a sort of "veto power" (Menkhaus 2004: 38). This provides challenges to peacemaking processes that are seen as changing the status quo.

➢ Contradiction between peacebuilding and statebuilding—Menkhaus et al have referred to this as one of the main challenges in resolving the conflict in south central Somalia

(Bryden 1999, Jama 2007, Leonard and Samantar 2011, Menkhaus 2004). In short, reconciliation between clans has not been achieved. Peacebuilding requires reconciliation, and "in the absence of reconciliation, statebuilding is perceived by faction leaders and their supporters as a way to wage war by other means" (CRD 2004:8). The process of statebuilding may take conflicts between warring groups from the battlefield and to the negotiation table with neither group willing to compromise due to the lack of reconciliation.[8] Furthermore when negotiations fail, the conflict repeats itself usually with increased violence as groups have had time to rearm and resupply[9].

➤ Representation and participation contradiction—Conflict analyses on Somalia have repeatedly highlighted the difficulty of representation in track one peace processes. Due to the ongoing conflict running over 20 years, Somalia lacks legitimate leaders who represent the Somali people.

➤ Risk-averse decision making—Menkhaus argues that business leaders, regional administrations, and warlords are willing to settle with statelessness because they see the risks of a revived central state as too great. This can include the closure of illicit businesses and loss of tax revenues that would usually be handled by the central government or local administration. This sort of decision making has been undertaken by actors in Somalia and produces sub-optimal outcomes with missed opportunities. "State collapse may be unpalatable, inconvenient and undesirable on any number of counts, but for political and economic actors who have survived and thrived in a stateless setting, embracing a state-building agenda appears to constitute a leap of faith they are unwilling to take" (Menkhaus 2004:47).

➤ Extreme individualistic mentality—The nomadic Somalis, who historically never had any form of centralized government, lived in societies with rules but without rulers, with a traditional governing system consisting of a set of contractual agreements adapted to nomadic culture and the harsh environment (Lewis 1999:1&29). Many Somali experts agree that a centralized government system is unfit for lineage-based politics as political competition turns into clannism and kinship rivalry (Bryden 1999, Menkhaus 2007).[10]

> ➤ Segmentation in society based on clan and kinship—Frequently referred to as the cancer of Somalia, Lewis highlighted the importance of lineage segmentation back in the 1950s and feared that it would be used in politics. Fifty years later Adam notes, like other post-colonial African governments, Somalia has also suffered the same problems caused by ethnic diversity. "Clannism is the Somali version of the generic problem of ethnicity or tribalism: it represents primordial cleavages and cultural fragmentation within Somali society" (Adam 1995: 70). Throughout the discourse on Somalia, clannism has been regularly used to explain the armed conflict. As highlighted in the next sub-section, Besteman and Cassanelli (2004) and Osman and Souare (ed 2007), amongst others, have challenged the prominence of clan divisions in the Somali conflict. That said, clannism remains a useful tool and approach for analyzing the armed conflict in Somalia.

The above issues, frequently referred to as root causes of the armed conflict in Somalia, provide a brief overview of the conflict dynamics and variables mentioned frequently in analytical reports, media articles, and policy papers. From a methodological perspective, the above issues easily fall victim to causal reciprocity but for the sake of parsimony they provide useful insights into the complex dynamics of the armed conflict in Somalia.

2.3.2 Two Schools of Thought on the Somali Conflict and Academic Contribution

When studying armed conflict in Somalia, analyses have tended to be broadly split into two schools of thought[11]: one approach that sees clan as the primary unit of analysis and foundation for understanding armed conflict and social and political organizations in Somalia; an alternative approach that sees other factors and variables at play in addition to the concept of clan. The first view has been championed by the father of Somali anthropology, Ioan M. Lewis (1998, 1999, 2010) and his supporters (Latin and Samatar 1987, Jama 2007); the second by a group of scholars such as Brons (2001), Besteman (1999, Besteman and Cassanelli 2004), Cassanelli (1982), Luling (2006), and Kapteijns (2011). Major critics of Lewis, such as Kapteijns, argue that "a substantial body of scholarship has documented that Somali society and Somali

33

sociopolitical organization in the past cannot be reduced to either narrow or broad constructions of clanship" (Kapteijns 2011:4) or to simply refer to violence in Somalia as "clan violence" (Kapteijns 2011:12).

On a geographical basis, one can argue that Lewis' approach is predominantly oriented towards sociopolitical dynamics of the northern clans whose social and economic livelihoods are primarily based on pastoralism. On the other hand, sedentary communities in south central Somalia along the two main rivers that cut across the region, including fishing communities along the coast, historically had different social and political structures in their communities with social norms of "clan" differing from their pastoralist peers (Besteman 1999, Besteman and Cassanelli 2004, Dracopoli 1914).

Despite the scholarly challenges towards Lewis' emphasis on clan, realpolitik in Somalia has embraced it when convenient. The "4.5 formula" has been numerously applied to the national political peacemaking process in Somalia since the state collapsed in 1991. The formula splits state power, such as parliamentary seats and ministerial posts, into the four major clan families of the Hawiye, Darod, Dir, Rahanweyn, with minority clans receiving half the number. It has also been used in mediation processes for selecting representatives and even for hiring national staff by international NGOs.

The 4.5 formula "appears to have originated at the Nationalities Institute in Addis from discussions on ethnic federalism in the 1980s" and was first adopted at the 1996 Sodere peace conference (Bradbury 2009:17). Separately, according to Menkhaus (2010:348), the "principle of rough clan proportionality [based on the 4.5 formula] has been in existence since the first government was formed in 1960 and is consistently used as one of a number of Somali yardsticks to judge the legitimacy of a national-level meeting or government. The specific 4.5 formula was first put into practice at the Arta peace talks in 2000." However, when political processes are locally driven, different types of clan representation formulas are applied based on perceived clan numbers, economic power, and clan strength. Furthermore, the role of clan elders, religious leaders, warlords, and cross-border alliances also come into play in various forms and levels affecting the distribution of political power and representation. The influence of clan elders, seen as the guardians and representatives of their respective clans during peace processes, may vary from region to district and the 4.5 formula can both empower and disempower them depending on the context.[12]

With social, political, economical, security, and humanitarian factors all at play simultaneously, Lewis' paradigm becomes epistemologically attractive for understanding the complex dynamics in Somalia and provides policy makers and pundits parsimonious narratives, especially when one is not able to visit Somalia due to security constraints. But with researchers from various disciplines, albeit a very small group, slowly conducting more fieldwork in south central Somalia since the state collapsed, Lewis' paradigm is increasingly facing challenges based on new and different research approaches.

My own research is one example. It uses detailed quantitative analysis related to violence for the first time and includes extensive fieldwork carried out in Mogadishu over nearly two years to study the armed conflict. It challenges Lewis' "epistemological prominence" (Kapteijns 2011:5) but at the same time paradoxically uses it to deconstruct local dynamics qualitatively. In short, the research inquiry presented in this discourse can be seen to use both paradigms: the quantitative approach attempts to challenge Lewis' epistemological prominence using inferential statistics while the qualitative approach utilizes the "clan paradigm" at times to decipher issues that are quantitatively unexplainable.

In terms of the contribution to Somali studies, with the exception of Mogadishu, four out of the five cities have not been researched from a scholastic perspective. For Mogadishu there have been a series of studies. Hansen (2007) and Marchal (2002&2011) have led the research in regard to Mogadishu, albeit with a focus on economic issues. Saferworld [13] (2012) and the Danish Refuge Council and UNICEF (Bryld and Kamau 2012) have also produced analytical pieces based on qualitative and quantitative approaches with the aim of providing a "snapshot" and mapping of the situation and context in Mogadishu. The National Democratic Institute for International Affairs conducted two qualitative opinion research polls in 2010 and 2011 focusing on citizen attitudes about peace, governance, and the future government (Levy 2010&2011). The United Nations and African Union conducted a mapping exercise of key stakeholders and actors for Mogadishu in 2012, however the findings were never made public. Security reports produced by DSS, which are not publicly accessible and are shared with United Nations staff and the diplomatic corps, are of an anecdotal nature and aim to provide details related to security incidents and trends.

In regard to the other cities, Interpeace carried out extensive "peace mapping" studies focusing on local peacemaking and mediation efforts (2008a & 2008b & 2008c & 2009, Bradbury 2009) and Bradbury and Healy (2010) collected a series of articles regarding the different actors involved in various Somali peace processes. Different United Nations entities have also conducted research at the national level on specific thematic issues such as health, education, sexual violence, and IDPs (Carr-Hill and Ondijo 2011, Paul 2012, UNHCR 2011, UNICEF 2006) covering the different five cities and regions. However none of these reports and assessments has ever looked into dynamics and variables related to social capital or have attempted to conduct a full analysis of violence and armed conflict.[14]

The only detailed conflict analysis in regard to the five cities were the conflict analysis reports produced by Saferworld consultants on the request of UNDP to substantiate the UNDP baseline study. Therefore, an inquiry into the social relations in the area of peace and conflict for these five cities will provide substantive insight into the overarching dynamics that previous analysts and researchers may have overlooked.

2.4 Social Capital in Somalia

For this research inquiry, social capital is treated as a mental resource which is utilized at the micro-level for interpersonal interactions within the community. A conscious effort is made to analyze social capital at the local-level (micro-level) to highlight the dynamism of these interpersonal exchanges versus the national level which are based on impersonal relations.[15] For Somalia, where variances of armed conflict exist between regions, social capital needs to be analyzed at the regional level versus national level to identify these important dynamics[16]. This approach allows the research inquiry to investigate the pockets of peace and violence. This section introduces the theory related to bonding, bridging, and linking social capital used for the purpose of the research inquiry.

2.4.1 Bonding and Bridging Social Capital – The Independent Variable

While studying armed conflict and social capital, it is crucial to differentiate between bonding and bridging social capital[17]. However clearly differentiating between bonding and bridging (and linking) social capital presents challenges. Furthermore, as will be highlighted later, analyzing bonding social capital has its own complications and suffers from a lack of clarity due to the issue of scalability and the level the analysis is conducted at[18]. With this caveat in mind, bonding and bridging social capital are used for the research inquiry.

Based on a variety of proxies, social capital for the quantitative approach is measured by using data from surveys and questionnaires. The answers to the questionnaires and surveys are interpreted as ordinal data to represent the various proxies related to social capital. For the qualitative approach, social capital is analyzed using secondary literature, focus group discussions, interviews, and a small-n survey.

The analytical framework used incorporates the models presented by Bhavnani and Backer (2007) in *Social Capital and Political Violence in Sub-Saharan Africa* and the World Bank's *Integrated Questionnaire for the Measurement of Social Capital* (Woolcock 2004). Bhavnani and Backer's model (figure 2.1) consists of five distinct dimensions related to social capital: associational membership, civic engagement, trust, social cohesion, and equality (2007:5). Armed conflict, the dependent variable, is represented as a function of these five dimensions of social capital and a standard set of socio-demographic factors are included as controls. In total there are six explanatory variables as seen on the left side of figure 2.

Five dimensions of social capital
Associational Membership
Civic Engagement
Socio-Demographic + Trust → Armed conflict
Attributes
Social Cohesion
Equality

Figure 2. Bhavnani and Backer's five dimensions of social capital, plus a standard set of socio-demographic attributes that are included as controls (2007:6)

For the analytical framework I borrow questions used by Bhavnani and Backer to measure only three social capital proxies—associational membership, trust, and social cohesion—and armed conflict (political violence as stipulated by Bhavnani and Backer), which originate from surveys of the *Round Two Afrobarometer Survey* (Afrobarometer 2002). However, limiting the survey to the questions used by Bhavnani and Backer leads to significant deficiencies when trying to measure bridging and bonding social capital in detail when using just their proxies.

For example, the proxy of associational membership is used by Bhavnani and Backer to measure both bonding and bridging social capital. Associational membership is differentiated by four categories. First, religious membership is used to represent bonding social capital with three other categories of organizations used to measure bridging social capital: union and farmers' associations; professional and business associations; and community development and self-help associations (2007:7). In my view, these rough categorizations of associations inaccurately represent bridging and bonding social capital as proxies. They lack robustness and make the proxies vulnerable to different interpretations. Bhavnani and Backer even admit in a footnote that the three types of organizations measuring bridging capital "could obviously be homogenous in other respects" and also portray bonding social capital characteristics (2007:7). Therefore additional independent variables are necessary to strengthen their framework to clearly distinguish the concepts of bonding and bridging social capital to make the analytical framework robust. With additional variables and questions added to their framework, the variances in the different types of social capital can be further distinguished.

The supplementary variables are based on the theoretical framework of the six dimensions introduced in the World Bank's *Integrated Questionnaire for the Measurement of Social Capital* (Woolcock 2004:5). The six dimensions introduced consist of: groups and networks; trust and solidarity; collective action and cooperation; information and communication; social cohesion and inclusion; and empowerment and political action. Despite the Bank's questionnaire overlapping with Bhavnani and Backer's theoretical framework, it provides additional proxies to clearly distinguish bridging and bonding social capital. Of the six dimensions used by the Bank, I use the dimensions of groups and networks, trust and solidarity, and social cohesion and inclusion.

In the process of attempting to quantify bridging and bonding social capital clearly, we come upon the issue of Somali identity. Here, proxies to distinguish between "them" and "us" are based on the useful theory by Sacks (1992) which makes the distinction between *"identity categories"* and *"category sets"* (Silverman 1998:74). "Identity categories are the group labels that people use to define who they are... Category sets, by contrast, are the broad axes of social division into which these categories can be sorted. They include religion, race, tribe, nationality, region, and language" (Posner 2005:15). The category sets used for analysis are, *inter alia*, clan, occupation, residence status, education level, and region of origin.

Regarding identity, clannism in the Somali context and academic discourse is seen as the main category set that Somalis readily use to differentiate themselves. The small-n questionnaire will analyze clannism in Somali society to see whether and how significant this category set is. The other category sets will also be analyzed to identify their significance in relationship to violence and armed conflict. By using this systematic process of identification based on Sacks, Posner, and the theoretical framework of Bhavnani and Backer, I attempt to make clear quantitative descriptions to highlight the cleavages and social networks that exist in Somalia.

But how to make a clear distinction between the different clans when clan identity is seen as an extremely fluid, situation bound, and at times an ad hoc arrangement? The issue of clan identity needs to be looked at in detail with its relationship to the different social capital proxies. Clannism is quantitatively analyzed and distinguished by asking questions about clan identity but also using proxies to create predictor variables to distinguish bridging and bonding social capital. Besides asking straightforward questions about clan identity, questions also investigate how Somalis see themselves in various situations relative to others and the degree of interaction with different clan members. By asking Somalis about their affiliations and actual interaction with their own clan and members of different clans, insight into bridging and bonding social capital can be determined not only through perception but also through cognition.

2.4.2 Linking Social Capital—The Other Independent Variable

In addition to bonding and bridging social capital, linking social capital is also used to further analyze armed conflict and go beyond the paradigm of horizontal inclusive and exclusive social networks. Where bridging social capital is essentially horizontal "(that is, connecting people with more or less equal social standing), linking social capital is more vertical, connecting people to key political (and other) resources and economic institutions—that is, across power differentials" (Woolcock 2004:4).

While literature on linking social capital focuses mainly on vertical relationships and networks with somebody in a position of higher authority—who can assist with access to private or public goods that are restricted—or higher economic status, I also look at the leadership positions in the community that may not have authority for enforcing decisions or providing economic goods. The research inquiry attempts to take into account that people with enforcement authority and sanctioning power, as seen in exclusive vertical networks between warlords and selected parts of the community, may have *hard power* but not necessarily have legitimate leadership roles within the broader community. On the other hand, people with a leadership role in the broader community—such as clan elders, civil society organization leaders, working professionals, religious authorities, teachers, and women group leaders—may lack economic status (to provide public or private goods) and enforcement authority[19] but instead have *soft power* and *legitimacy* within the wider community. This includes goodwill and trust from the community and thereby has "far greater potential to promote socialization and social cohesion" (Paffenholz 2010:429). In terms of inclusiveness, vertical relationships based on soft power tend to be more inclusive while relationships based on hard power are increasingly exclusive.

By making a clear distinction between linking social capital that is based on hard or soft power (exclusive and inclusive networks respectively), a demarcation between *elite* and *mass based civic relations* can also be established. Mass based civic associations revolve around soft power and have a following based on leadership qualities, trust, and legitimacy. For example, a clan elder in Somalia historically would become a leader if he was a talented poet or a religious expert and not simply because of his financial wealth and military power (1977:37).[20] Access to clan elders is mass based, that is any male and female will be allowed to seek consultation and advice from the clan elder.[21] Oppositely, elite based civic relations are exclusive consisting of hard power and sanctioning mechanisms. This consists of individuals with relationships to others in higher authority who can assist access to private or public goods and who are not accessible to everyone. Membership and access to these elite based civic relations are restricted and limited to only members of a particular group or community.[22]

Vertical relationships for connecting people to resources

Elite based civic relations—*exclusive* structures consisting of *hard power*/enforcement

---
Vertical leadership for connecting with people in community leadership positions
---

Mass based civic relations—*inclusive* structures consisting of *soft power*/non-enforcement

Figure 3. Linking social capital consisting of two sub-categories: hard and soft linking social capital

In sum, soft linking social capital will represent vertical civic relations that are mass based, lacking sanctioning power, and are inclusive relying on soft power. Hard linking social capital will represent elite based civic relations that are exclusive and have sanctioning power (hard power) from above.

In terms of the data collection, linking social capital is qualitatively analyzed by inquiring the identity of the leadership in the community, the ability of the leadership to mobilize the community, and the leadership's roles in the community. The small-n survey will specifically inquire whether people in higher political and economical authority (businessmen, political leaders, warlords and military persons) have leadership roles in the community. It will also look at the performing roles of community leaders.

Quantitatively, from the UNDP baseline data, trust is used as the main proxy for analyzing linking social capital. It looks at trust within the community towards clan and community leaders, religious leaders, and police in responding to violence and crime. Specifically, trust in clan and community leaders and police represent hard linking social capital while trust in religious leaders is representative of soft linking social capital. Clan membership and frequency of clan disputes are also used as proxies for hard linking social capital.

Although leadership by clan elders was earlier referred to as possessing soft power, for the quantitative analysis the issue of trust towards clan and community elders is treated as *possessing hard power* as the UNDP baseline study specifically asks respondents: "what is the level of trust you have towards clan/community elders in responding to violence and crime?" The question assumes elders have the capacity to respond to violence and crime, which would require hard power and sanctioning mechanisms.

The use of police, at first, to analyze linking social capital seems an unnatural fit as the police are the most visible representation of the state and seem unrelated to civic associations. However, in the case of Somalia, the police are not simply part of the state apparatus but may represent personal vested interests of selective groups within the community, similar to a "civil militia", and therefore can be used to analyze social capital in a "civil capacity" and not simply as a state function.[23]

For the quantitative analysis, the level of trust towards the police in responding to violence and crime represents two proxies related to social capital: bridging social capital and hard linking social capital. This is because the police in Somalia have multifaceted characteristics related to social capital and are not treated the same as police in liberal democracies; in one sense, from a utility perspective, they are the interface between the state and the community; in another, as individuals, they bridge different communities together; and as a group they represent hard power to coerce and apply sanctions. By treating the police as an armed group, irrespective of legitimacy, the police can be used to provide insight into hard linking and bridging social capital. However, because the status of the police is ambiguous, the predictive power tends to be weaker for this proxy.[24]

The concepts of hard and soft expand the mainstream definitions of linking social capital. Applying these new concepts in a complex armed conflict setting like Somalia provides both challenges and opportunities for the research inquiry. On the downside, the applicability of the concept is limited to certain constraints, such as difficulty in measurement and interpretation; on the upside, it provides further detailed analysis of vertical relationships. With that caveat in mind, hypotheses related to hard and soft linking capital are established including theoretical predictions related to the five cities.

2.5 Armed Conflict in Somalia

The term armed conflict has multiple definitions and has been analyzed in numerous settings ranging from inter-state and intra-state conflict, proxy wars, terrorism, organized crime, gang warfare, and social conflict. In the Somali context, "the distinction between criminal violence and acts of war was difficult to make" (Menkhaus 2007:77). That said, and as mentioned in chapter one, the research here concentrates on violence being used outside of the immediate family, therefore excluding domestic violence, and focuses on violence using small arms and light weapons (SALW), including knives and machetes, with the end purpose to inflict bodily harm.

Differentiating and recording violence in the Somali context between various actors has been conducted by security analysts, think-tanks, and organizations such as the United Nations Department of Security and Safety (DSS), and the Armed Conflict Location and Event Dataset (ACLED). During the time of research, DSS categorized incidents as armed conflict, terrorism, crime, and civil unrest in general terms and had a further 40 sub-categories. However, the DSS incident tracker data is not publicly available. ACLED, whose data is publicly available, differentiates incidents into eight types of events.

For the purpose of this research, various data sources are used to qualitatively and quantitatively compare the trends of armed conflict in the five cities. The ACLED data, UNDP baseline study, and UNSOA opinion surveys are used to quantify the degree of armed conflict and violence in each city. Qualitatively, the surveys administrated during my fieldwork in focus group discussion settings are used. By combining various data sets, armed conflict variances can be measured amongst the five cities.

2.5.1 Armed Conflict – The Dependent Variable

With a wide range of definitions and methods to categorize and measure armed conflict, violence using SALW is seen as dichotomous for the research inquiry and this provides a baseline to measure variances. Incidents are either violent or non-violent and this differentiation allows various types of violence to be accounted for. Despite some researches like Menkhaus (2007) differentiating between armed conflict and violent crime, I treat violent crime as part of armed conflict for the analysis. Furthermore, I do not distinguish between war and armed conflict based on the intensity levels of violence as stipulated by the Uppsala Conflict Data Program [25] where armed conflict is defined as at least 25 but less than 1,000 battle-related deaths per year and war is defined as having at least 1,000 battle-related deaths per year (Paffenholz 2010:403).

In terms of analyzing armed conflict qualitatively, this is measured by looking at violence and uses questions from Bhavnani and Backer (2007)—who applied data from the *Round Two of the Afrobarometer Survey*—and the World Bank questionnaire (Woolcock 2004). For the purpose of this study, the respondents are asked whether they agree that the use of violence is never justified in Somali politics. They are also asked whether they have ever experienced political violence and if in the past twelve months they were the victim of a violent crime. Importantly, respondents were not asked whether they had ever used force or violence for a political cause as pilot tests showed that respondents either refused to answer this question or overwhelmingly answered negatively[26].

Social cohesion and inclusion are the dimensions taken from the World Bank questionnaire to investigate the potential of conflict in a community. The Bank's questionnaire sees the "presence of conflict in a community or in a larger area is often an indicator of the lack of trust or lack of appropriate structural social capital to resolve conflicts, or both" (Woolcock 2004:13). Despite the Bank's questionnaire treating the presence of conflict as an independent proxy for social capital, I use eight questions from the Bank's survey (questions 5.16 to 5.21) to analyze the relationship between social capital and armed conflict (Woolcock 2004:37). By combining both questions from the Afrobarometer and World Bank, the research looks at possible causal relationships in detail.

In addition to the variables mentioned above, the following questions are also asked to analyze violence in the context of armed conflict:

> ➤ Scholars argue that the clan system is the cause of conflict. Would you agree with this view?
> ➤ How often do the following cause violence in your community? Differences in clan; differences in landholdings; economic differences; differences between diaspora and non-diaspora; differences in political party affiliations; differences in religious views (e.g. fundamentalism, liberalism).

In regard to quantitatively analyzing armed conflict, various questions from the large-n surveys are used to produce a statistical model to measure the relationship between the outcome and predictor variables. The questions used to measure armed conflict are elaborated in detail in the following chapter.

Importantly, I analyze armed conflict at the city level assuming there is no spillover effect of violence between cities. This approach makes the analysis regarding armed conflict increasingly manageable. In reality, this assumption is not farfetched and is justified by the large physical distances between the five cities with the two closest cities, Burao and Las Anod, being at least a six-hour drive by car (250 kilometers) separated by large areas of semi-desert terrain. Mogadishu, seen as having the highest levels of armed conflict, is over 700 kilometers from Galkayo. In addition the clan composition, political dynamics, and stateness of each city is unique (as will be seen in chapter three and four). Even media reports of violence or peace do not instigate or mitigate violence between the five cities as far as I can recall. Therefore, I treat armed conflict as being localized in each of the five cities and do not analyze linkages of armed conflict in one city to another.

2.6 The Analytical Framework

This section introduces the analytical framework in detail and the main proxies used to analyze social capital. It touches upon civil society and customary law, as both have a crosscutting effect on the various forms of social capital. The section also provides an overview of the socio-demographic attributes of the samples for both the quantitative and qualitative data and touches upon the statistical approach applied.

2.6.1 Analyzing Social Capital and Armed Conflict

Out of the many proxies that are used in social capital analysis, I choose the following six proxies for the analytical framework for both the quantitative and qualitative research inquiry: groups and group networks; trust; social cohesion and inclusion; personal networks; identity; and community leadership. The first four proxies come from the questionnaire of Bhavnani and Backer and the World Bank.

Each proxy is multifaceted and can be used to analyze the various types of social capital. For example, trust can be used to look at bridging, bonding and linking social capital simultaneously. The last two proxies, identity and community leadership, respectively look at analyzing the category set of clannism (treated as a proxy for bonding social capital) and linking social capital in detail. Armed conflict, the dependent variable, looks at how violence varies in the five cities. The analytical framework used throughout the research inquiry is shown below in figure 4.

Groups and Group Networks

Personal Networks

Socio-Demographic + Trust   → Armed conflict
Attributes

Social Cohesion & Inclusion

Identity

Community Leadership

Figure 4. Analytical framework used to analyze social capital and armed conflict in Somalia

For the quantitative approach, detailed analyses of the data sets and variables are undertaken to identify proxies in order to replicate the analytical framework. This is achieved by reviewing the questions and answers of the large-n surveys (the UNDP baseline study and UNSOA opinion polls) and choosing variables that represent the different types of social capital. Each individual proxy may represent several types of social capital depending on the relevant data available. Logistic regression is then conducted with armed conflict as the outcome variable. Due to the different structures and objectives of the two surveys, different data are used as proxies to apply the above analytical framework. The proxies and data selected for the quantitative analysis are elaborated in the next chapter.

In terms of applying the analytical framework qualitatively, a tailored questionnaire (the small-n survey) was developed for focus group discussions in the five cities. The questionnaire replicated the analytical model and was divided into the following eight parts: profile; belonging (identity); groups and group networks; personal networks; community leadership; trust; social cohesion and inclusion; and armed conflict. As previously mentioned, questions were taken from multiple sources, such as the World Bank's inquiry questionnaire and Afrobarometer survey, while others were developed primarily for the research inquiry to take into consideration important factors from the

Somalia context, such as the unique role of civil society, associational relationships and networks, and customary law. The following sections set out to explain how these factors—civil society, associational relationships, and customary law—are addressed within the analytical framework for the qualitative approach.

Finally, I am mindful that the direction of causality can be reversed with armed conflict influencing the social capital proxies. Throughout, the research inquiry takes into consideration this possibility and the qualitative approach, through detailed case studies of the five cities, allows the issue of reverse causality to be addressed.

2.6.2 Civil Society – Associational Relationships and Networks

This section does not go into the extensive literature related to civil society in conflict and post-conflict settings (Posner 2004, Paffenholz 2006). Neither does it delve into the academic discourses and debates surrounding the successes and failures of peacebuilding and statebuilding. Instead it focuses on the benefits and challenges of using civil society in the context of armed conflict and peacebuilding. For the purpose of the research inquiry, it applies the concepts of peacebuilding which over the years have been consolidated[27]. The research focuses on "track two" and "track three" peacebuilding where non-state actors are the main agents. Here, track two actors are organized civil society, such as unions, associations; while track three is the grassroots level groups which include local NGOs and community self-help groups (Paffenholz and Spurk 2006, UNDP 2012).

Since the collapse of the state in 1991, there has been a proliferation of civil society organizations (CSOs) in Somalia (Menkhaus et al 2010:331)[28]. Who and what is a CSO is debatable in the Somali context and Somalia is not short of controversies related to these actors who have filled in the role of the state (Menkhaus et al 2010:325). In short, CSOs can either (intentionally or unintentionally) contribute or mitigate conflict in Somalia. This can happen in a variety of ways, for example with CSOs intentionally or unintentionally reinforcing social cleavages, undermining or replacing formal gover-nance institutions, and monopolizing civic space in the community.

It is necessary to consider the unique paradigm that Somali CSOs operate in, that of statelessness and/or in an armed conflict setting, and that comparisons between CSOs as mentioned by Putnam in a non-war setting need to be treated differently. In Somalia, CSOs can readily be targets of the armed conflict, such as assassinations of the organizations' members, a situation that CSOs for example in Japan will not have to worry about. CSOs in Somalia, therefore, operate in a unique environment compared to their counterparts that are mentioned in the literature of Putnam (2002) and Lin (2002). Menkhaus et al highlight how CSOs in Somalia have the capacity "to protect themselves from threats and violence" and that the "typical workday of a civil leader in Mogadishu is devoted to tasks related to risk management" in ensuring the CSO's security (2010:347).

Outside of the Somali context, there is also no agreed definition regarding civil society or CSOs (Spurk 2010:3). However in terms of the roles from a peacebuilding perspective, civil society has been a key player in "support of peacebuilding, both during and after armed conflict... Put simply peacebuilding aims at preventing and managing armed conflict and at sustaining peace after large-scaled organized violence has ended" (Paffenholz 2010: viii). Paffenholz et al argue that civil society is seen as crucial in the peacebuilding context however the nexus between civil society and peacebuilding has been under-researched (2010: vii).

The development and emergence of CSOs is another area of interest and importance. The conventional thinking is that during an armed conflict the environment for CSO development is not benign (Forster and Mattner 2006). Furthermore, "trust disappears, and social capital beyond family, clan, or ethnic affiliation is destroyed" (Spurk 2010:18). Paffenholz notes that "the case of Somalia is a sad example of how extreme levels of violence become the biggest obstacle to civil society activities. The post-2006 warfare... made it almost impossible for most local NGOs to operate at all" (2010:402). Contradictively, she states that the absence of the state "favored various forms of civil society activism, in particular the delivery of basic services, such as education and health care" (2010:409). Spurk notes the paradox nature of state failure in Somalia which allowed civil society to actually flourish and that "disruptions to predatory or authoritarian states may help civil society" emerge (2010:4). My findings also show that the failure of the state and ongoing armed conflict created a unique opportunity for civil society to flourish in Somalia, even in the conflict-ridden city of Mogadishu. Counter-intuitively, the data analysis shows that regions in Somalia with high-levels of armed conflict are able to also have high levels of civil society activity compared to stable areas.

But what is civil society's role in peacebuilding? Paffenholz and Spurk present seven functions of civil society's peacebuilding functions: protection; monitoring; advocacy and public communication; in-group socialization; social cohesion; intermediation and facilitation; and service delivery (2010:67). Paffenholz (2009:197) notes that in-group socialization and social cohesion are crucial components for building social capital. Based on their framework, I view in-group socialization and social cohesion as the two most relevant functions of civil society in the context of armed conflict. Here, in-group socialization refers to socialization that "takes place only within groups and not between or among former adversary groups" while social cohesion focuses on "bridging ties across adversarial groups" (2010:70-72).

In the Somali context, Menkhaus et al argue that "Somali civil society has not been able to build adequate bridges across clan, regional, and ideological divides" (2010:341). He points out that CSOs tend to fall into four types: civic actors that reinforce social cleavages; "civic groups that try to build broader social cohesion but simply face too many obstacles"; civic actors "that have in fact succeeded in building genuine social cohesion at the national level"; and "civil society movements that succeed in building bridges that help overcome one social divide but that simultaneously contribute to the worsening of another social divide", such as Islamist movements (2010a:341). He concludes that "Somali civil society groups have had mixed success transcending clan, regional, and ideological divisions in the country, with certain types of social movements, networks, and organizations (such as business partnerships) better suited to bridging these divisions than others" (2010a:346). These four types of CSOs in Somalia challenge the conventional thinking of Putnam who argues that "participation in civil society is an act of building social capital" (Paffenholz et al 2010:414).

Considering the challenges and various roles of civil society, the analytical framework attempts to clarify how CSOs contribute to social capital being developed. Participants in focus group discussions are asked about their membership in groups and group networks. It attempts to analyze whether these groups have bridging or bonding social capital and looks at characteristics related to linking social capital based on the following questions:

> ➤ Are some members of the group richer or poorer than others, or do they all have mostly the same income level?
> ➤ Do you belong to any groups that consist of different clan members?
> ➤ Would you say that there is strong pressure in the group for members to obey the group's decisions?

Paffenholz et al highlight that "the higher the level of violence, the more the space for civil society is reduced; violence destroys social networks and organizations" (2010:409). The data from the focus group discussions and UNDP baseline study provides insight into whether the conventional literature arguing that civil society (and CSOs) development is indeed impeded by armed conflict. Correlations of the large-n data are used and interviews from the five cities reveal the challenges for CSOs.

Furthermore, the issue of causality needs to be looked at when considering the existence of civil society in an armed conflict setting. Chapman raises this important question: does "vibrant civic life make societies more peaceful" (2009:159)? Put succinctly, when discussing the issues of endogeneity, "one must determine whether civic institutions contribute to peace or are caused by peace" (Chapman 2009:161). Chapman points out that "individual attitudes and participation in civic institutions may be endogenous and without correcting for this endogeneity it is possible to falsely conclude that civic institutions play a large role in socializing their members to reject political violence, leading to more peaceful societies" (2009:166). Using a two-stage least squares approach to analyze statistical data, Chapman (2008:522) shows that membership in civic associations may be driven much more by pre-existing attitudes and socio-demographic factors and "the presence of vibrant social capital may be a product, not the cause, of peace and prosperity" (2009:168). In short, he argues, "it may be the case that civic institutions are simply created by individuals with characteristics that predispose them to reject political violence" (2008:528).

2.6.3 Customary Law – Xeer[29]

According to the Federal Republic of Somalia Ministry of Justice, Religious Affairs, Constitution, Federal and Reconciliation (2013:1), three parallel legal systems exist in Somalia:

> ➢ Magistrate Court – served as the formal mechanism for the administration of the rule of law by the Government of Somalia
> ➢ Aqil "Chieftain" Court – covered traditional community conflicts such as inheritance and property right issues through the application of Xeer Somali
> ➢ Qadi Court – handed family issues through the application of Sharia law

Known as Xeerdhaqamed or Xeer Somali (xeer going forward), Somali customary law continues to be the justice system used even today (Menkhaus 1999, Ministry of Justice 2013:1). The objective and mechanism behind xeer is deterrence and retaliation respectively.

Based on principles of Sharia law, but not strictly following the teachings of Sharia, xeer is a non-written set of "tariffs" that describe the compensation in monetary terms and/or livestock or other assets required to settle damages from one-party to another. Damages can be related for a wide range of grievances such as death and injury (intentional and accidental), theft, loss, contractual defaults, inheritance, property, and divorce. At the community level, the tariff is usually set between clans who live locally and can be based on norms of reciprocity, historical grievances, and past conflicts. At the family and extended family level the same tariffs used by the community can be applied to settle grievances. However field research shows that xeer can "collapse", disappear, or become irrelevant under certain circumstances between communities. It can also be non-existent between two communities who reside locally. Alternatively, xeer can exist and be "operational" between two clans who may not reside locally.

Importantly xeer payments are flexible. Even though a wide amount of literature refers to the compensation for the death of a man as fixed at 100 camels and 50 camels for a woman, field research shows that the tariffs for death can vary. During my fieldwork, participants highlighted that the tariff of 100 camels for the death of man was only a guiding principle and that the circumstances and situation of the incident provided flexibility to the amount of compensation for the death. Customary law in Somalia is extremely flexible and has dynamically changed overtime to be pragmatic and useful to the current context.

Xeer, in the context of social capital, needs to be taken into consideration when analyzing the different proxies and has the potential to address issues related to omitted-variable bias. Although not the objective of this research, epistemologically, xeer also allows a structural approach to be applied into the analysis of social capital and armed conflict. Elaborated in detail later, xeer can contribute to all three types of social capital and this must be taken into consideration during the analysis. Attempts have been made with the focus group survey to touch upon the concept of xeer.

In terms of data collection, participants were asked if they belonged to a diya paying group. Diya is blood-money, the tariff for compensation. Based on membership of a diya paying group, one can have insight to the extent xeer is applied in a community. Xeer applicability can also be viewed through the large-n data in regard to the degree respondents chose to address incidents through clan elders (since clan elders prescribe xeer and determine diya payments). Detailed analysis, both qualitatively and quantitatively, will be conducted taking into consideration the important concept of xeer.

2.6.4 Socio-demographic Attributes of the Quantitative and Qualitative Approach

Samples were taken from five cities in Somalia: Burao in Somaliland, Bosaso in Puntland, Las Anod in the disputed area between Puntland and Somaliland, Galkayo in Puntland and Galmudug, and Mogadishu in south central Somalia. The choice for these five cities was based on the availability of the large-n data collected by UNDP for their baseline study on violence in 2009 and 2010. The five cities provide a useful diversification and contrast for comparison and importantly are cases where field research was feasible, albeit with huge security challenges, to collect the necessary data. The cities are interesting case studies based on historical, political, economical, cultural, and regional dynamics.

In terms of security constraints for personally conducting fieldwork in these cities, Mogadishu proved most challenging, followed by Galkayo, and Bosaso. During the time of research, an active offensive was being undertaken by the TFG and AMISOM against anti-government elements in Mogadishu. Galkayo was experiencing a series of kidnappings and Bosaso was recovering from a series of assassinations. It was not possible to visit Las Anod due to the political sensitivities and security constraints and instead an enumerator and research coordinator conducted the focus group discussion survey. Burao was the easiest city to conduct research in terms of security however the logistics to reach the city proved challenging due to seasonal flooding making roads impassable at certain times.

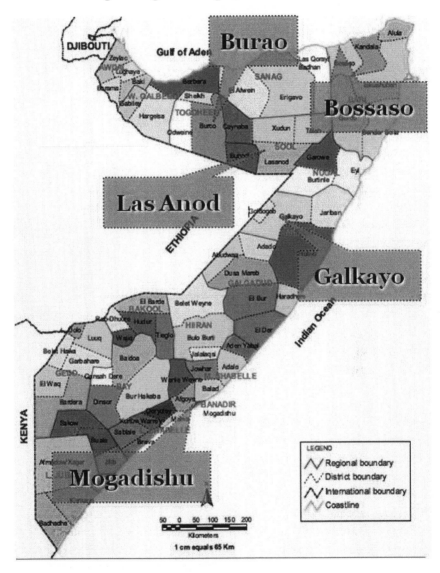

Map 1. Map of Somalia highlighting the five cities where the UNDP baseline study was conducted (courtesy of UNDP Somalia)

53

The participants for the small-n survey and focus group discussions were primarily a mixture of youth ranging from about 18 to 30 years old and also included members of the business community for Mogadishu. The small-n survey was pilot tested in Hargeisa and revised for ease of self-administration while trying to maintain academic rigor and value[30]. The method of self-administration of the questionnaire by the participants, under my supervision, was chosen to address the logistical and security challenges of conducting lengthy discussions in the security setting prevailing at that time. Simply put, the method of having participants fill out a questionnaire themselves had the best "cost effectiveness" to capture as much information on the research subject within the limited amount of time, which was usually three hours.

Based on experience working in Somalia, conducting a group workshop or intensive discussion in a structured format is usually effective and productive if it is kept under three hours. Gatherings usually take place in the mornings and need to finish before lunchtime prayers (based on the Islamic religion). Alternatively, interviewing in the afternoon from 15:00 is another option but this usually forces the discussions to be rushed since participants want to return to their homes before evening prayers or for security reasons. With the exception of Burao, where participants felt comfortable travelling during nighttime, the focus group discussions were timed to take into consideration participants' safety and security. In the process of arranging the logistics and meeting times for these discussions, this provided a useful insight and comparison regarding the security situation in the various cities.

Following an approach to maximize my time on the ground for research while taking into consideration the security constraints, the drawbacks to this approach are obvious. Based on the group discussions I had with participants, I was not able to meet on an individual basis for follow-up interviews. This was either because the security conditions did not permit it or simply because the logistics of "making it happen" were too challenging and financially costly. As an alternative, I would ask other Somalis the questions that I wanted to follow-up on. Other drawbacks to my approach in the field were the limited amount of time I had in each session, a maximum of three hours, and the selection of participants for the discussions.

The participants from the focus group discussions in Burao, Bosaso, Galkayo, and Las Anod mainly involved "youth" participants. With the definition of youth varying, and no universally accepted definition in place (UNDP 2012:5), I categorized youth in the age group until 25 years-old for the purpose of this research (and the statistical analysis). However participation in the focus groups targeted students intentionally and therefore included a wide range of ages. With the venue of the focus group discussions being within the universities in Burao, Bosaso, Las Anod, and Galkayo, participation was from enrolled students at the universities and students were chosen randomly from various faculties and departments. For the case of Mogadishu, participants were chosen by the research coordinator. For Burao and northern Galkayo, they also included youth NGO members and leaders.

There are several reasons university students and youth were used. First, to make the research feasible and to manage the security constraints and challenges on the ground. As mentioned previously, conducting fieldwork in Somalia consists of different security risk levels which can involve extremely fluid situations on the ground. For example in Galkayo and Mogadishu, kidnapping and assassination were rampant respectively. From earlier fieldwork in south central Somalia and Somaliland in 2004, I noticed that security on university campuses was generally adequate, allowing the researcher to visit and conduct work in a relative secure surrounding. In addition, targeting university students in urban settings increases the feasibility of the overall research as students tend to be located in central geographical locations, making them relatively accessible in large numbers at one time to achieve "economies of scale". A second reason is to maintain data sample conformity across the five cities. By using university students across the five cities, one is able to control certain variables such as age, educational background, and importantly clan make up. According to field research conducted in 2004, I was informed by local sources familiar with universities in Somalia that each city generally consisted of students from the specific region and clan. We could therefore expect the majority of students from Burao to originate from the Isaaq clan, the Darod clan in Bosaso and northern Galkayo, and the Hawiye clan in southern Galkayo. This clan concentration would therefore allow inter and intra-group networks to be looked at in detail.

University students also provide a detailed look into local affairs and represent social networks that reflect the realities of Somali society and politics at the grassroots level. With UNDP (2012:4) estimates accounting for 73 percent of the population as being under 29 years old, the youth population between 15 and 29 comprises around 27 percent of the total population (2.3 million). Based on this huge youth bulge, the youth in Somalia is the majority of the Somali population.[31]

One major criticism and bias that emerges from selecting university students is that they are a small elite group of individuals who are financially and socially better off than the majority of the population. Even though Somali university students are a minority in society, the networks students have are similar to the networks of the major actors who have influence in the Somali conflict and politics. For example, major stakeholders in the Somali politics are usually individuals with higher levels of education and wealthy backgrounds. Similar to university students, they are also a small elite group of individuals who do not represent the overall population but have influence on the overall political developments in Somalia. By choosing university students, they not only give a closer representation of the current leaders but are more likely to become and represent the future leaders of Somalia. History shows, since the colonization of Somalia, that they are better positioned in terms of influencing and having a major role in Somali politics in the future versus other actors such as the Somali nomad or farmer who makes up the majority of the population. Also, as victims of violence, university students and youth are more likely expected to be aware of the issues surrounding the armed conflict and the tensions within the community. By better understanding the Somali university student, new perspectives are expected to emerge regarding the armed conflict in Somalia.

As mentioned earlier, the focus group discussions in Mogadishu were supplemented with participation from the local business community. These were not the major business players conducting international trade and contracting companies that the United Nations would employ. Instead they were businesses who ran small shops and markets in Mogadishu and who did not speak any English. The purpose was to analyze the business community's social networks and relations in an environment that had experienced fierce combat and armed conflict.

Finally, the UNDP large-n data sample and UNSOA opinion poll data captures a wide representation within the five cities for the quantitative analysis. Through a detailed analysis of this representative data, the selection bias for primarily using youth and university students in the focus group discussions for the qualitative approach will be counterbalanced.

2.6.5 Statistical Analysis Method

The statistical analysis uses both descriptive and inferential statistics for the research inquiry. As the majority of the data is ordinal and categorical, Pearson's chi-square tests are used to look at the relationship between the various data. Cross-tabulations are first produced to analyze the different distributions between the five cities for proxies related to social capital. Correlations between the different proxies of social capital and the relationships between the social capital indicators and the dependent variable are analyzed using Spearman's Rho.

Logistic regression (multiple regression of a bivarate dependent variable) is used for analyzing the relationships and significance of the predictor variables onto the outcome variable. The logistic regression uses a "forced entry method" and will calculate odds-ratios (Exp (B)) and test for multicollinearity. Exp(B) is crucial to the interpretation of logistic regression and is an indicator of the change in odds resulting from a unit change in the predictor. Simply put, it highlights the effect of how a change in one variable affects another variable (Field 2005:225). Further details regarding the interpretation and variables of interest for the logistic regression are presented in chapter three.

Separately, discriminant function analysis [32] is used to see how discriminant function variates [33] allow groups of cases to be discriminated (Field 2005:729). The groups of cases are used to discriminate the five cities which are treated as the dependent variables. While the dependent variables used are the five cities, the independent variables are the social capital proxies and the armed conflict proxy (Field 2005:614). Simply put, discriminant analysis highlights the "uniqueness" of the five cities based on the social capital and armed conflict proxies.

2.7 Hypotheses

To recall, the research inquiry sets out to look at the issue of trust and social relations in the area of peace and conflict studies. Specifically, it looks at the relationships that exist between the six social capital proxies and armed conflict proxies at the aggregate level and at the city level to analyze the role of bridging, bonding, and linking social capital on armed conflict. The research inquiry attempts to answer the following questions based on the qualitative and quantitative data:

- ➢ Does social capital contribute to armed conflict or does it mitigate it, if so, how?
- ➢ Does armed conflict affect social capital, if so, how?
- ➢ What kinds of social capital—bonding, bridging, and linking—contribute to armed conflict and what types mitigate it?
- ➢ To what extent do the social capital proxies relate to peace and conflict?

To answer these questions, the following general hypotheses are proposed followed by theoretical predictions for the five cities separately.

2.7.1 Hypotheses on Social Capital and Armed Conflict

The following are the main hypotheses regarding the relationship between social capital and armed conflict.

- ➢ Hypothesis one: *Bridging social capital has a negative impact on armed conflict.*
- ➢ Hypothesis two: *Bonding social capital has a positive impact on armed conflict.*
- ➢ Hypothesis three: *Hard linking social capital has a positive impact on armed conflict.*
- ➢ Hypothesis four: *Soft linking social capital has a negative impact on armed conflict.*

The different social capital impacts on armed conflict are summarized in the following table. For example, a negative sign (-ve) for armed conflict versus bridging social capital (first column to the left in the table below) indicates bridging social capital having a negative impact on the likelihood of armed conflict occurring: when bridging social capital is high, the likelihood of armed conflict occurring will be low; when bridging social capital is low, the likelihood of armed conflict occurring will be high. Alternatively, a "+ve" symbol represents a positive impact on the likelihood of armed conflict occurring.

	Armed conflict vs. Bridging	Armed conflict vs. Bonding	Armed conflict vs. Hard Linking	Armed conflict vs. Soft Linking
Hypothesis	-ve	+ve	+ve	-ve

Table 1. Hypothesis regarding the relationship between social capital and armed

From the onset, it is important to make assumptions of the levels of armed conflict for the five cities. This is done before even looking at any quantitative data and is based on personal expert judgment from researching Somalia since 2004 and working as a United Nations professional officer on Somalia since 2008. The levels of armed violence for the five cities are assumed in the following order from highest to lowest:

1. Mogadishu
2. Las Anod
3. Galkayo
4. Bosaso
5. Burao

➢ Mogadishu has the highest levels of armed conflict.
➢ Burao has the lowest levels of armed conflict.

The hypotheses are tested by quantitatively analyzing the aggregated data for the five cities and then looking at the data separately for each city. Qualitatively, this would mean analyzing each city individually and comparing the four hypotheses with the findings of each city. This is achieved by extending the hypotheses into theoretical predictions, as highlighted in the next section.

In the social capital literature, as described earlier, bridging social capital are inclusive social networks and relations that promote social cohesion and trust across categorical sets. When bridges between various categorical sets exist, such as between different clans, a degree of symmetry is present thereby lowering the transaction costs for

59

engagement and negotiation. The opposite exists for bonding social capital, where socialization takes place only within the categorical set and social relations are exclusive leading to increased transactions costs for engagement and negotiation with adversary groups in an asymmetrical setting. In an armed conflict setting, bridging social capital creates a conducive environment to immediately mitigate the escalation of violence between two groups while bonding social capital contributes to suspicion and higher transaction costs between two parties because of the lack of regular communication and information exchange, thereby delaying conflicts being resolved[34].

While linking social capital is measured by using proxies that look at vertical social relationships, I argue that higher levels of hard linking social capital lead to an increased likelihood of violence as individuals with relationships to people in positions of authority are more likely to participate in armed conflict when instructed or pressured to. Reasons for participating in armed conflict due to such vertical social relations may include: maintaining patron-client relationships [35] ; financial pressure to follow a leader's orders; and maintaining one's access to public and private resources within the community. In addition, hard linking social capital consists of hard power enforcement mechanisms which can be used to coerce people through violent means. Hard power also seems to suggest a stronger amplifying effect for imposing the leader's wish onto others due to its sanctioning power.

On the other hand, soft linking social capital based on community leadership and legitimacy is less likely to lead to violence because economical incentives to follow orders and enforcement mechanisms are weak or lacking, making punishment for disobeying or applying sanctions difficult. With soft power in community leadership having a deficit of physical power to coerce people, orders to carry out violence are less likely to be observed. Also, community leadership involves mass based civic associations that are seen as being inclusive, having a wider variety of members, and optional therefore making it difficult for any hard power that exists in the relationships to be utilized for violent means. Furthermore, the desire of the leaders with soft power can be attenuated (or softened) through negotiations with various stakeholders.

2.7.2 Theoretical Predictions Related to the Cities
When analyzing social capital on a regional level, variances between regions are expected to be larger in Somalia which suffers from

different levels of chronic insecurity versus a country that has uniform levels of security. Based on the above four hypotheses, deductive reasoning is applied to develop theoretical predictions for the individual cities when looking at the three different types of social capital and variances in armed conflict. Based on the assumed levels of armed conflict for each city, the levels of social capital are worked backwards. The theoretical predictions are established on the assumption for armed conflict level being highest in Mogadishu and lowest in Burao. Using the above assumptions related to armed conflict levels and the four hypotheses, the following theoretical predictions are developed and highlight the variances of social capital by city.

> Prediction one: *Bosaso and Burao have relatively higher levels of bridging social capital versus Mogadishu, Galkayo, and Las Anod.*
> Prediction two: *Mogadishu, Galkayo, and Las Anod have relatively higher levels of bonding social capital versus Bosaso and Burao.*
> Prediction three: *Mogadishu has higher levels of hard linking social capital relative to the other four cities.*
> Prediction four: *Burao and Bosaso have higher levels of soft linking social capital relative to Mogadishu, Galkayo, and Las Anod.*

The above logical deductions are made based on the premise that Mogadishu has the lowest level of bridging social capital, high levels of bonding social capital, and high levels of hard linking social capital. Burao, alternatively, has the highest levels of bridging social capital and low levels of bonding social capital, and high levels of soft linking social capital. The theoretical predictions can be summarized for each city in the following table in terms of the individual social capital levels, which also include the assumed levels of armed conflict for the respective cities.

	Bridging (Prediction 1)	Bonding (Prediction 2)	Hard Linking (Prediction 3)	Soft Linking (Prediction 4)	Armed Conflict Level
Burao	H	L	L	H	L
Galkayo	L	H	L	L	H
Mogadishu	L	H	H	L	H
Las Anod	L	H	L	L	H
Bosaso	H	L	L	H	L

Table 2. Theoretical predictions for the five cities by type of social capital and assumed levels of armed conflict

To address the issue of causal ambiguity, the proxies in the analytical framework are analyzed in detail to grasp the underlying mechanisms. This process will also attempt to address possible omitted-variable biases. As mentioned earlier, the research inquiry will aim to provide answers and explanations into the relationship between social capital and armed conflict and address the direction of causality. It will also aim to answer the question of whether violence and armed conflict actually impedes civil society being developed as argued by Paffenholz et al (Paffenholz et al 2010:423, Spurk 2010:18).

2.7.3 Implications from the Results

Although not the primary objective of this research inquiry, policy implications and recommendations will be mentioned briefly based on the conclusions of the analysis. If the analysis supports the hypotheses, then the following consideration for policy makers can be made:

> *Somalia needs more bridging social capital; less bonding social capital; and less hard linking social capital.*

2.8 Limitations and Challenges to the Research Design

Conducting academic research in an insecure and challenging setting obviously has its limitations and challenges. But even with these limitations, academic research can provide interesting insights (Cohen and Arieli 2011). Since the armed conflict in Somalia prevents detailed qualitative fieldwork from being conducted (such as an ethnographic approach), analyses must therefore rely on available secondary and primary data that has been collected based on the prevailing security constraints. Applying a regional approach by studying five cities is a valid option to overcome the security constraints experienced and partially addresses the deficiencies of not being able to conduct detailed nationwide research.

In this respect I am mindful of the deficiencies related to the research design employed versus the results that detailed ethnographic fieldwork would produce. The limitations of using social capital theory are acknowledged throughout the research inquiry and applying social capital in "non-traditional" areas, such as armed conflict, immediately and rightfully exposes the inquiry to criticism. However, I intentionally focus on an approach that exclusively uses social capital theory and am conscious that there are many other factors and variables outside of the social capital arena that may mitigate and trigger armed conflict. While attempting to avoid becoming a hostage of criticism related to the social capital theory debate, I highlight the difficulties related to using social capital theory, especially in the areas of quantifying it.

As with any research based on empiricism, epistemological limitations exist in the analysis and theory building. Although the research design takes a dual-track approach to address the problem statement, that of a qualitative and quantitative approach, it does not encompass other epistemelogies such as critical theory or feminism. This is another area that researchers may want to consider in the context of sociology and social violence. Epistemological issues aside, the following limitations and challenges, some which have been already stated, are stated below:

> Finding appropriate measurements of social capital for the proxies used and measuring armed conflict (Chapman 2009:158, Halpern 2005:31, Lederman et al 2002);

> Using secondary data that was collected for a specific purpose and applying it to the analytical framework;

> Comparison of different large-n surveys conducted at different time periods;

> Analyzing data for Mogadishu that covers only six out of 16 districts[36];

> Identifying the direction of causality between social capital and armed conflict[37];

> Comparing fieldwork results of different time periods covering a span of two years;

> Not being able to visit Las Anod because of political sensitivities;

> Applying the findings to other cities and regions in Somalia;

> Conducting analysis that accurately reflects the relevant conflict and social variables in a dynamic armed conflict setting such as Mogadishu;

> Sample biases for the focus group discussions which targeted only urban youth.

As the large-n surveys were conducted at different times (between 2009 to 2013), the research inquiry needs to take into consideration the context and developments during these periods. For example, Mogadishu saw major political developments and security improvements during the period from 2010 to 2012. In this context using secondary data for the analytical framework requires identifying variables that "best fit" the social capital proxies. Although not a perfect fit, the descriptive analysis using these variables provides interesting insight into the social and conflict dynamics in the five cities.

In terms of primary data collection, I was able to visit four out of the five cities with the exception of Las Anod. Although wanting to visit Las Anod in my capacity as a researcher, international United Nations staff at the time of field research was prohibited from visiting the city because of the associated political sensitivities. Located in the disputed area between Somaliland and Puntland, security forces from Somaliland occupied the city while the majority of residents belonged to clans affiliated to Puntland. Visits by international United Nations staff were extremely rare, and my affiliation to the United Nations Political Office for Somalia, considered a highly political body of the United Nations, made any visit extremely difficult. If I had visited in my capacity privately, I would have had to waive all my privileges and immunities as an international civil servant which I personally found as too risky under the prevailing circumstances.

Despite the limitations and challenges related to addressing the problem statement, the research inquiry attempts to look at possible answers and provide further insight into the relationship between social capital and armed conflict in Somalia and hopes that this thesis provides a launch pad for other researchers.

Notes

1   For example, there is major disagreement between researchers as to whether the form of relationships between relative strangers is to be considered as social capital (Halpern 2005:14).
2   The objective is not to provide an exhaustive historical background on the history of Somalia. The aim is to provide a succinct background for readers not familiar with Somali history. There are numerous books and articles related to the history and process of state formation in Somalia. Elmi (2010), Harper (2012), and Lewis (2010) provide contemporary accounts. Bradbury (2008) provides a comprehensive history regarding Somaliland's emergence and Mahadallah (2008a) looks at the rise of Somali nationalism. This section is based primarily on material used from my Master's dissertation (Matsukawa 2006).
3   I am aware that Somali "culture" consists more than the northern pastoralists.

The point made here is that non-Somalis typically associate Somali "culture" with the northern nomads.

4   To this day the Darod clan, who were supporters of the Barre government, see themselves as having been expelled from Mogadishu while the Hawiye clan, who are most likely the majority of residents in Mogadishu following the collapse of the Barre government, see the Darod clan as having simply returned to their traditional clan territory in northern Somalia.

5   For a summary and overview on the Djibouti peace process, Kasaija (2010) provides a comprehensive account of events between 2008 and 2009.

6   In the early morning of 6 August 2011, Al Shabaab withdrew from the remaining parts of Mogadishu, claiming it was a tactical retreat. During the night of 5 August, there was a more than usual amount of gunfire and drone movement in the city which prompted speculation of an offensive by AMISOM and TFG troops (Fieldwork: 2 to 6 August 2011, Mogadishu). I was present in Mogadishu during that day and the local population openly celebrated the withdrawal of Al Shabaab.

7   Interview: FAO consultant 5 April 2013, Bosaso.

8   Fighting between different groups in Kismayo in June 2013 representing different "presidents" of Jubaland reiterates the challenges between statebuilding and peacebuilding.

9   Although no precise data exists, the number of casualties from the armed conflict in south central Somalia seems to have increased drastically from when I first visited Mogadishu in 2004 versus February 2014. Simply, the number of actors on the ground who possess lethal force have increased dramatically.

10   It must be noted that clans involved in agricultural production may have less of an individualistic mentality versus pastoralists. Communities based on sedentary are socially organized differently and have different cultural practices versus northern pastoralists (Fieldwork: 21 November, Baidoa; 23 March 2013 Beletweyne). For more details Besteman and Cassanelli (2004) provide a comprehensive insight into farming communities in south central Somalia.

11   Ladan (2002:20-23) further divides the literature on Somalia into three groups: traditionalists, materialists, and internationalists. In addition to Mahadalla's (1998a) division of traditionalists and materialists, which represent the Lewis and non-Lewis "camps" respectively, Ladan adds a third group, "internationalists" (2002:23). The internationalists analyze the conflict in Somalia through the United Nations and United States intervention in the early nineties. It also includes Somalia's role as a client state of both the United States and Soviet Union during the Cold War. Following AMISOM and Ethiopia's involvement in Somalia, which includes the regional states of Kenya and Djibouti, the foreign intervention could also be put in this category.

12   During the selection of the parliamentarians for the new Federal Government of Somalia, clan elders were for the first time given the role for selecting members of parliament. Following the principles of the 4.5 formula, clan elders paradoxically found themselves both restricted and empowered in their selection. They were also instructed to appoint female parliamentarians, creating an awkward situation for the clan elders who were used to the conception of only

men holding political power.

13 I thank Saferworld for providing access to their survey data. Unfortunately for the purposes of this research, the data was not used as variables and questions could not be applied to the inquiry.

14 The International Food Policy Research Institute looks at the relationship between extreme weather and civil war in Somalia. They estimate "that a temperature rise of around 3.2 degrees Celsius... would lower cattle prices by about four percent and, in turn, increase the incidence of violent conflict by 58 percent" (Maystadt et al 2013: v).

15 Personal communication: Nakamura 10 July 2013, Tokyo.

16 One could go as far and say that aggregated national data on social capital dampens or disguises the regional variances and should therefore be used as "secondary information at most" (Personal communication: Nakamura 10 July 2013, Tokyo).

17 Halpern states that in the United States there is a positive correlation between bonding and bridging social capital at the individual level, therefore diminishing the need to measure bridging and bonding social capital (2005:21).

18 Depending on the level of analysis, such as macro or micro, different results regarding bridging, bonding, and linking social capital will also emerge (Halpern 2005:26).

19 Traditional community leaders, such as clan elders or religious leaders, do not have enforcement mechanisms—for example private armies or access to a monopoly of violence—to implement their decisions or advice and rely instead on the communities to carry them out.

20 Based on the fieldwork conducted and literature review, I was unable to confirm whether women were also able to become poets and religious leaders.

21 In the case of females, depending on the age and the issue, a male relative may need to accompany the discussions with clan elders.

22 I do not look at the relationship characteristics between elites. Lin and others have shown in their study on Taiwan, acquaintance to persons in high prestige jobs are more common amongst people who have higher education levels—a characteristic of an elite based civic association—compared to people who are less educated (Lin et al 2001).

23 Personal communication: Thesis Committee 13 December 2013, Tokyo.

24 Personal communication: Thesis Committee 13 December 2013, Tokyo.

25 http://www.pcr.uu.se/research/ucdp/definitions/

26 As pointed out by numerous interlocutors, respondents were unlikely to admit they had used or participated in violence in the past and therefore this question was irrelevant for the purpose of this study.

27 I agree with Paffenholz (2006) who sees the theoretical discourse on peacebuilding having "matured" and "consolidated". Current debates and exchanges amongst practitioners and academics on peacebuilding have an increased focus on "lessons learned" and "best practices" and the United Nations Peacebuilding Fund has also undergone reviews of its activities and mandates. Furthermore, the peacebuilding discourse has been overtaken by the sustaining peace narrative.

28 Fieldwork: 13 to 20 September 2004, Mogadishu. Interview: CSOs 5 July 2011, Mogadishu.

29 Menkhaus (1999) provides a comprehensive overview of "traditional conflict management mechanisms" in Somalia.

30 In 2008 the research initially looked at conducting a large-n survey targeting only university students. However due to security and financial constraints, this approach was set aside and instead focus group discussions based on a structured survey and free discussion were chosen.

31 The last population survey for Somalia was conducted in 1985 however the results were not released (UNFPA 2012:5). EIU estimates for 2012 put the population around 9.8 million (EIU 2012:4), with a total of 1.1 million internally displaced persons and 990,378 refugees in neighboring countries for September 2013 (UNHCR 2013a).

32 I am grateful to Professor Akihiko Ohno of Aoyama Gakuin University for suggesting this analysis.

33 The discriminant function variate is "a linear combination of variables created such that the differences between group means on the transformed variable is maximized. It takes the general form $\text{Variate}_1 = b_1 X_1 + b_2 X_2 + ... + b_n X_n$" (Field 2005:729).

34 Bohara et al argue that social capital reduces the levels of violence: "higher levels of social capital create both fewer opportunities for insurgents and better managed and controlled government security forces... The higher the amount of social capital, the lower the level of government and insurgent violence" (2006:113).

35 Boix suggests that "ethnic groups are excellent conveyors of patron-client networks in underdeveloped countries. But that once economic relations and poverty decline, those networks fall in significance and violent conflict lessens as well" (2008:216).

36 Although the UNSOA opinion covers all 16 districts of Mogadishu, data for only six districts was analyzed based on the districts covered in the UNDP baseline study. Variances exist between districts in Mogadishu and the UNSOA data is used to attempt and provide further analytical insight into the variances.

37 Based on the secondary data available, it was not possible to conduct structural equation modeling or use an instrumental variable approach to deal with causality issues statistically.

CHAPTER 3. QUANTITATIVELY APPROACHING SOCIAL CAPITAL AND ARMED CONFLICT IN SOMALIA

3.1 Introduction

The objective of the statistical analyses is three-fold: to acquire an overall picture and context setting of social capital and armed conflict descriptively in the five cities and inferentially identify three cities for further qualitative research; to verify the robustness of the analytical framework by looking at the statistical significance of the chosen social capital proxies; and to look at the relationship between social capital and armed violence against the four hypotheses and four theoretical predictions. This chapter analyzes two large-n data sets for the inferential statistics: the UNDP baseline data set and UNSOA opinion poll. Proxies are identified from each data set to replicate the analytical framework for the research inquiry.

The chapter is laid out as follows in terms of research design. Background to the UNDP data set and social capital proxies selected are introduced. The analysis then first looks at the UNDP baseline data (n=4,638) covering the five cities of interest. It introduces the profile of the respondents, the community disputes, and perceptions of safety. Logistic regression is used on the aggregated data to identify significant variables and analyze the relationship between social capital and armed conflict at the national level incorporating two different dependent variables to create two models. Logistic regression is then carried out on the same five cities separately for the two models. Second, the analysis then looks at the UNSOA data[1], consisting of two opinion polls conducted in Mogadishu between 2011 (n=431) and 2012 (n=308), and uses the same analytical framework and logistic regression approach. Third, armed conflict data for each city is analyzed to establish the intensity of armed conflict for the five cities. Fourth, discriminant analysis on the UNDP baseline data at the aggregate level is carried out to identify three cities for further qualitative analysis. Finally, a discussion of the results and conclusions are presented. With inferential statistics primarily used for the analysis in this chapter, detailed descriptive analysis has also been carried out and relevant cross tabs and correlations are included in the Appendix.

The detailed historical, social, political and economical backgrounds of the five cities and regions are not discussed here and will be looked at separately for three cities in the next chapter. It is without saying though that historically Mogadishu, as widely reported in the media as the "most dangerous capital in the world", has been the epicenter for the armed conflict while the northern parts of Somalia have been relatively spared.

3.2 The Data Sets

The main data set originates from a baseline study undertaken by UNDP Somalia[2] from October 2009 to July 2010 in five cities to conduct evidence-based programming in the field of peace and security (UNDP 2010:1). Sample sizes consist of n=1,597 for Mogadishu, n=701 for Galkayo, n=800 for Las Anod, n=740 for Bosaso, and n=800 for Burao. In Mogadishu, the survey only covered six districts out of 16 due to security constraints during the data collection[3]. Consisting of over 140 questions,[4] the data set is an extensive victimization survey and aims to describe "not only criminal activities as stated by victims, but also the tools used in the perpetration of crimes, sociological information concerning the victim, and specific information regarding crimes themselves" (UNDP 2010:4).

Importantly, the data set is unique as it is most likely the first and only nation-wide detailed survey (at the time of writing in 2013) looking at crime, people's perceptions on security and threats, the response of state and non-state security providers, and other social structures that address these issues. In addition, the victimization survey looks at a broad range of issues concerning crime and sources of community disputes and conflicts. The data set consists of: sociological information and profiles, including clan, household composition, and education background; perceptions of safety; details of community disputes and conflicts; number of households experiencing a murder, assault, sexual assault, and property crime; availability and type of arms; types of weapons used; time and place of assault; number of witnesses of violence; and the level of trust in security actors. The survey also "aims at providing information on the characteristics of both criminal and non-criminal victimization and on the number and types of crimes not reported to law enforcement authorities for example violence from armed gangs... [it] allows measure/quantify qualitative data, such as the perception of the police, justice and other non-state security providers" (UNDP 2010:4).

The other data set is the UNSOA opinion poll from 2011, which looks at 350 issues through 150 questions, and the 2012 poll focusing on 425 issues. The 2011 poll was conducted from 14 December 2011 to 9 January 2012 and consists of 990 samples from all the 16 districts in Mogadishu and 56 samples from the "Afgoye Corridor"[5]. The 2012 opinion poll was conducted in December 2012 and consists of 1,046 samples covering all 16 districts of Mogadishu including other regions of south central Somalia[6]. Both opinion polls looked at issues related to the diaspora, media, local and international institutions, views on AMISOM and the international community, peace processes, piracy, constitution, elections, governance, and leadership. In addition, the 2012 poll looked at issues related to stabilization, livelihoods, and challenges facing Somalia. For the purpose of this analysis, data from only the same six districts in Mogadishu covered in the UNDP survey are used from the UNSOA opinion poll in order to maintain consistency. When only the same six districts for Mogadishu are considered, the 2011 and 2012 opinion polls have a relevant sample size of 431 and 308 respectively.

3.3 Proxies for the Analytical Framework

To recall, out of the many proxies that are used in social capital analyses I choose the following six proxies, including socio-demographic attributes, to quantitatively and qualitatively investigate the relationship between armed conflict and social capital: groups and group networks; trust; social cohesion and inclusion; personal networks; identity; and community leadership. Armed conflict, the dependent variable, looks at how violence varies between the five cities. As introduced in chapter two, the analytical framework used is shown below in figure 5.

Groups and Group Networks

Personal Networks

Socio-Demographic + Trust   →   Armed conflict
Attributes

Social Cohesion & Inclusion

Identity

Community Leadership

Figure 5. Theoretical framework used to analyze social capital and armed conflict in Somalia

Following a detailed analysis of the UNDP data set, specific variables are chosen to represent the above proxies to replicate the model. Although not a perfect "fit", the following variables from the questionnaire are chosen to replicate the analytical framework. The type of social capital (bonding, bridging, and linking) is highlighted in parentheses.

➢ *Armed Conflict Model 1:* Perception of Safety (dependent variable for armed conflict)
➢ *Armed Conflict Model 2:* Feeling of Threat from a Fanatic Group (dependent variable for armed conflict)
➢ *Socio-Demographic Attributes:* Age, Region, Gender
➢ *Groups and Group Networks:* Education-level (bridging)
➢ *Personal Networks:* Residence Status (bonding), Employment Status (bridging)
➢ *Trust:* Trust in Clan and Community Leaders (bonding, hard linking), Trust in Religious Leaders (bridging, soft linking), Trust in Police (bridging, hard linking), Trust in Courts (bridging)
➢ *Social Cohesion & Inclusion:* Gender Equality (bridging)
➢ *Identity:* Clan Membership (bonding, hard linking)
➢ *Community Leadership:* Clan Dispute Frequency (bridging, hard linking)

Two residual variables are added in order to look at the effects on both models and identify possible relationships: "Firearms Availability" and "Threat of Remote/Time Control Bombs" (improvised explosive device (IED) Threat).

Based on the above proxies, the statistical analysis will be looking at results and indicators that support or contradict the hypotheses and theoretical predictions at the aggregate and city level. To recall, I establish the argument that armed conflict is high in regions with strong levels of bonding social capital and conflict is low in areas with high levels of bridging social capital. In terms of linking social capital, armed conflict is high in regions with strong levels of hard linking social capital and conflict is low in areas with high levels of soft linking social capital.

As highlighted in chapter two (section 2.6.1), each proxy can represent different types of social capital simultaneously. Based on the questions asked in the UNDP data set, the following variables are used for the different proxies which represent the various types of social capital.

3.3.1 Quantitative Bridging Social Capital Proxies

For the quantitative analysis, five proxies from the analytical framework are used to represent bridging social capital as shown below. The following seven variables, based on questions from the UNDP data set, are used for the proxies to analyze bridging social capital.

Groups and Group Networks: Education-level
Personal Networks: Employment Status
Trust: Trust in Religious Leaders, Trust in Police, Trust in Courts
Social Cohesion & Inclusion: Gender Equality
Community Leadership: Clan Dispute Frequency

"Education-level" is treated as categorizing the respondents' household head as having or not having formal or informal education. Attendance in formal or informal schooling is seen as representing bridging social capital as schools provide exposure to a wide variety of groups and persons from different backgrounds. "Employment Status" looks at whether the respondents' household heads are employed or not. Employment is seen as leading to increased socialization and interaction across groups versus someone who is unemployed. "Trust in Religious leaders; Police; and Courts" in responding to violence and crime is seen as a bridging social capital trait. Religion is seen as inclusive and cutting across clan lines[7]; the police and courts represent an inclusive system where in theory all citizens are treated equally with group affiliation being disregarded. "Gender Equality" within a community is seen as being inclusive and possessing bridging social capital as there is increased participation amongst the community. "Clan Dispute Frequency" sees lower levels of inter-clan disputes representing higher levels of bridging social capital as clan groups have established networks and systems to manage disputes.[8]

3.3.2 Quantitative Bonding Social Capital Proxies

Three proxies from the analytical framework with one variable each are used to analyze bonding social capital. Two residual variables, "Firearms Availability" and "Threat of Remote/Time Control Bombs" (IED Threat), also look at bonding social capital.

> *Personal Networks*: Residence Status
> *Trust:* Trust in Clan and Community Leaders
> *Identity:* Clan Membership
> *Residual variables*: Firearms Availability, Threat of Remote/Time Control Bombs (IED Threat)

"Residence Status" looks at the respondent either being a permanent resident or a refugee/internally displaced person (IDP). A refugee or an IDP is seen as portraying increased bonding social capital as these groups are more vulnerable than a permanent resident and will be focused on building protective networks that are exclusive to deal with insecurity. "Trust in Clan and Community Leaders" looks at how much connectedness there is within a community. An increased sense of trust towards clan and community leaders reflects increased bonding social capital as members of the community have a stronger feeling of togetherness. "Clan Membership" is a categorical set differentiating individuals from each other and represents the feeling of "them" versus "us".

Both residual variables are related to bonding social capital. For "Firearms Availability", a proliferation of weapons represents increased bonding social capital as the community is seen as suspicious of outsiders making it difficult for inclusive networks to nurture. In regard to "IED Threat", high threat levels resemble a community that is also suspicious of strangers, thereby making the community inward looking.

3.3.3 Quantitative Linking Social Capital Proxies

Linking social capital is looked at through three proxies and five variables.

> *Trust:* Trust in Clan and Community Leaders (hard linking)
> Trust in Police (hard linking)
> Trust in Religious Leaders (soft linking)
> *Identity:* Clan Membership (hard linking)
> *Community Leadership:* Clan Dispute Frequency (hard linking)

As discussed in section 2.4.2, trust in clan and community leaders and police represent hard linking social capital while trust in religious leaders is representative of soft linking social capital. Although counterintuitive, "Trust in Clan and Community leaders" is treated as possessing hard power as the UNDP baseline study specifically asks respondents: "what is the level of trust you have towards clan/community elders in responding to violence and crime?" Here, the question assumes elders have the capacity to respond to violence and crime, which would require hard power and sanctioning mechanisms, thereby representing hard linking social capital. "Trust in Police" looks at the police in responding to violence and crime. As a group the police represent hard power to coerce and apply sanctions. As trust in police increases, their hard power within the community also increases leading to higher levels of hard linking social capital. As religious leaders lack sanctioning power and mechanisms to enforce their decisions and judgments, "Trust in Religious Leaders" represents soft linking social capital. Here, religious leaders are seen as the legitimate leaders of the community creating inclusive networks that go beyond social divides. "Clan Membership" focuses on vertical relationships within the clan. Mobilization of armed groups in Somalia is usually based on clan, with command and control of the group coming from above within the clan. "Clan Dispute Frequency" highlights the amount of hard power exerted in the community that leads to armed conflict between communities. An increased frequency of clan disputes indicates high levels of hard linking social capital.

3.4 Analysis of the UNDP Data Set

As mentioned previously, the data set covers five cities in five different regions of Somalia. To set the quantitative contextual scene, this section focuses on a descriptive statistical analysis of the UNDP data related to the respondents' profile. It looks at the important issue of clan membership, community disputes, and trust—an important social capital proxy. This is then followed by the inferential statistical analysis.

3.4.1 Profile of the Respondents

Overall the data set consists of 41% male (n=1871) and 59% female (n=2660). Bosaso, Las Anod, and Burao had female respondent rates of 65%, 64%, and 59% respectively[9]. Galkayo had 53% followed by Mogadishu having 55% female respondents. No clear explanation can be given for the variation in responses by gender. The average age of the respondents is 37.89 years old (n=4361) with a standard deviation of 13.34. When looking at age distribution, peaks were noticeable for respondents answering their age as 30, 40, 50, and 60 years old. This is probably due to the respondents not knowing their exact birthday and with many guessing their date of birth or rounding up (or down) the date. In terms of age groupings, 18 to 25 years old respondents made up 19% (n=805) of the population, followed by 26 to 35 years old range for 28% (n=1,228), and 36 to 45 years old range for 27%. Split by regions, Galkayo had the largest numbers in the age groups of 26 to 35 years old (31%) followed by the range 18 to 25 years old (27%).

			Marital Status				Total
			Single	Married	Divorced	Widowed	
Region	Bari-Bosaso	Count	64	608	22	28	722
		% within Region	8.9%	84.2%	3.0%	3.9%	100.0%
	Sool-Las Anod	Count	64	645	25	58	792
		% within Region	8.1%	81.4%	3.2%	7.3%	100.0%
	Togdheer-Burao	Count	133	490	44	62	729
		% within Region	18.2%	67.2%	6.0%	8.5%	100.0%
	Mudug-Galkayo	Count	134	474	20	16	644
		% within Region	20.8%	73.6%	3.1%	2.5%	100.0%
	Benadir-Mogadishu	Count	294	831	187	184	1496
		% within Region	19.7%	55.5%	12.5%	12.3%	100.0%
Total		Count	689	3048	298	348	4383
		% within Region	15.7%	69.5%	6.8%	7.9%	100.0%

Table 3. Region x Martial Status Crosstabulation

As shown in table 3.1, when split by region, there is a significant association between the region and the marital status of the respondents, χ^2 (12)=353, p<.001, and Cramer's V=.164, p<.001. Mogadishu has the lowest number of married respondents and the highest rates of divorce and being widowed. This highlights that approximately only one out of two respondents belong to a nuclear family in Mogadishu while respondents in Bosaso have the most number of those being married.

Clan identity, which is based on patrilineal lineage, is quantified by asking the respondents the clan of their household head. This is probably asked to the household head because women are able to have two primary clan identities, that of their father and husband. Primarily lineage will depend on the context and therefore by asking the woman's clan identity of the household head the identity focuses on the husband if the respondent is married or father if she is single. For divorced and widowed cases, female respondents could answer either way. When looking at the clan breakdown, the responses were looked at by region/city. Based on the expected counts in the crosstabulation, five cells (11.1%) have an expected count less than five, therefore meeting the assumptions of loglinear. The test statistic shows that there is a significant association between the region and the clan identity of the household head, $\chi^2 (32)=5,469$, $p<.001$, Cramer's V=.561, $p<.001$, and the Contingency Coefficient=.747, $p<.001$, highlighting a strong association between the two variables.

		Clan									Total
		Darod	Dir	Hawiye	Digil-Mirifile	Isaaq	Indian	Arab	Bantu	Others	
Bari-Bosaso	Count	536	25	30	16	16	0	25	55	36	739
	% within Region	72.5%	3.4%	4.1%	2.2%	2.2%	.0%	3.4%	7.4%	4.9%	100.0%
Sool-Las Anod	Count	738	3	20	8	10	0	0	12	7	798
	% within Region	92.5%	.4%	2.5%	1.0%	1.3%	.0%	.0%	1.5%	.9%	100.0%
Togdheer-Burao	Count	24	5	12	4	674	0	0	0	17	736
	% within Region	3.3%	.7%	1.6%	.5%	91.6%	.0%	.0%	.0%	2.3%	100.0%
Mudug-Galkayo	Count	313	48	156	30	27	0	24	37	10	645
	% within Region	48.5%	7.4%	24.2%	4.7%	4.2%	.0%	3.7%	5.7%	1.6%	100.0%
Benadir-Mogadishu	Count	144	110	524	230	36	14	79	230	60	1427
	% within Region	10.1%	7.7%	36.7%	16.1%	2.5%	1.0%	5.5%	16.1%	4.2%	100.0%
Total	Count	1755	191	742	288	763	14	128	334	130	4345
	% within Region	40.4%	4.4%	17.1%	6.6%	17.6%	.3%	2.9%	7.7%	3.0%	100.0%

Table 4. Region x Clan Crosstabulation

District		Clan									Total
		Darod	Dir	Hawiye	Digil-Mirifile	Isaaq	Indian	Arab	Bantu	Others	
Shangani	Count	12	10	104	76	9	0	23	74	2	310
	% within District	3.9%	3.2%	33.5%	24.5%	2.9%	.0%	7.4%	23.9%	.6%	100.0%
Hamarweyne	Count	42	23	71	23	4	5	14	19	53	254
	% within District	16.5%	9.1%	28.0%	9.1%	1.6%	2.0%	5.5%	7.5%	20.9%	100.0%
Waberi	Count	8	24	112	29	13	7	10	21	1	225
	% within District	3.6%	10.7%	49.8%	12.9%	5.8%	3.1%	4.4%	9.3%	.4%	100.0%
Dharkinley	Count	6	16	99	26	2	0	9	22	1	181
	% within District	3.3%	8.8%	54.7%	14.4%	1.1%	.0%	5.0%	12.2%	.6%	100.0%
Wadajir	Count	67	24	101	47	5	0	6	46	2	298
	% within District	22.5%	8.1%	33.9%	15.8%	1.7%	.0%	2.0%	15.4%	.7%	100.0%
Hamarjajab	Count	9	13	37	29	3	2	17	48	1	159
	% within District	5.7%	8.2%	23.3%	18.2%	1.9%	1.3%	10.7%	30.2%	.6%	100.0%
Total	Count	144	110	524	230	36	14	79	230	60	1427
	% within District	10.1%	7.7%	36.7%	16.1%	2.5%	1.0%	5.5%	16.1%	4.2%	100.0%

Table 5. Mogadishu Districts x Clan Crosstabulation

With the exception of Mogadishu, each city historically has a dominant clan in the city. Bosaso, located in Puntland, has a Darod majority; Las Anod which is controversially located in the border region of Puntland and Somaliland also has a Darod majority. Burao, located in Somaliland, has an Isaaq majority while Galkayo, in Puntland, has a large number of Darod (49%) followed by the Hawiye clan (24%). Mogadishu, which is considered as the most cosmopolitan city ethnically, has a very mixed clan composition. At first glance the data for Mogadishu suggests that the Hawiye clan is a majority (37%), however the survey was only conducted in six out of the sixteen districts in the Benadir region and when split by district, the clan composition can vary from district to district. The table below highlights how a wide variety of clans can inhabit one district. However the historical trends of the inhabitants or the type of governing body is not identifiable from the survey[10].

Statistically, based on the expected counts in the crosstabulation, eight cells (14.8%) have an expected count less than five, therefore meeting the assumptions of loglinear. The test statistic shows that there is a significant association between the district that one lives in Mogadishu and the clan identity of the household head, χ^2 (40)=470, p<.001, Cramer's V=.257, p<.001, and the Contingency Coefficient=.498, p<.001, highlighting a mild association between the two variables. In short, there is an association between clan identify and geographic habitation at both the regional/city level (macro-level) and the district-level (micro-level); in essence, variances in clan are observed by region.

3.4.2 Community Disputes

The issue of disputes within the community is a key focus for this research inquiry in the areas of studying violence and armed conflict. As in many countries, the reasons and dynamics for disputes vary based on different contexts. Each region in Somalia differs in terms of demographics, development, regional dynamics, and natural resources. The survey provides interesting insight into the frequency, reasons of dispute and whether these disputes led to violence. While perception is used for quantifying violence and safety, witnessing violence is also looked at.

Out of a total sample of n=4,638 for all five regions, there were 4,282 responses regarding "how often does your clan/community experience disputes with other clan/communities?" Excluding missing variables, 2,311 (58%) answered "Never/almost none" while 1,650 (42%) answered that they had experienced some form of dispute with other clan/communities on either a yearly, monthly or weekly basis. When broken down by region, 65% of responses in Galkayo noted some sort of clan/community dispute on a yearly, monthly, or weekly basis. This was followed by Las Anod (51%), Bosaso (39%), Mogadishu (37%), and Burao (21%). The statistical test showed that there was a significant association between the region and the frequency of clan/community disputes, χ^2 (12)=320.0, p<.001, and Cramer's V=.164, p<.001. Despite Mogadishu having a sample size twice as large as the other cities, 63% of the respondents interestingly stated that they "never" or had "almost none" experienced conflict. The data collected in Mogadishu covers six districts out of a total 16 districts.

			Frequency of clan/community disputes				Total
			Never/ almost none	Yearly	Monthly	Weekly	
(Region)	Bari-	Count	431	223	41	13	708
	Bosaso	% within B-1(Region)	60.9%	31.5%	5.8%	1.8%	100.0%
	Sool-Las	Count	358	312	46	12	728
	Anod	% within B-1(Region)	49.2%	42.9%	6.3%	1.6%	100.0%
	Togdheer-	Count	526	112	25	5	668
	Burao	% within B-1(Region)	78.7%	16.8%	3.7%	.7%	100.0%
	Mudug-	Count	215	293	81	28	617
	Galkayo	% within B-1(Region)	34.8%	47.5%	13.1%	4.5%	100.0%
	Benadir-	Count	781	345	76	38	1240
	Mogadishu	% within B-1(Region)	63.0%	27.8%	6.1%	3.1%	100.0%
Total		Count	2311	1285	269	96	3961
		% within B-1(Region)	58.3%	32.4%	6.8%	2.4%	100.0%

Table 6. Region x Frequency of clan/community disputes

Corresponding to this, 94% (n=1558) noted that the clan/community dispute resulted in physical violence with other clan/communities. A look at the Spearman's correlation shows there was a significant relationship between frequency of clan/community disputes and violence, r_s =.815, p<.001. Therefore one can conclude that the disputes noted in the survey led to some form of violence, with over two thirds of the disputes occurring at a yearly frequency rate. The statistical test showed that there was a significant association between the region and the frequency of clan/community violence, χ^2 (12)=77.6, p<.001, and Cramer's V=.125, p<.001, representing *a low association between the region and the frequency of clan/community violence.*

			Frequency of clan/community violence				Total
			Never/almost none	Yearly	Monthly	Weekly	
(Region)	Bari-	Count	9	210	45	17	281
	Bosaso	% within B-1(Region)	3.2%	74.7%	16.0%	6.0%	100.0%
	Sool-Las	Count	24	287	45	10	366
	Anod	% within B-1(Region)	6.6%	78.4%	12.3%	2.7%	100.0%
	Togdheer-	Count	23	117	11	0	151
	Burao	% within B-1(Region)	15.2%	77.5%	7.3%	.0%	100.0%
	Mudug-	Count	10	290	85	28	413
	Galkayo	% within B-1(Region)	2.4%	70.2%	20.6%	6.8%	100.0%
	Benadir-	Count	35	300	76	37	448
	Mogadishu	% within B-1(Region)	7.8%	67.0%	17.0%	8.3%	100.0%
Total		Count	101	1204	262	92	1659
		% within B-1(Region)	6.1%	72.6%	15.8%	5.5%	100.0%

Table 7. Region x Frequency of clan/community violence

A follow-up question asked "the most common reason of dispute between other clan/communities" and 1,557 responses were given as noted below.

	Frequency	Valid Percent
Resources	497	31.9
Family disputes	229	14.7
Crime	207	13.3
Power/cultural struggle	169	10.9
Revenge	440	28.3
Other	15	1.0
Total	1557	100.0

Table 8. Most common reason of dispute

The above data shows that resources and revenge, 32% and 29% respectively, were the most common reasons for disputes between clans and communities in the five cities, both highlighting areas where xeer is involved and variables for social capital come into play. When looking at the frequency of the dispute, 77% of disputes occurred on a yearly basis, 17% on a monthly basis, and a residual of 6% on a weekly basis. On a yearly basis, the most common reasons for disputes were resources (39%) and revenge (29%) followed by family disputes (14%).

			Most common reason of dispute					Total
			Resources	Family disputes	Crime	Power/ cultural struggle	Revenge	
Frequency of clan/Community violence	Yearly	Count	449	156	122	98	334	1159
		% within Frequency of clan/community violence	38.7%	13.5%	10.5%	8.5%	28.8%	100.0%
		% within Most common reason of dispute	91.3%	70.6%	61.6%	58.0%	79.0%	77.1%
	Monthly	Count	39	56	53	38	71	257
		% within Frequency of clan/community violence	15.2%	21.8%	20.6%	14.8%	27.6%	100.0%
		% within Most common reason of dispute	7.9%	25.3%	26.8%	22.5%	16.8%	17.1%
	Weekly	Count	4	9	23	33	18	87
		% within Frequency of clan/community violence	4.6%	10.3%	26.4%	37.9%	20.7%	100.0%
		% within Most common reason of dispute	.8%	4.1%	11.6%	19.5%	4.3%	5.8%
Total		Count	492	221	198	169	423	1503
		% within Frequency of clan/community violence	32.7%	14.7%	13.2%	11.2%	28.1%	100.0%

	% within Most common reason of dispute	100.0%	100.0%	100.0%	100.0%	100.0%	100.0%

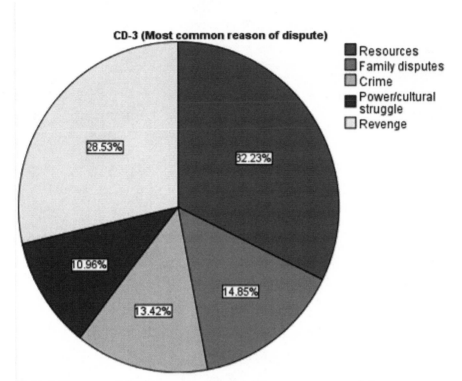

Table 9. Frequency of clan/community violence × Most common reason of dispute Crosstabulation

Figure 6. Most common reason of dispute

There is a significant association between the frequency of community/clan violence and the reason for the dispute, χ^2 (8)=165, p<.001, and with Cramer's V=.235, p<.001.

Split by city, the data shows that resources and revenge were the main cause of clan disputes in Las Anod, Bosaso, and Galkayo. Revenge and power/cultural struggle were the main causes of conflict in Mogadishu while Burao respondents noted that crime (35%) and family disputes (28%) were the main causes. Testing the data, there is a significant association between the region and the most common reason of dispute between clans and communities, χ^2 (16)=348, p<.001, and with Cramer's V=.235, p<.001.

		Most common reason of dispute					Total
		Resources	Family disputes	Crime	Power/ cultural struggle	Revenge	
Bari-Bosaso	Count	127	40	32	19	53	271
	% within Region	46.9%	14.8%	11.8%	7.0%	19.6%	100.0%
Sool-Las Anod	Count	160	60	27	9	66	322
	% within Region	49.7%	18.6%	8.4%	2.8%	20.5%	100.0%
Togdheer-Burao	Count	23	38	48	6	23	138
	% within Region	16.7%	27.5%	34.8%	4.3%	16.7%	100.0%
Mudug-Galkayo	Count	120	43	51	29	171	414
	% within Region	29.0%	10.4%	12.3%	7.0%	41.3%	100.0%
Benadir-Mogadishu	Count	67	48	49	106	127	397
	% within Region	16.9%	12.1%	12.3%	26.7%	32.0%	100.0%
Total	Count	497	229	207	169	440	1542
	% within Region	32.2%	14.9%	13.4%	11.0%	28.5%	100.0%

Table 10. Region x Most common reason of dispute Crosstabulation

The above data highlights some interesting patterns for further qualitative research. Burao, which has the lowest frequency for revenge and resources, has instead the highest frequency of family disputes and crime. This may suggest that Burao has "established" mechanisms to go beyond a zero-sum paradigm in regards to resource sharing. Appropriate mechanisms may have also been established for managing revenge, suggesting high levels of bridging social capital in Burao with xeer being effective. The high frequency of crime and family disputes may also support the paradigm that Burao has gone beyond "clan politics" and that it has progressively entered the ranks of other cities globally that also suffer from high crime rates and domestic violence. Dispute over resources and revenge in Bosaso, Las Anod, and Galkayo require further research to see whether these issues are unmanageable due to, inter alia, weak xeer and ineffective governance structures and low social capital.

3.4.3 Perception of Safety and Witnessing Violence

Perception of safety, one of the dependent variables used in the logistic regression, is looked at by asking respondents whether the community has become safe or unsafe compared to twelve months ago (responses varied from "become very unsafe", "become a little unsafe", "become a little safer", "become a lot safe"). On an aggregate base, 59% of respondents noted that their community had become a "little safer" or "a lot safer" compared to twelve months ago while 41% saw their communities become "very unsafe" or a "little unsafe". The responses

83

were split by region to create a crosstabulation with "very unsafe" and "a little unsafe" responses combined and "a little safer" and "a lot safer" combined. As expected, Burao has the highest perception of safety followed by Bosaso while 78% of respondents in Mogadishu feel either "very unsafe" or "a little unsafe" followed by Galkayo at 39%. Based on the responses, there is a significant association between the region and the perception of community safety over the past 12 months, χ^2 (4)=1,377, p<.001, and with Cramer's V=.566, p<.001, representing a strong association between the region and the perception of safety in the community.

			Community safety over 12 months		Total
			Unsafe	Safe	
Region	Bari-Bosaso	Count	194	541	735
		% within Region	26.4%	73.6%	100.0%
	Sool-Las Anod	Count	230	558	788
		% within Region	29.2%	70.8%	100.0%
	Togdheer-Burao	Count	6	723	729
		% within Region	.8%	99.2%	100.0%
	Mudug-Galkayo	Count	255	407	662
		% within Region	38.5%	61.5%	100.0%
	Benadir-Mogadishu	Count	1080	307	1387
		% within Region	77.9%	22.1%	100.0%
Total		Count	1765	2536	4301
		% within Region	41.0%	59.0%	100.0%

Table 11. Region x Community safety over 12 months Crosstabulation

When respondents were asked how often they felt a threat from a fanatic group, which is the other dependent variable, the responses were similar when compared regionally. Over 80% of respondents in Burao and Bosaso felt there was no threat from a fanatic group while 59% of Mogadishu respondents felt there was a high threat and 23% in Galkayo. A Spearman's correlation shows that there is a significant relationship between the perception of safety compared to twelve months ago and feeling threatened by a fanatic group, $r_s = -.520$, p<.001: when respondents feel safe, the threat from a fanatic group decreases. There is also a significant association between the region and whether respondents feel a threat from a fanatic group, χ^2 (8)=1984, p<.001, and with Cramer's V=.486, p<.001, representing a medium association between the region and threat.

			Feel threat from a fanatic group often			Total
			None	Low	High	
Region	Bari-	Count	592	125	10	727
	Bosaso	% within Region	81.4%	17.2%	1.4%	100.0%
	Sool-Las	Count	312	374	106	792
	Anod	% within Region	39.4%	47.2%	13.4%	100.0%
	Togdheer-	Count	582	58	60	700
	Burao	% within Region	83.1%	8.3%	8.6%	100.0%
	Mudug-	Count	311	178	143	632
	Galkayo	% within Region	49.2%	28.2%	22.6%	100.0%
.	Benadir-	Count	86	471	788	1345
	Mogadishu	% within Region	6.4%	35.0%	58.6%	100.0%
Total		Count	1883	1206	1107	4196
		% within Region	44.9%	28.7%	26.4%	100.0%

Table 12. Region x Feel threat from a fanatic group often Crosstabulation

The results for Mogadishu are unsurprising when considering that the survey was conducted in July 2010, after the peak of the armed conflict between anti-government elements and the TFG and AMISOM allies. During this period, anti-government elements were still controlling large swathes of Mogadishu and were continuing their attempt to overthrow the TFG. The districts where the survey was carried out were under the relative control of the TFG[11] however the "spillover" effect from the ongoing armed conflict in neighbouring districts would have had an influence on the respondents.

The issue of perception unavoidably provides biases that are intrinsic of questions related to views on safety and violence. This can be overcome by taking an empirical approach and asking respondents whether they have witnessed violence. The survey asks respondents whether they have witnessed with their own eyes any crime or violence against someone outside their own household during the last twelve months. Out of n=4,179, 21% of respondents (n=861) said they had witnessed crime or violence in the last twelve months. When split by region, Galkayo surprisingly had the highest number of witnesses of violence and crime (36%) followed by Mogadishu (25%). This was followed by Burao (18%), Las Anod (14%), and Bosaso (9%). When conducting a statistical test, there is a significant association between the region and whether respondents witnessed crime or violence outside the household in the last twelve months, χ^2 (4)=191.94, p<.001, and Cramer's V=.214, p<.001.

			Have witnessed crime/violence outside household in 12 months		Total
			Yes	No	
Region	Bari- Bosaso	Count	69	671	740
		% within Region	9.3%	90.7%	100.0%
	Sool-Las Anod	Count	108	691	799
		% within Region	13.5%	86.5%	100.0%
	Togdheer- Burao	Count	131	580	711
		% within Region	18.4%	81.6%	100.0%
	Mudug- Galkayo	Count	235	421	656
		% within Region	35.8%	64.2%	100.0%
	Benadir- Mogadishu	Count	318	955	1273
		% within Region	25.0%	75.0%	100.0%
Total		Count	861	3318	4179
		% within Region	20.6%	79.4%	100.0%

Table 13. Region x Have witnessed crime/violence outside household in 12 months Crosstabulation

When split by clan, respondents whose household head belonged to the Digil-Mirifile clan had the highest rate for witnessing violence or crime (36%) followed by "others" (32%), and the Hawiye clan (28%). As highlighted previously, the Digil-Mirifile and Hawiye respondents mainly live in Mogadishu, which have a high rate of crime or violence witnesses, while the Darod clan, with the largest number of respondents (n=1,718), had one of the lowest rates of witnesses (14%) of crime or violence. The low rate for the Darod clan is in line with the previous table where both Bosaso and Las Anod, inhabited mainly by the Darod clan, had the lowest rates of those witnessing crime.

		Have witnessed crime/violence outside household in 12 months		Total
		Yes	No	
Darod	Count	239	1479	1718
	% within Clan	13.9%	86.1%	100.0%
Dir	Count	34	137	171
	% within Clan	19.9%	80.1%	100.0%
Hawiye	Count	182	473	655
	% within Clan	27.8%	72.2%	100.0%
Digil- Mirifile	Count	82	148	230
	% within Clan	35.7%	64.3%	100.0%
Isaaq	Count	139	594	733
	% within Clan	19.0%	81.0%	100.0%
Indian	Count	1	13	14
	% within Clan	7.1%	92.9%	100.0%
Arab	Count	32	84	116
	% within Clan	27.6%	72.4%	100.0%
Bantu	Count	72	217	289

	% within Clan	24.9%	75.1%	100.0%
Others	Count	41	89	130
	% within Clan	31.5%	68.5%	100.0%
Total	Count	822	3234	4056
	% within Clan	20.3%	79.7%	100.0%

Table 14. Clan x Have witnessed crime/ violence outside household in 12 months Crosstabulation

When conducting a log linear statistical test, there is a significant association between the clan identity of the household head and whether respondents witnessed crime/violence outside the household in the last twelve months, χ^2 (8)=119.8, p<.001, and Cramer's V=.172, p<.001.

3.4.4 Trust as a Social Capital Proxy

One of the most used variables in the study of social capital is trust. The survey asks what level of trust the respondents have towards certain entities in responding to violence and crime. The various entities are: clan/community elders; religious leaders; police; and courts. The responses use a four-point ordinal scale of: very low; relatively low; relatively high; very high. For future modeling purposes, the answers related to "very low" and "relatively low" are merged into one as "low level of trust". The same is conducted for the remaining answers.

As highlighted in the previous sub-sections (2.4.2, 3.3.2, and 3.3.3), for the purpose of analysis and comparison in the context of social capital, trust in clan and community leaders is used as a proxy for *bonding social capital* – social networks that do not cross major clan lines – and *hard linking social capital.* In regard to trust towards religious leaders to respond to violence and crime, I use this as a proxy for *bridging social capital* – social networks that are inclusive and cut across clan lines – and *soft linking social capital* (as described in detail in sub-sections 3.3.1 and 3.3.3). Religious leaders, based on the tenets of Islam, widely cut across clan lines in Somalia and historically various political Islamic movements, such as Al Itahad and Alhu Sheikh[12], have also crossed different clan lines.

Looking at the level of trust towards clan/community, religious leaders, police, and courts in responding to violence and crime by region showed various results for the different actors. Respondents in Mogadishu had the lowest level of trust towards clan and community elders (78%) and Bosaso had the highest level of trust (85%) followed by Galkayo (76%) in responding to violence and crime. There is a significant association between the region and the level of trust towards clan/community elders, χ^2 (4)=1,128, p<.001, and Cramer's V=.520, p<.001, highlighting a strong association between the two variables.

| | | Level of trust towards clan/community elders in responding to violence and crime | | Total |
		Low level of trust towards clan/ community leaders	High level of trust towards clan/ community leaders	
Bari-Bosaso	Count	113	620	733
	% within Region	15.4%	84.6%	100.0%
Sool-Las Anod	Count	200	591	791
	% within Region	25.3%	74.7%	100.0%
Togdheer-Burao	Count	195	504	699
	% within Region	27.9%	72.1%	100.0%
Mudug-Galkayo	Count	160	496	656
	% within Region	24.4%	75.6%	100.0%
Benadir-Mogadishu	Count	1007	291	1298
	% within Region	77.6%	22.4%	100.0%
Total	Count	1675	2502	4177
	% within Region	40.1%	59.9%	100.0%

Table 15. Region x Level of trust towards clan/community elders Crosstabulation

Similar results were found for religious leaders as in the case regarding trust towards clan and community leaders, with Mogadishu having the lowest level of trust (71%) and Bosaso and Galkayo having the highest levels of trust (91%) for religious leaders to respond to violence and crime. There is a significant association between the region and the level of trust towards clan/community elders, χ^2 (4)=1,148, p<.001, and Cramer's V=.530, p<.001, highlights a strong association between the two variables.

| | | | Level of trust for religious leaders' response to violence/crime | | Total |
			Low level of trust towards religious leaders	High level of trust towards religious leaders	
Region	Bari-Bosaso	Count	69	666	735
		% within Region	9.4%	90.6%	100.0%
	Sool-Las Anod	Count	192	542	734
		% within Region	26.2%	73.8%	100.0%
	Togdheer-Burao	Count	329	347	676
		% within Region	48.7%	51.3%	100.0%
	Mudug-	Count	57	601	658

	Galkayo	% within Region	8.7%	91.3%	100.0%
	Benadir-Mogadishu	Count	885	363	1248
		% within Region	70.9%	29.1%	100.0%
Total		Count	1532	2519	4051
		% within Region	37.8%	62.2%	100.0%

Table 16. Region x Level of trust for religious leaders in responding to violence/crime Crosstabulation

These results show that high levels of bridging social capital exist in regions where there is strong bonding social capital and vice versa. The results are in line with the social capital theory that argues that a certain degree of bonding social capital is initially required before bridging social capital can develop (Cox 2009:172). In this case, Mogadishu lacks the foundations for bridging social capital to develop due to a lack of bonding social capital.

Trust towards police to respond to crime and violence, treated as a proxy for *bridging social capital* and *hard linking social capital*, was again lowest in Mogadishu (79%) followed by Las Anod (62%) and Galkayo (59%). In terms of high levels of trust towards the police, Bosaso and Burao were identical at around 51%. Trust in police is used as a proxy for bridging social capital as the police force can be an actor that crosses clan lines. However, depending on the city or town, the police can also be monolithic.

			Level of trust for police response to violence/crime		Total
			Low level of trust towards police	High level of trust towards police	
Region	Bari-Bosaso	Count	344	366	710
		% within Region	48.5%	51.5%	100.0%
	Sool-Las Anod	Count	485	302	787
		% within Region	61.6%	38.4%	100.0%
	Togdheer-Burao	Count	342	360	702
		% within Region	48.7%	51.3%	100.0%
	Mudug-Galkayo	Count	376	261	637
		% within Region	59.0%	41.0%	100.0%
	Benadir-Mogadishu	Count	1022	274	1296
		% within Region	78.9%	21.1%	100.0%
Total		Count	2569	1563	4132
		% within Region	62.2%	37.8%	100.0%

Table 17. Region x Level of trust for police in responding to violence/crime Crosstabulation

Statistically, there is a significant association between the region and the level of trust towards the police, χ^2 (4)=267, p<.001, and Cramer's V=.254, p<.001, highlighting a medium association between the two variables.

Trust in courts to respond to violence and crime is used as a proxy for *bridging social capital*. The direct translation used for court is maxkamada, literally translated as court. It is not clear whether the court system referred to is secular, traditional, or Sharia-based[13]. The data tends to suggest that the court in reference is secular however the perception of the respondents can be at question. In terms of the proxy being used to represent bridging social capital, this should not matter because in all three systems the court can cut across clan lines. For example, one is never clearly sure whether he or she will be judged by one's clansmen, and when incidents occur between two different clans a third clan will be asked to intervene in the traditional system to avoid favoritism of one particular clan.

The data shows that the courts in all five regions have a low level of trust for responding to violence and crime, with 82% of respondents in Mogadishu and Burao having the lowest levels of trust in the courts. Bosaso has the highest rate of those trusting the courts (46%) and Mogadishu with the lowest rate at 18%. Meeting the assumptions of the loglinear analysis, there is a significant association between the region and the level of trust towards the courts to respond to violence and crime, χ^2 (4)=264, p<.001, and Cramer's V=.256, p<.001, highlights a medium association between the two variables.

			Level of trust for court for responding to violence/crime		Total
			Low level of trust towards courts	High level of trust towards courts	
Region	Bari-Bosaso	Count	381	328	709
		% within Region	53.7%	46.3%	100.0%
	Sool-Las Anod	Count	478	295	773
		% within Region	61.8%	38.2%	100.0%
	Togdheer-Burao	Count	509	119	628
		% within Region	81.1%	18.9%	100.0%
	Mudug-Galkayo	Count	499	142	641
		% within Region	77.8%	22.2%	100.0%
	Benadir-Mogadishu	Count	1039	221	1260
		% within Region	82.5%	17.5%	100.0%
Total		Count	2906	1105	4011
		% within Region	72.5%	27.5%	100.0%

Table 18. Region x Level of trust for court for responding to violence/crime Crosstabulation

When looking at the Spearman's correlation between the trust in the courts and accessibility in terms of physical distance, there was a positive correlation of $r_s = .657$, at the $p < .01$ significance level (two-tailed), showing that the level of trust increased as accessibility improved. The relationship was strongly positive in terms of speed of response, $r_s = .801$ at the $p < .01$ significance level (two-tailed), indicating a relationship where the trust in the courts increased as the speed of response increased. Further research needs to be conducted into comprehending what influences the trust in courts and whether this can accurately reflect bridging social capital across the five regions.

In terms of trust amongst the various clan groups, the trust levels of the four major clans (Darod, Hawiye, Isaaq, and Digil/Mirifile) generally resembled the trust levels by city based on geographical residence of the clan groups. For example, Darod respondents, who compromise the majority of residents in Bosaso, saw similar levels of trust towards clan elders with responses from Bosaso (clan by trust levels crosstabulations are located in the Appendix).

3.5 Analyzing Social Capital and Armed Conflict

To recall, the objective of this chapter is to *quantitatively* analyze the relationship between social capital and armed conflict in Somalia and to also provide a deeper understanding of the various dynamics and variables pertaining to armed conflict and violence in the five selected cities in Somalia. Having reviewed over 140 questions and answers for a sample size of 4,638, I have attempted to extract data that is relevant from the UNDP baseline study. I have also reviewed data from the two UNSOA opinion polls.

As the first step for any quantitative study, I identified potential relevant variables through the use of crosstabulation and correlations and identified statistically significant relationships. Detailed descriptive analyses can be found in the Appendix. The next step is to create a model that captures the complex relationship between social capital and armed conflict based on the data on hand and the analytical framework proposed in figure 3.1. The model first uses aggregate data at the "national level", combining responses from all five cities, and then analyzes data at the city level. This is followed by discriminant analysis for the aggregated data to identify three cities for further qualitative analysis. Data from the two UNSOA opinion polls are then looked at to further analyze social capital and armed conflict in

Mogadishu. The section ends with armed conflict levels for each city being compared based on various proxies and data.

3.5.1 Social Capital and Armed Conflict at the National Level

As mentioned earlier in section 3.3, the social capital proxies used for the independent variables are: region, age group, gender, clan membership, residence status, employment status of the household head, education-level of the household head, female participation in village meetings, clan dispute frequency, clan community trust, religious leaders trust, police trust, and court trust. Two residual variables are also added: Firearms Availability and Threat from a Remote Control Bomb (IED Threat).

From the available data, which is primarily a victimization survey, challenges emerge to identify a reliable proxy to measure armed conflict. Several possible candidates emerge: Perception of Safety (based on the question of whether the community has become safe of unsafe compared to twelve months ago); Perception of Threat from a Fanatic Group (asking the question how often one feels a threat from a fanatic group); Experience of Assault (whether any member of the household experienced assault or physical attack within the last twelve months); and Witnessing Violence (whether crime or violence against someone outside the household has been witnessed by the respondent in the last twelve months).

For the purpose of this study two dependent variables from the above candidates were analyzed separately to create two models to represent the armed conflict proxy: Perception of Safety; and Perception of Threat from a Fanatic Group. The other two candidates, Experience of Assault and Witnessing Violence, are statistically difficult to use for inferential statistics because the results are skewed significantly to one answer (only 13% experienced assault and only 21% have witnessed crime outside the household).

First, the Perception of Safety variable, which is a four-point scale[14], is used as a dependent variable and converted into a binominal non-ordinal variable with zero as "become unsafe" and one as "become safe". The second dependent variable used is Perception of Threat from a Fanatic Group and is also converted into a binominal non-ordinal variable with zero representing "feel no threat" and one as "low or high threat". Based on the available UNDP data, these variables are used as proxies and are seen as most relevant in representing the dynamics of armed conflict in Somalia while allowing inferential statistical analysis to be conducted.

For both models logistic regression[15] (forced entry method) is used to calculate the Cox and Snell's R^2 and the Nagelkerke's R^2. In terms of interpretation, both the Cox and Nagelkerke's R^2 provide a "gauge of the substantive significance of the model" (Field 2005:223). The crucial values from the logistic regression are the change in odds resulting from a unit change in the predictor, Exp (B)[16], and identifying the significant variables with a 95% confidence level, $p<.05$ (Field 2005:225).

Results of Model One: Perception of Safety as the dependent variable

Using the aggregated data, the results of the logistic regression using *Perception of Safety* as the dependent variable are summarized below.

"Perception of Safety" Model Summary

Step	-2 Log likelihood	Cox & Snell R Square	Nagelkerke R Square
1	2527.633[a]	.368	.496

a. Estimation terminated at iteration number 7 because parameter estimates changed by less than .001.

"Perception of Safety" Hosmer and Lemeshow Test

Step	Chi-square	df	Sig.
1	4.599	8	.799

							95.0% C.I.for EXP(B)	
	B	S.E.	Wald	df	Sig.	Exp(B)	Lower	Upper
Step 1[a] Region – Bosaso			124.727	4	.000			
Region – Las Anod	.620	.165	14.051	1	.000	1.859	1.344	2.571
Region – Burao	3.541	.590	35.953	1	.000	34.486	10.840	109.711
Region – Galkayo	-.070	.183	.146	1	.702	.933	.652	1.334
Region – Mogadishu	-1.186	.214	30.592	1	.000	.305	.201	.465
AgeGroup – 0 to 17			24.039	6	.001			
AgeGroup – 18 to 25	.369	.445	.686	1	.408	1.446	.604	3.461
AgeGroup – 26 to 35	.447	.441	1.026	1	.311	1.563	.659	3.710

AgeGroup – 36 to 45	.810	.442	3.359	1	.067	2.248	.945	5.347
AgeGroup – 46 to 55	.939	.454	4.274	1	.039	2.557	1.050	6.228
AgeGroup – 56 to 65	.375	.475	.623	1	.430	1.454	.574	3.687
AgeGroup – 66 upwards	.027	.530	.003	1	.960	1.027	.364	2.901
Gender – Male	-.034	.104	.107	1	.744	.967	.788	1.185
Clan – Darod			33.204	8	.000			
Clan – Dir	-.102	.252	.164	1	.685	.903	.552	1.479
Clan – Hawiye	.698	.182	14.686	1	.000	2.009	1.406	2.871
Clan – Digil/Mirifile	.809	.241	11.244	1	.001	2.246	1.400	3.605
Clan – Isaaq	.625	.321	3.790	1	.052	1.869	.996	3.506
Clan – Indian	-.671	1.094	.376	1	.539	.511	.060	4.364
Clan – Arab	.777	.291	7.115	1	.008	2.174	1.229	3.846
Clan – Bantu	.527	.226	5.422	1	.020	1.694	1.087	2.639
Clan – Others	-.601	.339	3.138	1	.076	.548	.282	1.066
HouseholdStatus – IDP/Refugee	-.124	.124	.998	1	.318	.884	.693	1.126
HouseholdHead – Employed	-.075	.109	.471	1	.493	.928	.749	1.149
HouseholdHead – Educated	.444	.102	18.792	1	.000	1.558	1.275	1.904
FemaleParticipation – Yes	.016	.119	.019	1	.890	1.017	.805	1.284
ClanDisputeFrequency – Yes	.088	.105	.700	1	.403	1.092	.889	1.342
ClanCommunityTrust – High	.714	.118	36.890	1	.000	2.042	1.622	2.571
ReligiousLeadersTrust – High	.365	.128	8.181	1	.004	1.441	1.122	1.851
PoliceTrust – High	-.284	.125	5.130	1	.024	.753	.589	.962
CourtTrust – High	.032	.133	.056	1	.813	1.032	.795	1.340
FirearmsAvailability – Same	-.176	.148	1.419	1	.234	.838	.627	1.120
FirearmsAvailability – Increase	.364	.145	6.279	1	.012	1.439	1.082	1.912
IEDThreat – Low	-1.376	.169	66.047	1	.000	.252	.181	.352
IEDThreat – High	-2.084	.173	145.172	1	.000	.124	.089	.175
Constant	.124	.505	.060	1	.806	1.132		

a. Variable(s) entered on step 1: Region, AgeGroup, Gender, Clan, HouseholdStatus, HouseholdHeadEmployment, HouseholdHeadEducation, FemaleParticipation, ClanDisputeFrequency, ClanCommunityTrust, ReligiousLeadersTrust, PoliceTrust, CourtTrust, FirearmsAvailability, IEDThreat.

Table 19. Model 1: Perception of Safety as the dependent variable

In table 3.17, the variables highlighted in yellow are significant variables at the 95% confidence level. Overall, based on the Cox and Narelkerke R^2, the model accounts for 36.8% to 49.6% of the variance in the Perception of Safety. As a brief summary, the following findings highlight the relationship of the different variables in predicting the Perception of Safety and the significance and strength[17].

- *Regions:* Regions were overall significant in predicting Perception of Safety except for Galkayo (p>.05). Relative to Bosaso, Burao respondents were more likely to see their community become safer compared to twelve months ago while Mogadishu residents were more likely to see their community become unsafe.

- *Age:* Grouped into different age-brackets, age was statistically non-significant at the 95% confidence level (p>.05) for all age-brackets except for the age group 46 to 55.

- *Gender:* Gender was non-significant at the 95% confidence level (p>.05).

- *Clan Membership:* Out of the nine different categories of clan, and excluding the reference clan (Darod), only four clans were significant (p<.05). The respondents belonging to the three clans of Hawiye, Digil/Mirifile, Bantu, and Arab were more likely to perceive their community as being safer compared to twelve months earlier.

- *Residence Status (Household status):* Using permanent resident status as the base, the status of being a refugee or IDP was non-significant (p>.05).

- *Employment Status (Employment status of household head):* The occupation of the household head was categorized as either being unemployed or employed in some form of work. This was non-significant in determining Perception of Safety in the community (p>.05).

- *Education-level:* Respondents whose household head had received some form of either formal or informal education were more likely to have a safer perception of their community versus those who had no formal or informal education.

- *Gender Equality:* The issue of female household members allowed to participate in village meetings was non-significant (p>.05) in predicting community safety perceptions.

- *Clan Dispute Frequency:* The frequency of clan/communities experiencing disputes with other clans and communities did not predict the perception of community safety (p>.05).

- *Trust in Clan and Community Leaders*: As the level of trust towards clan/community leaders in responding to violence and crime increases, the community is predicted to be perceived safe.

- *Trust in Religious Leaders:* As the level of trust towards religious leaders in responding to violence and crime increases, the community is predicted to be perceived safe, albeit at a lower odds ratio than clan and community leaders.

- *Trust in Police:* As the level of trust towards the police in responding to violence and crime increases, the community is predicted to be perceived unsafe.

- *Trust in Courts:* The trust towards courts in responding to violence and crime does not predict the perception of community safety (p>.05).

- *Firearms Availability:* Contrary to expectations, as the availability of firearms increases the community is predicted to be perceived as safe. When there is no change in terms of the availability of firearms, this does not predict the perception of community safety (p>.05).

- *Threat of Remote/Time Control Bombs (IED Threat):* As the threat of IED increases, the community is predicted to be perceived increasingly unsafe.

Testing for multicollinearity, collinearity diagnostics were conducted using linear regression. All tolerance values were above .1 and all variance inflation factors (VIF) were below ten. A VIF above ten indicates that an independent variable has a strong linear relationship with other independent variables while a tolerance statistic below .1 indicates serious multicollinearity issues (Field 2005:175).

Results of Model Two: Feeling of Threat from a Fanatic Group as the dependent variable

For model two, logistic regression was conducted using *Feeling of Threat from a Fanatic Group* as the dependent variable[18] and the previously used independent variables. The dependent variable was converted into a binominal non-ordinal variable with zero as "no threat" and one as "low or high threat".

The regression results show the overall fit of the model accounts for 44.4% to 59.4% of the variance in predicting Feeling of Threat from a Fanatic Group. However the Hosmer & Lemeshow's goodness-of-fit test[19] indicates the model is not predicting the data that well as the test statistic (16.298) is significant at .038 level, p<.05.

"Feeling of Threat from a Fanatic Group" Model Summary

Step	-2 Log likelihood	Cox & Snell R Square	Nagelkerke R Square
1	2189.154a	.444	.594

a. Estimation terminated at iteration number 6 because parameter estimates changed by less than .001.

"Feeling of Threat from a Fanatic Group"
Hosmer and Lemeshow Test

Step	Chi-square	df	Sig.
1	16.298	8	.038

The significant variables for the logistic regression in model two are highlighted below.

- *Regions:* Relative to Bosaso all regions, apart from Burao, were significant in predicting the fear of fanatic groups. Mogadishu had the highest odds ratio, Exp (B) = 26.87 with a 95% confidence interval of 16.12 to 44.79, implying that respondents in Mogadishu predicted an increased feeling of threat.

- *Clan Membership:* Relative to the Darod clan, the Hawiye and Indian clans were significant. The Hawiye and Indian clan members predicted a decreased feeling of threat from a fanatic group relative to Darod clan members.

- *Clan Dispute Frequency:* The frequency of clan disputes predicted the feeling of threat from a fanatic group increasing. As frequency of clan disputes increases, the feeling of threat increases.

- *Trust in Clan and Community Leaders:* As the level of trust towards clan/community leaders in responding to violence and crime increases, the feeling of threat from a fanatic group is predicted to decrease.

- *Firearms Availability:* The same availability of firearms predicts the feeling of threat from a fanatic group increasing. When the availability of firearms increases, the feeling of threat from a fanatic group is predicted to increase.

- *Threat of Remote/Time Control Bombs:* As the perceived threat of remote control bombs increases, the feeling of threat from a fanatic group is predicted to increase.

	B	S.E.	Wald	df	Sig.	Exp(B)	95.0% C.I.for EXP(B) Lower	Upper
Step 1ᵃ Region – Bosaso			193.758	4	.000			
Region – Las Anod	1.516	.175	74.906	1	.000	4.552	3.230	6.416
Region – Burao	.289	.372	.601	1	.438	1.335	.643	2.768
Region – Galkayo	1.580	.197	64.218	1	.000	4.854	3.298	7.143
Region – Mogadishu	3.291	.261	159.354	1	.000	26.868	16.119	44.786
AgeGroup – 0 to 17			5.242	6	.513			
AgeGroup – 18 to 25	.426	.491	.754	1	.385	1.532	.585	4.012
AgeGroup – 26 to 35	.442	.486	.826	1	.363	1.556	.600	4.035
AgeGroup – 36 to 45	.201	.487	.169	1	.681	1.222	.470	3.174
AgeGroup – 46 to 55	.450	.499	.814	1	.367	1.569	.590	4.170
AgeGroup – 56 to 65	.308	.522	.348	1	.555	1.360	.489	3.781
AgeGroup – 66 upwards	.685	.595	1.323	1	.250	1.983	.618	6.369
Gender – Male	-.151	.116	1.684	1	.194	.860	.685	1.080
Clan – Darod			20.319	8	.009			
Clan – Dir	-.540	.300	3.243	1	.072	.583	.324	1.049
Clan – Hawiye	-.813	.212	14.729	1	.000	.444	.293	.672
Clan – Digil/Mirifile	-.666	.343	3.763	1	.052	.514	.262	1.007
Clan – Isaaq	-.440	.324	1.852	1	.174	.644	.342	1.214
Clan – Indian	-1.955	.823	5.640	1	.018	.141	.028	.711
Clan – Arab	-.268	.394	.462	1	.497	.765	.353	1.657
Clan – Bantu	-.367	.305	1.448	1	.229	.693	.381	1.259
Clan – others	-.718	.401	3.214	1	.073	.488	.222	1.069
HouseholdStatus – IDP/refugee	.054	.155	.121	1	.728	1.055	.779	1.429
HouseholdHead – Employed	.037	.122	.094	1	.759	1.038	.818	1.318
HouseholdHead – Educated	-.063	.114	.307	1	.579	.939	.750	1.174
FemaleParticipation – Yes	-.176	.133	1.739	1	.187	.839	.646	1.089
ClanDisputeFrequency – Yes	.382	.115	11.063	1	.001	1.465	1.170	1.836
ClanCommunityTrust – High	-.786	.135	33.947	1	.000	.455	.350	.593

ReligiousLeadersTrust – High	-.196	.148	1.770	1	.183	.822	.615	1.097
PoliceTrust – High	.009	.133	.005	1	.946	1.009	.778	1.308
CourtTrust – High	-.109	.142	.588	1	.443	.897	.679	1.185
FirearmsAvailability – Same	.564	.159	12.595	1	.000	1.757	1.287	2.400
FirearmsAvailability – Increase	.400	.150	7.108	1	.008	1.492	1.112	2.002
IEDThreat – Low	2.130	.158	181.172	1	.000	8.411	6.168	11.469
IEDThreat – High	2.582	.170	230.281	1	.000	13.218	9.470	18.449
Constant	-2.693	.557	23.392	1	.000	.068		

a. Variable(s) entered on step 1: Region, AgeGroup, Gender, Clan, HouseholdStatus, HouseholdHeadEmployment, HouseholdHeadEducation, FemaleParticipation, ClanDisputeFrequency, ClanCommunityTrust, ReligiousLeadersTrust, PoliceTrust, CourtTrust, FirearmsAvailability, IEDThreat.

Table 20. Model 2: Feeling of Threat from a Fanatic Group as the dependent variable

In table 3.18, the variables highlighted in yellow are statistically significant variables at the 95% confidence level. Collinearity diagnostics were conducted using linear regression to test for multicollinearity. All tolerance values were above .1 and all variance inflation factors (VIF) were below ten. Interestingly the variables of trust towards religious leaders and police were non-significant for model two while these variables were significant in model one using Perception of Safety as the dependent variable.

3.5.2 Social Capital and Armed Conflict at the City Level

Applying the same analytical framework based on model one and model two (with Perception of Safety and Feeling of Threat from a Fanatic Group as the dependent variables), the logistic regression for each city[20] showed a variance in terms of significant variables and the odds ratio. The variances highlight the different types and levels of social capital in each city related to the two armed conflict proxies. As expected, and supporting Durlauf and Fafchamps argument[21], the individual results by city clearly show a variance versus the logistic regression using the aggregated data at the national level in terms of significant proxies.

The significant variables for each city in model one and model two are highlighted in the two tables. The plus and negative signs represent the direction of the odds ratio: a positive odds ratio for model one indicates a prediction that the Perception of Safety increases; a negative sign indicates that the Perception of Safety decreases. For model two, a positive odds ratio predicts that the feeling of Threat from a Fanatic Group increases while a negative odds ratio predicts that the feeling of threat decreases.

	Mogadishu	Bosaso	Las Anod	Burao	Galkayo
AgeGroup-0 to 17					
AgeGroup-18 to 25					+
AgeGroup-26 to 35					
AgeGroup-36 to 45					+
AgeGroup-46 to 55					+
AgeGroup-56 to 65					
AgeGroup-66 upwards					
Gender-Male		--			--
Clan-Darood					
Clan-Dir					
Clan-Hawiye					+
Clan-Digil/Mirifile					
Clan-Isaaq					
Clan-Indian					
Clan-Arab					
Clan-Bantu					
HouseholdStatus-IDP/Refugee					--
HouseholdHead-Employed		--			
HouseholdHead-Educated	+				+
FemaleParticipation-Yes					
ClanDisputeFrequency-Yes		--	+		
ClanCommunitytrust-High		+	+		+
ReligiousLeadersTrust-High	+		+		
PoliceTrust-High		--			
CourtTrust-High			+		
Firearms Availability-Same					+
Firearms Availability-Increase	+	--	--		+
IEDThreat-Low	--	--	--		
IEDThreat-High	--	--	--		--
District-Shangani					
District-Hamarweyne	--				
District-Waberi	--				
District-Darkinely	--				
District-Wadajir					
District-Hamarjabjab	--				

Cox R2	.269	.335	0.248	.101	.268
Nagelkerke's R2	.407	.482	0.357	1.00	.359
Hsomer&Lemeshow Test (Chi	5.573	5.357	5.209	.000	5.626
Hsomer&Lemeshow Test (sig.)	.695	.719	.735	1.000	.689

Table 21. By City--Model 1: "Perception of Safety" as the dependent variable

	Mogadishu	Bosaso	Las Anod	Burao	Galkayo
AgeGroup-0 to 17					
AgeGroup-18 to 25					
AgeGroup-26 to 35					
AgeGroup-36 to 45					
AgeGroup-46 to 55					
AgeGroup-56 to 65					
AgeGroup-66 upwards					
Gender-Male					
Clan-Darood					
Clan-Dir					
Clan-Hawiye					
Clan-Digil/Mirifile					
Clan-Isaaq	--				
Clan-Indian	--				
Clan-Arab					
Clan-Bantu					
Clan-Others					
HouseholdStatus-IDP/Refugee					
HouseholdHead-Employed					
HouseholdHead-Educated					
FemaleParticipation-Yes			+	--	--
ClanDisputeFrequency-Yes			+		+
ClanCommunitytrust-High			--		
ReligiousLeadersTrust-High			--		
PoliceTrust-High		+			
CourtTrust-High			--		+
Firearms Availability-Same			+		
Firearms Availability-Increase			+		
IEDThreat-Low	+	+	+	+	+
IEDThreat-High	+	+	+	+	+
District-Shangani					
District-Hamarweyne					
District-Waberi					
District-Darkinely					
District-Wadajir					

District-Hamarjabjab	--				
Cox R²	.080	.133	.378	.210	.305
Nagelkerke's R²	.216	.219	.507	.356	.409
Hsomer&Lemeshow Test (Chi	6.514	7.885	13.957	5.997	3.553
Hsomer&Lemeshow Test (sig.)	.590	.445	.083	.648	.895

Table 22. By City--Model 2: "Threat from a Franatic Group" as the dependent variable

Based on the various significant variables highlighted above for each city, the results clearly show the different social capital dynamics at play. As predicted, the variances indicate that different relationships between armed conflict and social capital exist in each city and provide interesting insight for the qualitatively analysis.[22] In addition the logistic regression using aggregated data and then analyzed at the city level shows different variables being significant, an expected result for this research inquiry that allows us to justify further analyses into the variances of social capital in Somalia[23]. The quantitative analyses indicate that each city has unique local dynamics and this will be looked into further detail qualitatively to understand the variances highlighted by the analytical framework. The following section takes a brief look at the UNSOA opinion data, which focuses on Mogadishu.

3.5.3 Social Capital and Armed Conflict in Mogadishu

For the purpose of analysis, data from the UNSOA opinion poll for only the same six districts in Mogadishu as covered in the UNDP survey was used in order to maintain consistency. Based on this criterion, the UNSOA opinion poll data for 2011 had a relevant sample size of 431 and the 2012 data had 308 samples. The analysis presents the results of the logistic regression for only these same six districts and uses only one dependent variable.

Once again, relevant proxies were identified for the analytical framework based on the questions used by the two opinion polls. Similar to the UNDP baseline data, although not a perfect "fit", the variables chosen from the UNSOA opinion poll attempt to replicate the analytical framework to compare the logistic regression results from the UNDP data for Mogadishu. It must be highlighted, however, that the questions used from the UNSOA opinion poll were different from those used in the UNDP survey. Every attempt has been made to identify similar questions between the two surveys however differences between the two questionnaires forces the selection of relevant variables to create a similar best "fit".

In terms of the dependent variable, I have chosen the question: "How, if at all, has the current conflict in Somalia affected you personally? Lost friends/relatives in violence?" Respondents answered either "no" (y=0) or "yes" (y=1). The distribution of answers makes an interesting comparison based on the six districts analyzed. In 2011, 39% answered that they had lost friends or relatives due to violence while in 2012 this number increased to 66%.

The following proxies[24] for the predictor variables were chosen from the UNSOA opinion polls to best replicate the analytical framework and conduct a comparison with the logistic regression results from the UNDP data. No residual variables were added to the model and no similar proxies related to "Firearms Availability" and "Threat of Remote/Time Control Bombs" was identified.

> *Armed Conflict (dependent variable):* Experience loss of friends/relatives from violence due to the current conflict in Somalia
> *Socio-Demographic Attributes:* District; Gender; Age; Living conditions compared to others[25]
> *Groups and Group Networks:* Education-level (bridging)
> *Personal Networks:* Residence Status (bonding); Employment status (bridging)
> *Trust:* Trust in clan and community leaders (bonding, hard linking); Trust in religious leaders (bridging, soft linking); Trust in politicians and government officials (bridging, hard linking); Trust in people from other clans (bridging); Trust politicians only from own clan (bonding)
> *Social Cohesion & Inclusion:* Vote for a better qualified candidate from a different clan (bridging); Talk until everyone agrees in community to make a decision (bridging, soft linking); Political power should be shared by all clans (bridging)
> *Identity:* Political parties organized on clan or political basis (bonding, bridging)
> *Community Leadership:* Effectiveness of clan leaders, religions men, business leaders in improving the situation in Somalia (bonding, bridging, hard linking, soft linking)

The logistic regression results for the 2011 and 2012 opinion polls show the following significant variables for the six districts with the respective Cox & Snell's R^2 and the Nagelkerke's R^2:

> ➤ **2011 Opinion Poll:** Region (Waberi only versus Dharkenley); Gender; Age (26 to 35 age group); Living conditions compared to others; Residence status; Willing to share political power

Model Summary for 2011 Opinion Poll

Step	-2 Log likelihood	Cox & Snell R Square	Nagelkerke R Square
1	452.725[a]	.243	.329

Hosmer and Lemeshow Test for 2011 Opinion Poll

Step	Chi-square	Df	Sig.
1	7.682	8	.465

The 2011 data shows, based on the odds ratios, that respondents in Waberi were less likely to have lost friends/relatives compared to Dharkenley; the age group 26 to 35 years old was more likely to have lost friends/relatives compared to the age group 18 to 25 years old; respondents who saw their living conditions better than other Somalis were more likely to have lost friends/relatives compared to those who felt they were worse off; residents who were displaced were more likely to have lost friends/relatives; and respondents who agreed that political power should be shared by all clans were more likely to have lost friends/relatives.

> ➤ **2012 Opinion Poll:** Region (Waberi and Wadajir versus Hamarweyne); Employment status

Model Summary 2012 Opinion Poll

Step	-2 Log likelihood	Cox & Snell R Square	Nagelkerke R Square
1	154.547a	.335	.471

Hosmer and Lemeshow Test for 2012 Opinion Poll

Step	Chi-square	Df	Sig.
1	8.146	8	.419

The 2012 data showed only the district and employment status as being statistically significant. Residents in Wadajir were less likely to have lost friends/relatives compared to residents in Hamarweyne; while residents in Waberi were more likely to have lost friends/relatives versus Hamarweyne and Wadajir residents. Respondents who were employed or students were more likely to have lost/friends versus those who were unemployed or were not students.

There were slight differences between the two opinion polls for individual answers with only two questions having notable differences:

> In 2011 only 3% of respondents thought that political parties should be divided on a clan basis. This increased to 30% in 2012.

> In 2011 60% of respondents viewed business leaders as effective in improving the situation. This number decreased to 39% in 2012.

Compared to the UNDP data results, the number of significant variables and social capital proxies from the 2011 UNSOA data was much less and decreased dramatically for 2012. This result indicates the unique dynamics at play for Mogadishu. The results from the UNSOA data for Mogadishu will be used when analyzing social capital and armed conflict qualitatively, especially for the districts of Waberi and Wadajir.

3.5.4 Armed Conflict at the City Level

Using the UNDP data, the trends in armed conflict by city are first compared using a simple count based on percentage terms of the following variables: Perception of Safety (question PV1); Feeling of Threat from a Fanatic Group (PV8); Frequency of Clan/Community Disputes (CD1); Frequency of Witnessing Violence (WV1); Frequency of Property Crime (PC1); and Experience of Forced Detention (OV1). A comparison of the data by city summarizes the following in order of "highest" armed conflict levels:

Armed conflict proxy/Ranking	1	2	3	4	5
Perception of safety	Mogadishu	Galkayo	Las Anod	Bosaso	Burao
Feeling of threat from a fanatic group	Mogadishu	Galkayo	Las Anod	Burao	Bosaso

Frequency of clan/ community disputes	Galkayo	Las Anod	Bosaso	Mogadishu	Burao
Witnessing violence	Galkayo	Mogadishu	Burao	Las Anod	Bosaso
Property crime	Mogadishu	Galkayo	Las Anod	Burao	Bosaso
Experience of forced detention	Mogadishu	Las Anod	Galkayo	Burao	Bosaso

Table 23. Ranking of cities based on percentage terms of various armed conflict proxies

A second count, using the results of the logistic regression for both models at the national level, looks at the change in odds (Exp(B)) for the different statistically significant regions. Relative to Bosaso, Mogadishu has the largest odds of the outcome decreasing for Perception of Safety while the likelihood of Feeling a Threat from a Fanatic Group increasing is the highest. Put simply, respondents in Mogadishu have the highest likelihood of feeling a threat from fanatic group while the least likelihood of feeling safe relative to Bosaso. Las Anod is ranked second for model one and Galkayo for model two. Galkayo is non-significant for model one and Burao is non-significant in model two in predicting the dependent variables.

Dependent variable/City and change in odds (Exp(B))	1	2	3	
Perception of safety relative to Bosaso	Mogadishu (.305)	Las Anod (1.859)	Burao (34.486)	Galkayo (non-significant)
Feeling of threat from a fanatic group relative to Bosaso	Mogadishu (26.868)	Galkayo (4.854)	Las Anod (4.552)	Burao (non-significant)

Table 24. Change in odds (Exp(B)) ranking for significant cities based on the logistic regression of the two models

Another set of data used to measure armed conflict on a nationwide scale is the Armed Conflict Location and Event Dataset (ACLED) which codes the dates and locations of all reported political violence events based on public news sources. The data contains information on (ACLED 2013):

➢ Dates and locations of conflict events
➢ Specific types of events including battles, civilian killings, riots, protests and recruitment activities
➢ Events by a range of actors, including rebels, governments, militias, armed groups, protesters and civilians
➢ Changes in territorial control
➢ Fatalities

The time period of October 2009 to July 2010 is used as the reference period to match the timeframe when the UNDP survey was conducted. Conflict events were counted at a *regional* level. Based on this specific timeframe, the ACLED data showed the following trend.

Region	Number of political violence events from Oct 2009 to July 2010
Benadir	394
Bari	64
Sool	48
Mudug	37
Togdheer	16

Table 25. Ranking of violence based on ACLED data for the five regions

What is clear from both the UNDP and ACLED data is that the Benadir region, city of Mogadishu, has the highest number of incidents related to armed conflict. Otherwise, the discrepancies in the data become difficult to interpret and the level of armed conflict becomes subjective. In the next chapter, based on the focus group discussion and small-n survey, more details related to the level of armed conflict are touched upon.

3.5.5 Discriminant Analysis

As mentioned in section 2.6.5, discriminant analysis is used to see how discriminant function variates [26] allow groups of cases to be discriminated. The groups of cases are used to discriminate the five cities which are treated as the dependent variables. While the dependent variables used are the five cities, the independent variables are all the social capital proxies used in the logistic regression from the UNDP baseline data. Wilks' Lamba [27], standardized canonical discriminant function coefficients, and the structure matrix (which provides canonical variate correlations coefficients) are included in the Appendix (Field 2005:610).

For the purpose of identifying three cities for further qualitative work, a combined-groups plot is used to highlight the differences of the group centroids (which are the average variate scores of each group). Simply put, the discriminant analysis allows us to visually picture the differences between the five cities (the dependent variables) based on the social capital proxies used earlier (independent variables) and identify three candidate-cities for further qualitative analysis.

The functions at group centroids are shown below for each city (table 3.24) and the combined-groups plot uses the coordinates of only the first two functions. Based on the group centroids of variates one and two, Mogadishu and Burao are clearly separated from the other three cities (plot 3.1). Thereby Mogadishu and Burao are selected as candidates for further qualitative research because of the large variances of the group centroids from the other three cities' group centroids. Galkayo is selected as the third city, or the "middle case" relative to Burao and Mogadishu, even though the differences in average variate scores relevant to Mogadishu are Burao are less than Bosaso.

Galkayo is preferred over Bosaso for two reasons in terms of research choice: the city is split in two both politically and by clan composition; the armed conflict levels for Galkayo, as highlighted in the previous section, place the city in between Burao and Mogadishu. To recall, based on the UNDP and ACLED data, Mogadishu is seen as having the highest levels of armed conflict while Burao is seen as having relatively low levels. The armed conflict levels for Galkayo conveniently fall in between the two cities, making the city an interesting candidate as the middle case for further qualitative analysis.

Functions at Group Centroids

Region	Function			
	1	2	3	4
Bari-Bosasso	1.028	.271	.435	.507
Sool-Las Anod	.977	-.328	.461	-.414
Togdheer-Burao	-.353	1.781	-.295	-.155
Mudug-Galkayo	.941	-.660	-.869	.044
Benadir-Mogadishu	-1.715	-.447	.088	.045

Unstandardized canonical discriminant functions evaluated at group means

Table 26. Average variate scores of each group represented as functions

Canonical Discriminant Functions

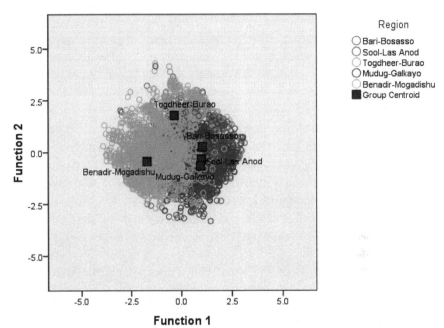

Function 1

Figure 7. Combined-groups plot illuminating the variate scores of each city and group centroids

3.6 Discussion of Results

This section reviews the results of the logistic regression for both models at the national and city level and examines the robustness of the analytical framework by looking at the statistical significance of the social capital proxies. The next and final section looks at the relationship between social capital and armed violence against the four hypotheses and theoretical predictions.

3.6.1 Comparing Model One and Model Two at the National Level

At the national level, the results of the logistic regression for the two models show that the *regional* variable significantly predicts the variance in the levels of Perception of Safety and Feeling of a Threat from a Fanatic Group. The regions of Las Anod and Mogadishu are significant in predicting both dependent variables. In terms of other social demographic attributes, *age* is significant only for the age group 46 to 55 in predicting the Perception of Safety. In terms of Identity as a specific social capital proxy, *clan* in general was significant for both models with variances seen amongst the two models. Household heads in the Hawiye clan were significant predictors for both models. For the social capital proxy related to Personal Networks, *household status in terms of residence* and *employment status* of the household head were non-significant for both models. *Education level* was significant only in predicting Perception of Safety. The Social Cohesion and Inclusion proxy for social capital, *female participation in village and town meetings*, was non-significant for both models. *Frequency of clan disputes*, a Community Leadership proxy, was only significant for predicting Feeling of Threat from a Fanatic Group variable. *Trust in community and clan elders* was significant for both models while *trust in religious leaders* and *police* was only significant in predicting Perception of Safety. *Trust in courts* was non-significant for both models. The residual variables, *level of firearms availability* and *feeling of threat from a remote control bomb*, were significant for both models.

Based on the results of the logistic regression using the aggregated data for both models, the analyses validate four out of the initial six social capital proxies. The four statistically significant proxies from the original analytical framework of figure 3.1 are highlighted below as a revised analytical framework.

Groups and Group Networks

Socio-Demographic +   Trust   →   Armed conflict
Attributes
                      Identity

                      Community Leadership

Figure 8. Revised analytical framework based on logistic regression using Model 1 and 2 based on aggregate data

To summarize, in terms of the specific proxies, the following variables were significant:

> *Socio-Demographic Attributes:* Region (Las Anod and Mogadishu for both models), Age (only for the age group from 46 to 55 in predicting Perception of Safety)
> *Groups and Group Networks:* Education Level (only for predicting Perception of Safety)

> ➤ *Trust:* Trust in Clan and Community Leaders (for both models); Trust in Religious Leaders and Trust in Police (only in predicting Perception of Safety);
> ➤ *Identity:* Clan Membership (Hawiye clan membership were significant predictors for both models)
> ➤ *Community Leadership:* Clan Dispute Frequency (only for predicting Feeling of Threat from a Fanatic Group)

Personal Networks (Residence Status and Employment Status) and the proxy *Social Cohesion and Inclusion* (Gender Equality) were non-significant for both models.

Table 3.25 provides a snapshot of the statistically significant variables for both models and highlights the relevant social capital proxies in terms of bonding, bridging, and linking. Overall the table highlights four variables representing bridging social capital, two for bonding social capital, and five for linking social capital as statistically significant.

The plus and negative signs represents the direction of the odds ratio (B): a positive odds ratio for model one indicates a prediction that Perception of Safety increases; a negative sign indicates that Perception of Safety decreases. For model two, a positive odds ratio predicts that the feeling of Threat from a Fanatic Group increases while a negative odds ratio predicts that the feeling of threat decreases. We would therefore expect the direction of the odds ratio to be opposite for each variable. For example, the negative odds ratio in model one predicts Perception of Safety decreasing while the positive odds ratio in model two predicts the Threat from Fanatic Group increasing. Put shortly, respondents in Mogadishu are more likely to predict feeling unsafe and feel a threat from a fanatic group. Based on this logic, expectations would be for the direction of the odds ratio for model one and two to be opposite, as seen in the case of Mogadishu. However Table 3.25 shows two variables with the same direction of odds ratio: the Las Anod region and Firearms Availability increasing.

Two possible explanations are suggested here but will require further verification and analysis. First, the northern region of Somalia, where Las Anod is located, has seen a slow infiltration of Al Shabaab affiliated groups. This may have led to Las Anod predicting an increase in Threat from a Fanatic Group even though Las Anod was perceived as safe. Second, in terms of Firearms Availability, the positive odds ratio in model one implies that an increase of firearms leads to an increased perception of safety. On the other hand model two indicates that an increase in firearms predicts a higher threat from a fanatic group. Based on the two results, it seems contradictory for an increase of firearms predicting an increased feeling of safety. However, this could come from feeling safer when one's group is increasingly armed and readily prepared to fend off attacks or threats.

	Variables	Model 1 Perception of Safety	Model 2 Threat from Fanatic Group	Social Capital Type
Socio-demographic attributes	Region-Bosaso (reference)			
	Region-Las Anod	+	+	
	Region-Burao	+		
	Region-Galkayo		+	
	Region-Mogadishu	--	+	
	AgeGroup-0 to 17			
	AgeGroup-18 to 25			
	AgeGroup-26 to 35			
	AgeGroup-36 to 45			
	AgeGroup-46 to 55	+		
	AgeGroup-56 to 65			
	AgeGroup-66 upwards			
	Gender-Male			
Identity	Clan-Darod (reference)			Bonding, Linking
	Clan-Dir			
	Clan-Hawiye	+	--	
	Clan-Digil/Mirifle	+		
	Clan-Isaaq			
	Clan-Indian		--	
	Clan-Arab	+		
	Clan-Bantu	+		
	Clan-Others			

		Model 1	Model 2	Type
Personal Networks	Household Status-IDP/Refugee			Bonding
	Household Head-Employed			Bridging
Group Networks	Household Head-Educated	+		Bridging
Social Cohesion	Female Participation-Yes			Bridging
Community Leadership	Clan Dispute Frequency-Yes		+	Bridging, Linking
Trust	Clan Community trust-High	+	--	Bonding, Linking
	Religious Leaders Trust-High	+		Bridging, Linking
	Police Trust-High	--		Bridging, Linking
	Court Trust-High			Bridging
Residual Variables	Firearms Availability-Stay same		+	
	Firearms Availability-Increase	+	+	
	IED Threat-Low	--	+	
	IED Threat-High	--	+	

Table 27. Significant variables for Models 1 and 2

3.6.2 Comparing Model One and Model Two at the City Level

As mentioned earlier, the logistic regression for each city exemplifies unique "local dynamics" that will be further looked at qualitatively using the analytical framework. The variances between the two models at the city level highlight the strengths and weaknesses of the analytical framework. Model one, using Perception of Safety as the dependent variable (table 19), seems more robust than model two (table 20) as the number of significant variables is higher. Model one is more robust for Mogadishu and Galkayo however it has no significant variables for

Burao[28]. This is a very interesting finding as it could suggest that certain aspects of social capital in Burao have been replaced by state institutions, warranting further qualitative analysis[29]. The results for Las Anod in model two are more robust than model one, since model two has more significant variables and higher values for Cox R^2 and Nagelkerke's R^2.

Overall the robustness of both models can be highlighted in terms of the direction of the odds ratio for the two models. Favorably, the opposite directions of the odds ratio are present in all significant variables that overlap for each city with one exception, Clan Dispute Frequency for Las Anod. Model one, for Las Anod, implies that increased clan disputes in the community predict an increased perception of safety, which is counterintuitive. Excluding this occurrence, both models at the city level highlight interesting dynamics that will be analyzed in the next chapter.

3.7 Conclusions and Areas for Future Research

To recall, the objective of this chapter is three-fold: to acquire an overall picture and context setting of social capital and armed conflict in the five cities descriptively and inferentially identify three cities for further qualitative research; to verify the robustness of the analytical framework by looking at the statistical significance of the chosen social capital proxies; and to look at the relationship between social capital and armed violence against the four hypotheses and theoretical predictions.

Based on the two models, a variety of significant variables for social capital was identified as statistically significant predictors of armed conflict. At the national level, the quantitative analysis confirmed the importance of: *region; clan identity; education-level; frequency of clan disputes; and trust in community/clan elders, religious leaders, and police.* Although not exactly proxies for social capital, but having characteristics similar to bonding social capital, the variables related to *firearms availability* and the *feeling of threat from a remote/time control bomb* were also both significant. At the city level, the relevant variables included *age, gender, residence status, employment status, female participation, and trust in courts.*

In terms of the analytical framework, the logistic regression using the UNDP data at the national level suggests that only four out of the original six proxies for social capital were significant: *Identity, Group Networks, Community Leadership,* and *Trust.* When the analytical framework using the UNDP data was applied at the city level, various results emerged for each city providing useful insight for future qualitative analysis for each city. The logistic regression at the city level showed an increased number of proxies being significant for each city, highlighting the relevance of the analytical framework even at the city level. However, the significance of the model decreased when the data from the UNSOA opinion poll for Mogadishu was used, highlighting the complicated local dynamics at play in the six districts and the need for qualitative research to analyze the district level dynamics.

Obviously the results of the analyses have their limitations and are strongly influenced by the selected variables from the data sets. Although the selected questions used from the UNDP data set were not a perfect "fit" with the analytical framework proxies, the research inquiry provides useful insight into the complex dynamics between social capital and armed conflict at the national and city level.

Based on the large-n data available, it was not possible to address the issue of causality, which would have required using different statistical methods such as structural equation modeling or instrumental variables approach. The statistical analyses do not provide any specific insight into the direction of causality between social capital and armed violence and the effects of armed conflict on social capital require further research.

Using the logistic regression results from the UNDP data for the two models, the four hypotheses are looked at, as stipulated below.

Hypothesis one: *Bridging social capital has a negative impact on armed conflict.*

Hypothesis two: *Bonding social capital has a positive impact on armed conflict.*

Hypothesis three: *Hard linking social capital has a positive impact on armed conflict.*

Hypothesis four: *Soft linking social capital has a negative impact on armed conflict.*

From the results of the logistic regression at the *national level*, the following relationships between armed conflict and social capital emerge.

> ➢ **Bridging social capital** has a *negative* impact ("-ve" as stipulated in Table 3.26) on armed conflict based on the proxies related to Group Networks and Trust in religious leaders, thereby supporting the hypothesis. However Community Leadership and Trust in police have a *positive* impact (+ve) on armed conflict, contradicting the hypothesis.
> ➢ **Bonding social capital** has a *negative* impact (-ve) on armed conflict based on the Identity and Trust in clan leaders proxies, contradicting the hypothesis. It also has a negative impact based on the Firearms Availability variable which has bonding social capital characteristics.
> ➢ **Hard linking social capital** based on Community Leadership and Trust in police has a *positive* impact (+ve) on armed conflict as predicted. However Identity and Trust in clan leaders have a *negative* impact (-ve) on armed conflict.
> ➢ **Soft linking social capital** has a *negative* impact (-ve) on armed conflict based on the proxy related to Trust in religious leaders, supporting the hypothesis.

The results of the logistic regression at the national level only fully supports the fourth hypothesis and partially supports the third hypothesis as shown in table 3.26. Hypothesis one displays both negative and positive impact. Hypothesis two is rejected as the data shows that the proxies related to bonding social capital predict armed conflict to decrease in both models.

	Armed conflict vs. Bridging	Armed conflict vs. Bonding	Armed conflict vs. Hard Linking	Armed conflict vs. Soft Linking
Hypothesis	-ve	+ve	+ve	-ve
Quantitative results	-ve/+ve	-ve	-ve/+ve	-ve

Table 28. Hypotheses against the quantitative results based on the aggregated UNDP baseline data for impact on the likelihood of armed conflict occurring

The social capital proxies that contradict hypothesis one, Community Leadership and Trust in police, may suggest omitted-variable bias and reverse causality respectively. The variable for Community Leadership looks at the frequency of clan disputes predicting the feeling of threat from a fanatic group (model 2). The results show that as frequency of clan disputes increases, the feeling of a threat from a fanatic group increases. Mogadishu had the largest number of respondents who felt there was a low or high threat from a fanatic group (54%) and also a high frequency of clan/community disputes compared to the other regions. As Mogadishu has seen the brunt of combat against Al Shabaab, this result would be expected. The relationship between the relatively high number of clan/community disputes in Mogadishu and the widespread feeling of threat from a fanatic group in the capital city could suggest an omitted-variable since the most common reason of disputes in Mogadishu (table 3.8) is revenge (32%) followed by power/cultural struggle (27%). Trust in police could suggest a reverse causality where a decreased perception of safety from armed conflict creates a sense of insecurity within the community, thereby increasing reliance and trust towards the police to provide security.

Hypothesis two is rejected based on the Identity and Trust in clan leaders proxies, both which have clan as the central tenet. Clan Membership is the variable representing the Identity proxy and both the Hawiye and Digil/Mirifle, which are large clan families, predict an increased perception of safety (compared to the Darod clan) contrary to the hypothesis. Since both of these groups are considered as "large" clans, an increased perception of safety could be originating based on the feeling of "safety in numbers". However, interestingly, the smaller minority clans (Arab and Bantu) also have an increased perception of safety despite the conventional thinking that minority clans are victimized and should be prone to feeling insecure. Further research will be required in this area. The analysis shows high levels of trust in clan community leaders in responding to violence and crime predict an increased perception of safety. This could be based on respondents feeling a sense of safety when their clan elders are seen as providing security and order in the community.

The above quantitative research results related to bonding and bridging social capital, albeit contradictory to the expectations, support the literature that bonding social capital is crucial in the development of bridging social capital and must exist a priori in sufficient amounts for bridging social capital to be developed.

Hypothesis three, regarding hard linking social capital, initially shows mixed results. Identity and Trust in clan leaders indicate a negative impact on armed conflict which is contrary to the predictions. Although Clan Membership, representing the Identity proxy, predicts

117

an increased perception of safety contrary to the hypothesis, its reliability as a proxy for hard linking social capital is questioned as membership in the *large* Hawiye clan family may simply be reinforcing the perception of safety and decreasing the feeling of threat from a fanatic group based on "safety in numbers", as highlighted earlier. When excluding the Identity proxy from the analysis, the results suggest hard linking social capital having an overall positive impact on armed conflict with only high levels of Trust in clan leaders predicting less armed conflict possibly due to improved community security arrangements.

In regard to reviewing the theoretical predictions, two approaches emerge to measure and compare the levels of social capital for the five cities. The first approach involves comparing the logistic regression results for each city and the significant proxies between the five cities, specifically the odds ratio and Exp(B). This approach however is not feasible as the logistic regression results at the city level show different variables being significant for each region, indicating that each city has unique and localized dynamics at play (see section 3.5.2 for more detailed analysis). The second approach, which is more practical for this research inquiry, is to compare the results of the crosstabulations by city for the statistically significant social capital proxies resulting from the logistic regression of both models at the nationwide level. The crosstabulations are used to identify the order of the cities in regard to the level of social capital and is determined by comparing the proportions within each specific city and ranking them against all five cities[30]. Based on table 3.25 we have four proxies to look at: Identity, Group Networks, Community Leadership, and Trust (for Clan Leaders, Religious Leaders, and Police). Socio-demographic attributes and the residual variables are left outside of the analysis.

> ➤ Prediction one: Bosaso and Burao have relatively higher levels of *bridging social capital* versus Mogadishu, Galkayo, and Las Anod.

Looking at the significant bridging social capital proxies by city for Group Networks, Community Leadership, and Trust, the following results were noted in order of highest to lowest:

- Group Networks (most "educated") – Bosaso, Las Anod, Burao, Galkayo, Mogadishu

- Community Leadership (in order of most clan dispute) – Galkayo, Las Anod, Bosaso, Mogadishu, Burao
- Trust in Religious Leaders (most trust towards religious leaders) – Galkayo, Bosaso, Las Anod, Burao, Mogadishu
- Trust in Police (most trust towards the police) – Bosaso, Burao, Galkayo, Las Anod, Mogadishu

Bosaso and Burao showed high levels of trust towards the police (table 3.15) and low amounts of clan disputes (table 3.4) as predicted. However Las Anod also showed high levels of bridging social capital based on group networks and trust towards religious leaders (table 3.14). Results for Mogadishu suggested low levels of bridging social capital relative to the other four cities. Galkayo indicated low levels of bridging social capital overall with the exception of high levels of trust towards religious leaders (table 3.14). *The results partially support the theoretical prediction.*

> ➤ Prediction two: Mogadishu, Galkayo, and Las Anod have relatively higher levels of *bonding social capital* versus Bosaso and Burao.

The significant proxies for bonding social capital are Identity and Trust. The Trust proxy focused on levels of trust towards clan and community leaders to respond to violence and crime.

- Identity – Mogadishu has the highest percentage of Hawiye and Digil/Mirifle clan members followed by Galkayo (table 3.2)
- Trust in Clan Leaders (most trust towards clan/community leaders) – Bosaso, Galkayo, Las Anod, Burao, Mogadishu

In regard to Identity, clan membership in the Hawiye, Digil/Mirifle, Indian, and Arab were seen as statistically significant variables portraying bonding social capital. Las Anod had the highest number of Darod in terms of percentage but this is not statistically significant as it is used as a reference for the logistic regression. The results for Identity support prediction two for Mogadishu and Galkayo suggesting high levels of bonding social capital in these two cities. However Bosaso, Las Anod, and Burao saw high levels of trust towards clan elders (table 3.13) contradicting the prediction where trust towards clan elders was

119

at their lowest for Mogadishu. The specific results for Galkayo and Las Anod support prediction two however the remaining results for the other cities challenge the prediction or contradict it, such as Burao. *The results for the data are mixed and the theoretical prediction is rejected.*

➤ Prediction three: Mogadishu has higher levels of hard linking social capital relative to the other four cities.

Identity, Community Leadership, and Trust are the significant hard linking social capital proxies.

- Identity – Mogadishu has the highest percentage of Hawiye and Digil/Mirifle clan members followed by Galkayo (table 3.2)
- Community Leadership (in order of most clan dispute) – Galkayo, Las Anod, Bosaso, Mogadishu, Burao
- Trust in Clan Leaders (most trust towards clan/community leaders) – Bosaso, Galkayo, Las Anod, Burao, Mogadishu
- Trust in Police (most trust towards the police) – Bosaso, Burao, Galkayo, Las Anod, Mogadishu

The results for Identity and Community Leadership support prediction three with Mogadishu indicating high levels of hard linking social capital. However Mogadishu had low levels of hard linking social capital based on Trust in Clan Leaders (table 3.13) and Police (table 3.15). Instead Bosaso and Burao showed relatively high levels of hard linking social capital based on the Trust proxy. When looking at the logistic regression results at the city level, interestingly the only city that has Trust in Police as significant is Bosaso, predicting an inverse relationship for both outcome variables. This will looked at in more detail in the qualitative analysis. *The results for the data are mixed and the theoretical prediction is rejected.*

➤ Prediction four: Burao and Bosaso have higher levels of soft linking social capital relative to Mogadishu, Galkayo, and Las Anod.

The proxy used for measuring soft linking social capital is Trust, specifically towards religious leaders.

- Trust (most trust towards religious leaders) – Galkayo, Bosaso, Las Anod, Burao, Mogadishu

The results for this proxy are mixed. Galkayo and Bosaso have high levels of soft linking social capital based on trust towards religious leaders (table 3.14). *Overall the results do not support prediction four.*

For the four theoretical predictions, the challenges of quantifying the different types of social capital are demonstrated. Putting aside the issue of "data fit" for the proxies, the results from the analyses clearly show the limitations and difficulties of identifying significant relationships between social capital and armed conflict. Table 3.27 highlights the quantitative results from this chapter against the respective theoretical predictions and the highlighted cells in gray denote results that are contradictory to the predictions.

		Bridging (Prediction 1)	Bonding (Prediction 2)	Hard Linking (Prediction 3)	Soft Linking (Prediction 4)	Armed Conflict Level
Burao	Theoretical Prediction	H	L	L	H	L
	Quantitative results	H	H	H	L	L
Galkayo	Theoretical Prediction	L	H	L	L	H
	Quantitative results	L	H	L	H	H
Mogadishu	Theoretical Prediction	L	H	H	L	H
	Quantitative results	L	L	L	L	H
Las Anod	Theoretical Prediction	L	H	L	L	H
	Quantitative results	H	H	L	H	H
Bosaso	Theoretical Prediction	H	L	L	H	L
	Quantitative results	H	H	H	H	L

Table 29. Theoretical predictions against the quantitative results based on the UNDP baseline data

Furthermore, the results highlight the issue of "scalability" related to bonding and bridging social capital; in other words distinguishing the (moving) dividing line that determines which social networks and trust relations are inclusive and exclusive between groups. The problem of scalability is clearly seen in regard to bonding social capital during the quantitative analysis. But as seen in the next chapter, the issue of scalability in social networks is also an issue encountered in the qualitative approach.

Overall, the analyses based on the results of the logistic regression using the analytical framework support only the third and fourth hypotheses and the first (albeit partially) theoretical prediction as seen in table 3.26 and 3.27. In conclusion, the results show that Mogadishu has the highest levels of armed conflict, low levels of bridging social capital and a mixture of different levels of bonding social capital[31]. For Bosaso and Burao, the data shows low levels of armed conflict and high levels of bonding and bridging social capital. The levels of social capital for Galkayo and Las Anod are inconclusive. For this discourse, further qualitative research will be required to support the argument that regions with high levels of bonding and low levels of bridging social capital have increased levels of armed conflict; and that armed conflict is low in regions with high levels of bridging social capital. One clear conclusion from the descriptive and inferential statistics is that Mogadishu and Burao are at opposite ends of the spectrum, suggesting interesting case studies to further analyze social capital.

Notes

1   I am grateful to Simon Davies of UNSOA who provided access to the data and Bronwen Morrison of AU/UN IST for compiling the data for analysis.
2   I am indebted to Daniel Ladouceur of UNDP Somalia who provided access to the data.
3   During the time of the data collection, control of Mogadishu was split between Al Shabaab and AMISOM/TFG and would therefore had made data collection extremely difficult in Al Shabaab areas.
4   The full questionnaire can be found in the Appendix.
5   The Afgoye Corridor is the main artery road between Mogadishu and the southern town of Afgoye and is about 30 kilometers in length. IDP camps were established along the road to escape the fighting in Mogadishu.
6   Lower Juba n=230, Bay n=344, and Hiran n=457 were also surveyed.
7   Al Shabaab has presented themselves as a religious movement that disregards clan affiliation.
8   This could also be treated as a variable for bonding social capital: an increased frequency of inter-clan disputes represents higher levels of bonding social capital.
9   For the ease of reading, the "%" mark is used instead of "percent".
10   A detailed analysis of the 16 Mogadishu districts is excluded in this paper. The dynamics within and between the different districts are complex. For example the issue of the Mayor's role and the District Commissioners (DCs) is unclear as Mogadishu, at the time of research, lacks a Municipal Council law while both positions are appointed unilaterally as political appointees.
11   A detailed analysis of which districts were under anti-government elements control during the survey is not presented in this paper.
12   Historical details of the various Islamic movements in Somalia have not been included intentionally.
13   The complementarities and contradictions of the three systems vary depending on the issue. In short, quotidian criminal offences, such as burglary and public disorder, are usually dealt by the secular courts; traditional courts tend to deal with divorce, family disputes, and land issues; Sharia courts are usually

operational in areas where the government run secular courts are absent in territories controlled by Islamic fundamentalist groups. In all three systems, the way murder and rape is handled and punished is different.

14 The question is: "Has your community become safe or unsafe compared to twelve months ago?" The answers are: "become unsafe; become a little unsafe; become a little safer; become a lot safer".

15 Logistic regression is used to predict the probability that a certain case belongs in a certain bi-nominal category (Field 2005:220).

16 "If the value (Exp (B)) is greater than 1 then it indicates that as the predictor increases, the odds of the outcome occurring increase. Conversely, a value less than 1 indicates that as the predictor increases, the odds of the outcome occurring decrease" (Field 2005: 226).

17 It is beyond the scope of this paper to calculate the individual odds ratios as the interest and focus is in the variables and relevant proxies.

18 The question asks how often one feels a threat from a fanatic group with the following answers offered: none, low, or high.

19 "This statistic tests the hypothesis that the observed data are significantly different from the predicted values from the model. So, in effect, we want a non-significant value for this test (because this would indicate that the model does not differ significantly from the observed data)" (Field 2005: 254).

20 For the case of Mogadishu, the six districts were included as a socio-demographic proxy.

21 Durlauf and Fafchamps (2004:52-62) argue that social capital studies using aggregate data have not been successful in analyzing the effects of social capital and that analysis needs to be done at the micro-level, such as the city or town level versus the national level.

22 Personal communication: Shimizu 27 July 2013, Tokyo.

23 If the results of the logistic regression at the aggregated level and city level had been similar, this would have indicated minimal variances in social capital and armed conflict within the country; suggesting a situation where social capital and armed conflict were uniform across Somalia.

24 Specifically, the following questions were chosen from the 2011 UNSOA opinion poll: A8, A12, D3, D2 for Socio-demographic Attributes; D5 for Groups; Q59, D7 for Personal Networks; Q17, Q56 for Trust; Q56, Q34 for Social Cohesion and Inclusion; Q53 for Identity; Q19 for Community Leadership. For 2012, the following questions were used: X12, A1, A2.1, A13 for Socio-demographic Attributes; A6.1 for Group; L1, A8 for Personal Networks; F2, K5 for Trust; K5, H2 for Social Cohesion and Inclusion; K2 for Identity; F4 for Leadership. The questionnaires for both surveys can be found in the Appendix.

25 The formulation of this question was suggested by Professor Mitsugi Endo in 2011.

26 Discriminant analysis is also known as discriminant function analysis. The discriminant function variate takes the general form of Variate1 $= b_1 X_1 + b_2 X_2 + \ldots + b_n X_n$ (Field 2005:729).

27 Wilks' Lamba is statistically significant therefore indicating that the group of predictor variables will provide predictions to the dependent variable that are

statistically significant.

28 The responses for the dependent variable Perception of Safety were skewed: 0.8% (n=6) said community safety became "a little unsafe"; 98.1% (n=715) "became a little safer"; and 1.1% "became a lot safer" (n=8).

29 Personal communication: Shimizu 27 July 2013, Tokyo.

30 For example table 3.15, which looks at Trust in Police, shows Bosaso having the highest level of trust as a proportion by city compared to other cities: 51.5% of respondents in Bosaso had high levels of trust. The next city with the highest level of trust is Burao (51.3%). It is important to note that the comparison is based by city and not as an aggregate.

31 Separately, although not used in the logistic regression, the UNDP data for Mogadishu showed a proliferation of organized armed groups that represent high levels of bonding social capital.

CHAPTER 4. QUALITATIVELY APPROACHING SOCIAL CAPITAL AND ARMED CONFLICT IN SOMALIA

4.1 Introduction

Following the quantitative analysis in chapter three, the results highlight the need for further research at the city level to understand the relationship between social capital and armed conflict. Using this time a qualitative approach, the research inquiry looks at the relationship between social capital and armed conflict based on the selected three cities from the discriminant analysis—Burao, Galkayo, and Mogadishu—and tests them against the four theoretical predictions. As highlighted in the research design, the research inquiry does not attempt to uncover the "root causes" of the armed conflict in Somalia and focuses on analyzing the dynamics between social capital and armed conflict and comparing the qualitative results against the four theoretical predictions. The four theoretical predictions for the three selected cities are stipulated in the table below.

	Bridging (Prediction 1)	Bonding (Prediction 2)	Hard Linking (Prediction 3)	Soft Linking (Prediction 4)	Armed Conflict Level
Burao	H	L	L	H	L
Galkayo	L	H	L	L	H
Mogadishu	L	H	H	L	H

Table 30. Theoretical predictions for the three selected cities by type of social capital and assumed levels of armed conflict

This chapter consists of four sections. The first three sections undertake a qualitative analysis of each city (Burao, Mogadishu, and Galkayo) and review the levels of social capital and armed conflict based on the analytical framework. The final section summarizes the findings of the qualitative analyses for the three cities to provide a comprehensive overview of the dynamics and relationships between social capital and armed conflict based on the four theoretical predictions.

In terms of organization, the first three sections are split into four parts for each city. The first part provides a contextual setting and gives a brief history and background for each city to establish the scene for analysis. The second part focuses on the conflict setting for each city. In the conflict setting, "root causes" of armed conflict, or more specifically "conflict variables", as highlighted in previous literature and research are presented. These conflict variables are compared with the findings of my own fieldwork related to armed conflict. The third part, which is the core of the section, looks at the dynamics related to social capital for each city using the analytical framework. It is based on interviews, focus group discussions, and the small-n surveys conducted in the three cities. The fourth and final part of each section ends with a conclusion in regard to the levels of armed conflict and social capital and compares them against the above theoretical predictions.

In terms of research design, as mentioned previously in chapter one (section 1.4.2), the qualitative approach involves a desk review and analysis of secondary data related to the three cities; analyses of the small-n survey conducted by myself in a focus group setting and focus group discussions; and review and reference to field work interviews with individuals in the three cities.

4.2 Burao – A Qualitative Approach

This section provides a contextual background and conflict setting for Burao based on primary data and secondary information. It highlights the roots causes and variables related to conflict. It then presents the fieldwork findings related to armed conflict and social capital and compares the results against the theoretical prediction relevant to Burao. To recall, based on the four theoretical predictions, social capital levels and armed conflict for Burao would be as follows:

	Bridging (Prediction 1)	Bonding (Prediction 2)	Hard Linking (Prediction 3)	Soft Linking (Prediction 4)	Armed Conflict
Theoretical prediction	H	L	L	H	L

Table 31. Theoretical predictions for Burao by type of social capital and assumed level of armed conflict

126

4.2.1 Burao – Contextual Background

The written material related specifically to Burao is limited, mainly focusing on anecdotal reports of local peacemaking initiatives (Bradbury and Healy 2010) and historical references to the Somaliland statebuilding process (Bradbury 2008, Hoehne 2009&2011a&2011b, Interpeace 2008a, Renders 2012). Saferworld (Ramadhan and Rynn 2010) and OCVP (2011a) have produced detailed reports supporting the UNDP baseline study for Burao that includes data from focus group discussions and the results of the UNDP large-n survey.

Burao is most well known as the place where a decision was taken at a conference in May 1991 for clans located in the region to secede from the rest of Somalia and create Somaliland[1]. Consisting mainly members of the Isaaq clan (as reflected in the UNDP survey, 92%[2] of the respondents answered they belonged to the Isaaq clan family), Burao's clan composition makes an interesting comparison with Las Anod which consists of mainly one clan family, the Darod.

Located on the main trading route between Ethiopia and the port city of Berbera, Burao is a transit point for cattle export and import of goods from abroad. The city is a five-hour drive from Somaliland's capital city of Hargeisa on fairly good paved roads and is located above a plateau rising over 1,000 meters, therefore providing a relatively cooler climate compared to the coastal towns. During my visit in April 2013, Burao had very limited international presence with only one United Nations security national staff permanently based there and with the majority of international aid organizations visiting Burao from Hargeisa for limited periods[3].

As the regional capital of Togdheer, Burao is in the traditional lands of the Isaaq clan with an approximate population of 400,000 residents[4]. However to use the clan system to understand political clan dynamics, one needs to go to the sub-clan level where the Isaaq clan splits into several sub-clans. In the case of Burao, the identity categories used in the category set of clannism are the Habar Jeclo and Habar Yonis clans who live in the east and west parts of the city respectively. During the fieldwork, my interlocutors rarely referred to this identity category and instead focused on being Isaaq versus the other large clan families of the Hawiye, Darod, and Rahanweyn who were seen as "outsiders". The Isaaq sub-division was only referred to when I raised specific questions and contexts regarding clan relations between the Habar Jeclo and Habar Yonis. Even though Burao is split in terms of residence between the two clans, this division was never referred to in the focus discussions and interviews unless I specifically raised or referred to it.

The actual split of the city, in terms of clan residence, passes through the commercial center which was not seen as an area of tension. This suggests the commercial center is seen as an area of "neutral space" (similar to the central market and business areas in Galkayo). In regard to communal tensions with IDPs, who live on the periphery of the town, no reference was made by the Burao permanent residents. Historically though, Burao has seen armed conflict between the Habar Jeclo and Habar Yonis clans and also with other non-Isaaq and Isaaq clans.

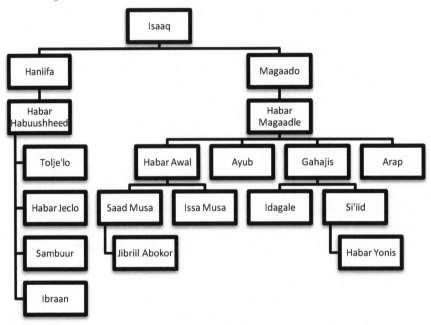

Figure 9. Clan genealogy of the Isaaq clan family (Renders 2012)

In 1988, during the civil war between the Barre government and the Somaliland independence movement SNM (Somali National Movement), Burao and Hargeisa were bombed from the air by the central government. This led to a huge exodus of the local population to refugee camps in Ethiopia, leaving Burao completely empty with the exception of Barre's army (Renders 2012:78). Importantly for Somaliland history, this aerial bombing united the various Isaaq clans against the Barre regime who then fought for independence against the rest of Somalia.

However this unity did not last for long. In January 1992, fighting broke out in Burao between the Habar Yonis militia who supported Somaliland's newly elected president and Habar Jeclo militias who were in opposition. The conflict lasted for a week and saw 300 people killed in Burao when the Habar Yonis president tried to take control of Habar Jeclo militias in the city (Bradbury 2008:89). Several peace conferences were convened thereafter from October 1992 to early 1993 however in July 1993 the Habar Yonis announced that they would not cooperate with the new government of President Egal (Quero 2011a:14).

In May 1995, the Habar Yonis and Habar Jeclo militias waged battles again in Burao over a one-month period with no clear winner emerging (Renders 2012:138). According to Renders, the conflict was seen as a wider political war between national political groups within Burao versus a simple clan conflict between the two groups. She notes how the two clans in rural areas outside of Burao coexisted with each other peacefully, albeit uneasily (2012:139). In July 1996 a peace deal was brokered and according to OCVP the conflict was only completely settled after a five-month National Peace Conference held in Hargeisa in February 1997 (2011a:14).

Lewis also notes how Burao has historically been a scene of conflict between the two clans (2002:285). However in April 2013, when I visited Burao, the historical cleavages were not mentioned with any of the interlocutors. Instead the issue of peace and stability was highlighted and it was only during in-depth interviews that I was able to discuss the issue of armed conflict and cleavages within the community.

Renders describes in detail how trust between clans and formal governance structures were rebuilt in Burao, including the challenges, following the 1994 to 1996 civil war in Somaliland (2012:160). She notes how ad hoc Peace Committees were established by clan elders from the Habar Yonis and Habar Jeclo with government participation limited to an observer role. These committees of clan elders "would resolve land, commercial disputes, or other disputes that turned violent, according to existing xeer laws between the two clans involved" (Renders 2012:161).

The elders who participated in the Peace Committees also dealt with conflict resolution within their own clan. The xeer laws that were practiced by the elders between the two clans were not aligned with the administrative law and the police rarely interfered in the Peace Committees unless requested by the elders. Once diya, blood money, was agreed then the perpetrator would be usually set free if held by the police. The police would rarely arrest anyone if it was related to a clan conflict and Renders highlights, similar to my own findings in 2013, that "in order to avoid a shoot-out—wrongdoers were apprehended by their own clansmen and then (sometimes) left in police custody so the elders of the involved clans could start conducting their negotiations" (2012:162).

My interlocutors explained further that the perpetrator was usually arrested and jailed for their own protection while discussions related to diya payment were being discussed! During the time in detention, the clan of the perpetrator would have to feed the accused and provide payment to the police[5] for providing custody[6]. The Peace Committees that Renders mentions were still active according to my fieldwork[7] in Burao and will be discussed further in the next section.

According to residents, Burao has gone through major reconstruction with funding provided by the diaspora and local business community following the massive destruction caused by the civil wars where between 70 to 90 percent of the buildings had been destroyed. When I visited in April 2013, the city's central market and business center was bustling with activity during the day and night and restaurants and teashops remained open for business in the evenings and nighttime. People from both the Habar Yonis and Habar Jeclo clans were able to visit different parts of the cities irrespective of their clan identity.

The city's infrastructure consists of an airport (under renovation during the time of visit), a central power grid running the main parts of the city, and has reliable water resources. Several bottling plants produce bottled water for export to neighbouring regions, including to Somaliland's capital city Hargeisa. The city has several governmental entities, including the mayor and governor's office, a police station, prison, court house, and public hospital. During my visit to the mayor's office, security was minimal with only several guards protecting the area and residents were able to freely come and go.

Economically, Burao is reliant on the livestock industry including livestock trading. Its strategic central location, on the transit route between Ethiopia and the seaport city of Berbera, makes it a convergence point for rural producers (Ramadhan and Rynn 2010). Besides water bottling, the city and region boast several large trading firms and construction companies, veterinary clinics and schools, universities and technical schools, hotels, light industry (brick making, concrete producer, and detergent factory), money transfer and banking, and telecommunications.

4.2.2 Conflict Setting and Fieldwork Results on Armed Conflict in Burao

This section first summarizes the main findings related to armed conflict of seven focus group discussions conducted by Saferworld (Ramadhan and Rynn 2010) in Burao in mid-June 2010 as part of the qualitative study supporting the UNDP baseline study and the DDG small arms report (2009). It provides a general profile of the conflict and security issues, and underlying causes of violence in the city. It also reviews armed conflict management systems briefly. Furthermore it focuses on the armed conflict variables in Burao based on my fieldwork conducted in the city in April 2013. The results refer to interviews, focus group discussions, and the small-n survey based on the questionnaire used in all five cities. The major causes of conflict as highlighted in the Saferworld focus group discussions are compared with my fieldwork results. The comparison highlights the relevance of the Saferworld findings and provides additional conflict variables for consideration. In sum, *the primary and secondary data indicate low levels of armed conflict in Burao.*

According to the Saferworld report, participants in the focus group discussions in 2010 referred to the historical animosities ("civil wars") between the Habar Yonis and Habar Jeclo but "when asked about the current level of safety in the area, respondents were overwhelmingly positive about recent trends... the absence of political violence during election campaigning, and the hiring of private security guards and creation of village security committees" (Ramadhan and Rynn 2010:6).

Based on the Saferworld focus group discussions, the following issues were highlighted as the major causes of violent conflict among families and clans in Burao (Ramadhan and Rynn 2010:7-8):

> ➤ Land disputes—This included rural and urban land. Residents highlighted how they were monitoring territorial incursion by other clans regarding rural land, while competition for land in the city was increasing due to urbanization.
> ➤ Livestock threat—Seen as a phenomenon in rural areas, groups of young men were seen as the perpetrators.
> ➤ Revenge killings—Although usually related to land disputes, the killings were related to disputes over compensation payments in which the perpetrator's clan delays payment or does not pay the full amount of diya. This included biased support to individuals by clansmen, leading to revenge killing within and across clan lines.
> ➤ Muggings and burglaries—This was seen as an urban phenomenon.
> ➤ Rape of women—This can lead to violence between clans when the perpetrator belongs to a different clan versus the victim.
> ➤ Hostility between the host community and IDP community—Waste disposal and poor sanitation by IDPs was seen as aggravating tensions with the host community due to the spillover effect from the sewage.
> ➤ Al Shabaab—A few respondents highlighted the threat of this terrorist group as a threat to Somaliland.

The causes underlying the above issues were highlighted by the participants as: clannism; consumption of qat; poverty and unemployment; extensive rural-urban migration; failures of traditional compensation mechanisms; political rivalry; weak legal and security systems; and widespread ownership of firearms by civilians. The Saferworld analysis highlights economic issues as causal factors, especially poverty and unemployment, and resource scarcity (Ramadhan and Rynn 2010:13, Quero 2011a:26).

In terms of armed conflict management, traditional elders and religious leaders were viewed as crucial actors in maintaining social harmony in partnership with the state. The weak judicial system was seen as the main reason for people to rely on traditional elders and the police were called upon first for mainly criminal issues and community violence. Accordingly, Burao "has an actively engaged citizenry who are keen to support local initiatives as much as the national independence project and a set of well-respected traditional and religious leaders that provide guidance and conflict management services" (Ramadhan and Rynn 2010:13).

Participants noted that traditional elders were also involved in enforcing decisions in addition to conflict resolution decision-making. Traditionally, this is quite unusual as clan elders are normally seen as only providing decisions with no enforcement power in the community. "Civilian security committees" were established in crime hotspots with the objective to deter crime through patrolling by community volunteers. As a fee based arrangement, where each household pays 5 U.S. dollars per month, the communities saw these security committees as effective and beneficial in decreasing crime within the neighborhoods (Ramadhan and Rynn 2010:11).

Comparing the above causes of conflict from the Saferworld focus group discussions, my fieldwork and relevant UNDP data showed the following results:

> Land disputes—Disputes over rural land amongst pastoralists still occurred in the Togdheer region but urban land disputes in Burao were considered a thing of the past.
> Livestock threat—The issue of livestock being stolen in rural areas by young men was not mentioned in the interviews.
> Revenge killings—Disputes over compensation payments in which the perpetrator's clan delays payment or does not pay the full amount of diya continues to be a problem. Furthermore, in some murder cases, diya can be refused by the victim's relatives who will instead want vengeance by death. Diya could be refused by the clan when the victim is considered to be a huge loss for the community or is a person of high social standing in the community. The clan of the perpetrator will argue that xeer should be applied uniformly based on past incidents, however this can be rejected by victim's clan and lead to a collapse of the xeer system. When the perpetrator is not handed over then other clansmen from the perpetrator's clan can be murdered in retaliation, setting off a spiral of inter-clan violence. Delays in compensation were also noted however this was seen as infrequent. Diya payments were formalized through written agreements and signed by clan chiefs specifying the amount and deadlines, including payment by installments. The role of

the court in handling delayed payments was highlighted. Cases involving payment delay, usually related to death, were taken to the court and the judge would specify a new date for the diya to be paid.

➤ Muggings and burglaries—This was not mentioned by respondents and the small-n survey showed only 7% (n=2), including members of their household, had been the victim of violent crime, such as assault of mugging (Q7.9)[8].

➤ Rape of women—This was seen as a cause of conflict when the victim's family, usually brother or father, sought revenge in terms of death. The issue of the victim marrying the rapist was not highlighted for protecting family honor, but instead the issue of livelihood support to the victim by the perpetrator was highlighted since nobody would marry the victim after she lost her dignity and was seen as "spoiled" (in the context of losing her purity). No longer able to marry in the future, due to her status as a spoiled woman, the perpetrator would be threatened with punishment of death if he refused to marry his victim.

➤ Hostility between the host community and IDP community— Interviewees did not highlight any tensions between IDPs and the host community, as IDPs were not trying to grab land. The issue of sewage from IDP communities was not seen as a major issue of conflict.

➤ Al Shabaab—Reference was not made directly to Al Shabaab and instead respondents noted increasing tensions between various religious groups over the past ten years. However on 21 August 2013 suspects related to Al Shabaab, who had attempted to attack the City Plaza Hotel in Burao where I had stayed during my fieldwork, were arrested by the Somaliland police, highlighting the ongoing threat from this extremist group (DSS 2013b).

Additional conflict variables that emerged from my interviews were the issue of resource distribution, such as humanitarian and developmental aid distribution, and job opportunities related to oil exploration[9]. Distribution of aid and resources by NGOs and the government led to arguments and tensions between communities as distribution was seen as uneven. Recruitment for government positions and NGOs in the locality was expected to be based on clan quotas versus hiring individuals based on merit. Companies exploring for oil were also expected to provide job opportunities to local communities based on clan quotas and not on the education or skills of the local populace.

The small-n survey from Burao highlighted the following trends related to armed conflict and other conflict related variables. When participants were asked whether the neighborhood they lived in was generally peaceful or marked by violence, 96% (n=27) said it was peaceful with only one respondent answering it was moderately violent (Q7.6). Again, all but one participant (96%, n=27) answered that they felt very safe from crime and violence when at home alone (Q7.8). In terms of walking alone after dark, 89% (n=23) answered they felt very safe, while the remaining respondents responded as "moderately safe" or "neither safe nor unsafe" (Q7.8).

As mentioned above, only two out of 27 participants said they or someone from their household had been a victim of a violent crime, such as assault or mugging, in the past 12 months (Q7.9). In regard to personally experiencing political violence in the past year, 64% (n=18) replied negative while a total of 18% either replied "yes, often" and "yes, several times" (Q8.2). Compared to the other four cities, the responses from Burao indicated the city as being the safest and having the lowest degrees of violence.

4.2.3 Fieldwork Results on Social Capital in Burao

Applying the analytical framework, this section focuses qualitatively on the six proxies related to social capital: identity; groups and group networks; personal networks; community leadership; trust; and social cohesion and inclusion. *The findings of the fieldwork in Burao demonstrate high levels of bonding and bridging social capital* with references made particular to clan elders. The section looks at the individual social proxies in turn based on interviews, focus group discussions, and the results of the small-n survey.

Identity

As mentioned previously, the category set of clannism is the Habar Jeclo and Habar Yonis clans who live in the east and west parts of the city respectively and are both part of the Isaaq clan family. Participants did not highlight this category set within Burao. Some participants referred to the issue of clan when comparing Burao to other cities in Somalia in the context of Isaaq versus the other larger clan families of the Hawiye, Darod, and Rahanweyn who were viewed as "outsiders" but were welcome in Burao. When discussing variables related to conflict, participants did not refer to a Habar Jeclo and Habar Yonis divide causing conflict. Instead they used the term "clan" in general terms, without highlighting specific lineages. In given examples of conflict between clans, it was never clear at what level in terms of sub-clan or sub sub-clan the conflict occurred.

The small-n survey showed that 88% (n=24) of participants belonged to the Isaaq clan, including their father and spouse, highlighting Burao as a relatively homogenous place in terms of division at the upper-end of the clan system (Q2.1). In terms of clan identity helping to differentiate who to trust, only 33% (n=7) agreed that this was useful. Clan identity was seen as a basis for social life by only 32% (n=7) of respondents (Q2.5). Interestingly Burao had the highest number of participants by percentage (39%, n=11) who answered that they were able to have multiple clan identities (Q2.9). In terms of marriage, 59% (n=16) said that clan identity was a concern followed by 26% who said it matters only a bit (Q2.6).

Excluding the issue of marriage, the survey suggests that clan is not a major variable of division within the community. Focus group discussions also did not refer to clannism as a source of cleavage within the community. Whether this was intentional or unintentional is unclear however divisions between the Habar Jeclo and Habar Yonis seem to be a thing of the past with participants emphasizing Burao as a place of harmony between clans.

Groups and group networks

In general, focus group discussants noted high levels of trust by the community towards civil society organizations. Interlocutors did not refer to groups and CSOs playing a leading or contributing role in conflict resolution or mediation in Burao. However SOYDAVO, a CSO based in Burao, did mention their role in resolving conflict disputes in the areas bordering Togdheer region and Ethiopia, where conflicts focused on land issues.

While in the past civil society groups were active in promoting peace and reconciliation, such as organizing peace caravans and workshops (DRC 2004:24), the prominence of civil society in regard to conflict resolution in recent years may have subsided following peace consolidation in Burao after the armed conflict in the 1990s. With recent outbreaks of armed conflict in Burao not being reported in my discussions with interlocutors, the role for CSOs, groups, and associations may simply not be necessary in this area. However the preventive role of these entities, as social capital in mitigating armed conflict, is unclear. As a CSO leader pointed out, society needs a foundation to work off from to promote peace[10]. Whether informal or formal organizations, networks, and associations provide this foundation requires further analysis.

The small-n survey focusing on the social capital proxy related to groups and group networks displayed characteristics of relatively high bridging social capital. In terms of occupation, 82% (n=19) of the participants were students, a bridging social capital trait, while the remaining youth described themselves as professionals working in the community (Q1.4). When asked about membership in groups or organizations, networks, and associations, 41% (n=12) said they were a member of some form of informal or formal group (Q3.1). The type of groups they belonged to were related to community development, advocacy, youth and student associations with the community seen as the main beneficiary of the group (Q3.2,Q3.3). Group membership consisted of different clan members in 65% of the groups, highlighting inclusivity.

In regards to linking social capital, 53% of respondents noted that they did not feel strong pressure from the group for members to obey the group's decisions, indicating a mixture of hard and soft linking social capital (Q3.5, Q3.6). Regarding neighborhood composition, 82% (n=22) said their neighborhood consists of an equal mixture of different clans and also 82% (n=23) said they would not mind if their next door neighbor was from a different clan (Q3.7, Q3.8).

Personal networks

Focus group discussions and interviews did not mention the importance of personal networks to "get things done" in Burao. With a certain degree of state institutions present in the city, such as the governor and mayor's administration, the impersonal networks of state bureaucracy may paradoxically be part of the personal networks of individuals in Burao. The small-n data shows Burao as having the most number of respondents, 57% (n=16), who said they or their families have connections with people in political authority from the same clan while 79% said they have connections with people in political authority from different clans (Q4.3,Q4.4). When it came to suddenly borrowing a small amount of money (equal to about one week's wages) beyond the immediate household and close relatives, 73% said they "definitely" or "probably" could do so (n=19).

Community leadership

As mentioned in the analytical framework, community leadership focuses on hard and soft linking social capital. The small-n survey with focus group discussants first asks who the leaders in their community are. Clan elders and political people/government officials were community leaders for 43% (n=12) and 39% (n=11) of responses respectively, highlighting a mixture of hard and soft linking social capital in the community (Q5.1). Compared to the other four cities, community leaders were seen as having the most power to mobilize the community (Q5.2). A cross tabulation analysis showed that both clan elders and government officials had the ability to mobilize the community.

Community leaders were seen as "always, often, and sometimes" important in times of emergency, such as settling conflicts (91%, n=21, Q5.3). Similar responses were given in regard to community leaders providing guidance (91%, n=21) and security (87%, n=20). Community leaders were from the same clan for 70% (n=16) of participants (Q5.4). The results highlight a mixture of hard and soft linking social capital and the important role of community leaders in settling conflicts, providing security, and mobilizing the community in Burao.

Trust

The issue of trust was repeatedly raised by interlocutors in the context of conflict management. The key actors mentioned in resolving conflict were clan elders, secular courts, religious leaders, and the police, all which were referred to as having high levels of trust. The small-n survey also reflects similar findings as shown in table 4.1 (Q6.4). Relative to the other four cities, the small-n survey shows that Burao had the highest levels of trust towards clan elders, religious leaders, police, and NGOs run by Somalis.

		1. A lot	2. A little	3. Not at all
A	People from your clan	64	32	5
B	People from other clans	48	48	4
C	Teachers	83	13	4
D	Clan elders	48	43	9
E	Businessmen/businesswomen	35	50	15
F	Politicians, government officials	38	43	19
G	Military persons	50	33	16
H	Religious leaders (Ullaama U Ddin/ Culuma)	82	4	14
I	Police	54	37	8
J	NGOs run by Somalis	71	24	5

Table 32. How much do you trust the following people? (in percentage terms)

For the question: "Generally speaking, would you say that most people can be trusted, or that you cannot be too careful in your dealings with other people", 59% (n=17) answered that "most people can be trusted" while 41% chose "you cannot be too careful" (Q6.3). The results were similar for south Galkayo (57%, n=15, answered most people can be trusted) while Mogadishu displayed the least of amount of general trust (63%, n=20, responded "you cannot be too careful").

In Burao, there are 140 *agaals* (traditional clan chiefs) recognized by the government. It was highlighted that the residents of Burao "have historically lived under the *control* of elders"[11]. The issue of "control" may be linked to the notion of how elders also have a role in enforcing decisions, with threat of banishment from the clan's protection system most likely as an effective enforcement mechanism for implementing decisions. In addition to the unusual role of elders enforcing decisions, which is not mentioned in existing literature related to clan elders (Gundel, Le Sage, Lewis, and Menkhaus to mention a few), I conclude that the role of the clan elders in Burao is similar to the services of a "defense lawyer" during times of conflict and dispute:

> Your elder will defend you even if you are in the wrong, however the religious leader will base his decision on what is right. If you killed intentionally, the religious leader could support the relatives of the victim's request that the perpetrator be killed and that diya be declined. If [the killing was] unintentional, then the sheikh will recommend diya be accepted... [If the killing was intentional] your elder will try to convince the other clan to take the diya. The elder is trying to save your life. However if you go to the religious leader, he will do what is right.[12]

139

Interviews in Burao suggested that the police on the other hand have two specific roles: acting as a stopgap measure when conflict resolution processes managed by clan elders get stuck or simply did not operate; and facilitating and supporting the clan elders' conflict resolution process by providing protection and "safekeeping" to the perpetrator (or suspect). As noted by one of the interviewees, "People strongly trust elders, but go to police when elders don't act… There is good trust in the police. The police are called to register the violence and record evidence for the court. The police are used to capture the killer for the protection of the [perpetrator's] clansmen to avoid retaliation by the victim's relatives"[13]. In essence, the perpetrator's clansmen willingly handover the individual to the police for safekeeping and as an indication to the victim's clansmen that they are eager to settle the issue through dialogue and avoid the incident escalating into violence.

With the perpetrator in the custody of the police, this provides protection to the perpetrator and to his clansmen from retaliation while discussions between clan elders proceed to find a settlement for compensation under xeer agreements. Simply put, once the perpetrator is identified by the victim's clansmen, every male belonging to the same clan as the perpetrator, regardless of age, becomes a legitimate target for revenge. The intention is that by imprisoning the perpetrator, retaliation from the victim's clansmen can be avoided while clan elders discuss the issue of compensation.

In this context, "the police act as the middleman between clans" to facilitate the process for settlement between elders but are not seen as the first choice for settling conflicts[14]. This is due to the perceived disadvantage that the police may not be your clansmen and could be (un)biased against the victim or perpetrator.

With interlocutors expressing trust towards the police, the question arises why parties to a conflict prefer to settle using clan elders versus reporting the incident to the police. Interlocutors suggested that choosing elders over police seems to rest on the perception that settling conflicts through clan elders will lead to an advantageous decision for both parties while going through the police may follow a process of settlement that is impartial and based on secular law, or is (un)biased due to clan affiliation[15]. This is similar to clan elders being preferred over religious leaders, where decisions based on Sharia may be disadvantageous to the perpetrator, especially for incidents related to death.

While interlocutors mentioned courts as being too costly and timely to manage disputes, where appeals were also seen as slowing down rulings, the courts have a unique role in facilitating and supporting the settlement process led by clan elders. The role includes managing conflicts between clans when xeer agreements collapse or are not existent[16]. A participant noted how "the clan conflict was mitigated by courts even when xeer collapses between clans or clans that don't have xeer"[17].

In principle, the court system is seen as a last source for conflict resolution and is used to mediate between elders "when the xeer breaks down" in situations where there is a lack of agreements to handle land disputes or killings. The courts are used when the conflict resolution becomes "unmanagemable" or when the clan elders themselves also become part of the conflict, as elders themselves have a vested interest in protecting their clan's interests versus coming to an agreement that provides justice. In these situations, the court becomes an arbitrator, attempting to settle difference between clan elders and providing solutions.[18] Interviewees noted that in the past when the court system was not "strong enough", the role of the court was limited.[19] In recent years, however, newly trained judges and lawyers from Hargeisa University were seen as having improved the judicial system.[20]

The choice of secular law, Sharia law, and customary law (xeer) depends both on the victim and perpetrator, where each side may have their own specific preference based on the perceived benefit of each process. The controlling factor though is that both the victim and perpetrator's representatives need to agree on the system of due process.[21] When there is disagreement on the process to be used, this could lead to conflict escalating to the clan level and becoming violent.

As diya is a primary component of customary law, the agreement of compensation by both parties and timely payment from the perpetrator to the victim is crucial to settling disputes peacefully and mitigating armed conflict. In Burao, interlocutors highlighted the limitations of the xeer system in settling conflicts.[22] The first was when the xeer payment was too large for the perpetrators' clansmen to pay. This would occur in situations related to death of a large number of people, such as more than ten, and when the community had limited resources to make payment. Therefore, it was crucial to make sure that diya payments were realistic and not simply agreed for the sake of agreement.

Secondly, the success of the xeer system depended on whether "unique xeer" existed between the parties versus "general xeer". Unique xeer was seen as a system in place between two parties (usually at the sub-clan level) based on previous transactions related to compensation. Previous transactions related to diya payment fostered trust and reciprocity between parties, addressing issues of asymmetry. This unique xeer, between specific clans, is built upon repeated transactions and importantly supported by the community elders leading to improved conflict resolution settlements. On the other hand, general xeer refers to the customary agreed amounts of compensation, such as payment of 100 camels[23] for the death of a man, and excludes specifics, such as whether the killing was intentional or accidental, or how to handle settlements if the victim's relatives refuse diya payment. Importantly it does not have support from the wider community and makes enforcement, and therefore collection of payment difficult.

In regard to collecting diya payment, for situations where unique xeer exists, this is managed by an "administrative committee" which consists of clan members of the perpetrator. [24] The committee's responsibility is to collect diya payment from clan members and ensure that the compensation is made by the agreed deadlines. The committee will decide which clan members are responsible for payment, including the amount payable by each individual, and will also seek payment from clan members of the diaspora. The amount of payment will depend on the clan member's earnings, such as whether he has a stable salary or is operating a successful business. He may also have to pay on behalf of his unemployed male relatives and closeness to the perpetrator.

As collection of diya payment can be a time consuming and complex process, the administrative committee charges an administrative cost for its services, which is paid by both the victim and perpetrator's clansmen. Enforcement of payment is unchallenged as the obligation to pay is based on the perpetrator's clansmen knowing that they may also require the clan's protection and insurance in the future. Refusing payment means exclusion from the clan's security network, leaving one with no "insurance" against future liability.

In terms of the relationship between the regional administration and clan elders, the Togdheer governor is responsible for all matters related to security and works closely with the clan elders to resolve conflicts and provide security to the region. Importantly, the governor involves clan elders on issues related to dispute resolution. Administratively, the elders come under the governor and are registered with the Somaliland Ministry of Interior[25]. Meanwhile the mayor of Burao is primarily responsible for development, while also dealing with land disputes related to land registration and municipal issues within Burao's city limits. Interlocutors highlighted good relations between the clan elders and the administration, including cooperation between the state and the community. An example given was the successful public-private partnership for the construction of the Debooh bridge which crosses the river that divides Burao. The bridge was financed by both the state and the local community. The small-n survey showed 83% of respondents (n=24) viewing the current government as either resolving conflicts between communities as "very well" or "fairly well" (Q6.1).

Social Cohesion

As mentioned previously, Burao's residents can generally be divided primarily into three clan groups: Habar Jeclo, Habar Yonis, and outsiders/others. Although these three groups can be used as a basis for analyzing social cohesion, this approach omits the social dynamics within these three category sets. The small-n survey attempts to address this deficit by analyzing social cohesion within these three groups.

From the survey, Burao had the highest percentage (52%, n=14) of respondents agreeing that "each person should put the well being of the community ahead of their own interests" versus the alternative choice of "everybody should be free to pursue what is best for themselves as individuals" (Q7.1). Burao also had the most responses favoring consensus building when asked which statement they agreed with: "in order to make decisions in our community, we should talk until everyone agrees" (71%, n=20); versus "since we will never agree on anything, we must learn to accept differences of opinion within the community" (Q7.2).

Interestingly, the strength of feeling of togetherness or closeness in the respondents' neighborhood was relatively low compared to the other four cities. Only 53% (n=15) answered "very close" or "somewhat close" while Las Anod had the highest percentage regarding the feeling of togetherness or closeness as seen in the table below (Q7.4).

			Feeling of togethernewss or closeness			
			Distant	Neither	Close	Total
Region	Benadir-Mogadishu	Count	8	7	23	38
		% within Region	21.1%	18.4%	60.5%	100.0%
	Togdheer-Burao	Count	9	3	15	27
		% within Region	33.3%	11.1%	55.6%	100.0%
	Bari-Bosaso	Count	12	3	17	32
		% within Region	37.5%	9.4%	53.1%	100.0%
	Las Anod	Count	4	2	25	31
		% within Region	12.9%	6.5%	80.6%	100.0%
	North Galkayo	Count	3	0	3	6
		% within Region	50.0%	.0%	50.0%	100.0%
	Galmudug - South Galkayo	Count	3	3	20	26
		% within Region	11.5%	11.5%	76.9%	100.0%
Total		Count	39	18	103	160
		% within Region	24.4%	11.2%	64.4%	100.0%

Table 33. Region versus feeling of togetherness or closeness. The answer "close" incorporates responses of "somewhat close" and "very close"; "distant" incorporates "somewhat distant" and "very distant".

To examine the relationship between social cohesion and violence in the community, participants were asked how often certain differences in the community caused violence (Q7.5). Relative to other cities, differences in clan, landholdings, and political party affiliations were seen as causing violence in Burao while economic differences were the least cause of violence.

	1. A lot	2. A little bit	3. Not at all
A. Differences in clan	61	30	9
B. Differences in landholdings	48	35	17
C. Economic differences	33	29	36
D. Differences between diaspora and non-diaspora	39	34	26
E. Differences in political party affiliations	39	17	13
F. Differences in religious views (eg fundamentalism, liberalism)	35	25	40

Table 34. How often do the following cause violence in your community? (in percentage terms)

The small-n data displays a mixed picture of social cohesion for Burao. While consensus building and community well-being are seen as a priority for Burao respondents, the feeling of closeness and togetherness in the neighborhood is relatively low. In addition, clan divisions are seen as causes of violence in the community.

Focus group discussions also displayed a mixed picture of social cohesion[26]. Burao is generally divided into two areas between the Habar Jeclo and Habar Yonis with the business district and market dividing the two clans geographically. IDPs and other clans live on the periphery of the town. Choosing location of residence is primarily based on being next to one's clan for two reasons. First, residents simply feel uncomfortable living in an area that is not their own clan. This was described by participants as "living on the wrong side of town" and would be a security issue during times of conflict between the two clans. For example, a Habar Jeclo residing in a Habar Yonis neighborhood could find himself being targeted by his neighbors when relationships between the two clans were tense, simply because he belonged to the Habar Jeclo clan and lived amongst the Habar Yonis despite having no involvement to the incident that was causing tension between the two clans. Second, the pragmatic issue of being close to your family and clan for daily support and protection was another reason not to live in a neighborhood away from one's relatives or clansmen. Simply, living away from your relatives meant difficulty in receiving daily support and protection during an emergency. In difficult times people rely on their clan and family for support. While during tension they are differentiated by their clan identity and can be a target due to their clan affiliation.

However the small-n survey painted a different picture with 82% (n=22) of respondents saying their neighborhood consisted of an equal mixture of different clans instead of consisting of mainly the same clan (Q3.7). The responses could be based on respondents considering clan identity at the sub sub-clan level and below, even if the neighborhood was primarily inhabited by clan members at the same sub-clan level (Habar Jeclo or Habar Yonis).

The relationship between land disputes and social cohesion can be analyzed through the concept of deegan, which refers to how traditional clan territory is managed between parties. Deegan[27] is part of dhaqasho, the civil code of xeer, which also consists of regulating matters related to family (xilo), private property (xoolo), and hospitality (maamuusa) (Norton 2008:158). Focus group participants highlighted how deegan was clear to all, thereby mitigating conflicts related to clan ownership of land.

145

Whether agreements between clans over deegan contributed to social cohesion, or whether social cohesion is a basis for deegan agreements to succeed is unclear. Strong social cohesion may contribute to deegan agreements being formulated smoothly and quickly through the existence of trust and reciprocity (which are other components of social capital). Alternatively, a lack of deegan agreements could contribute to social cohesion (and trust and reciprocity) deteriorating between clans.

The conflict mitigation effects of deegan agreements are put under strain in circumstances when temporary settlements of people, such as IDPs, emerge and over time transform into permanent settlements. As these settlements infringe upon traditionally owned land by clans, deegan agreements can be disputed leading to the possibility of violent conflict emerging between the settlers and the traditional owners of the land. Disputes may become harder to resolve when over time some members of the settlers, such as young clansmen, may not be aware that they were temporarily granted permission to reside. The death of older clansmen from the settlers' side, who may have first made the agreement decades ago, could also create a situation where the settling community's clansmen conveniently "forget" they were temporary allocated land. In such situations, land ownership disputes arise and deegan agreements do not function.

Another example of the relationship between conflict management and social cohesion is highlighted in Burao's District Safety Committee [28]. The purpose of the Committee is for civil society organizations to contribute to peace and conflict resolution by supporting the local administration that is perceived as weak. The Committee acts as a mediation standby team to resolve conflicts or initialize peace processes. Consisting of lawyers, teachers, civil society leaders, and local administration officials, the Committee also attempts to develop structures and frameworks for nurturing peace by focusing on developing bridging social capital. This involves activities such as bringing schools from the two clans together through sporting events. Public spaces are shared by students from both clans in the hope of promoting social cohesion [29].

Interlocutors continuously highlighted the readiness and willingness of the community, civil society organizations, and the local administration to contribute to peace processes. Three explanations emerge regarding the dynamics and relationships between social cohesion and conflict resolution: various community actors can be seen as creating a foundation for promoting peace, which in turn could contribute to social cohesion; alternatively pre-existing social cohesion within the community could be the foundation for these actors to work together in promoting peace and conflict resolution mechanisms; finally, a combination of both dynamics could be at play, highlighting equifinality between the various actors and dynamics related to promoting peace.

4.2.4 Summary of Armed Conflict and Social Capital in Burao

Based on the focus group discussions, interviews, and small-n survey, Burao qualitatively displays high levels of bonding *and* bridging social capital with very low levels of armed conflict. Trust and social cohesion were two social capital proxies that were referred to repeatedly in the context of conflict resolution, prevention, and management. Traditional and secular institutions (such as police and courts) worked closely together, supporting each other in the process of addressing conflict within the community. Specifically, the police and courts were seen as supporting traditional processes which were led by traditional elders or religious leaders. In terms of linking social capital, Burao highlights a mixture of hard and soft linking social capital. Clan elders and political/government officials were considered as community leaders. The role of community leaders included settling conflicts, providing security, and mobilizing the community. Clan identity, treated as a bonding social capital proxy, suggested that clan is not a major variable of division within the community. The fieldwork results can be summarized as follows and are compared with the theoretical prediction related to Burao.

	Bridging (Prediction 1)	Bonding (Prediction 2)	Hard Linking (Prediction 3)	Soft Linking (Prediction 4)	Armed Conflict
Theoretical Prediction	H	L	L	H	L
Qualitative results	H	H	H	H	L

Table 35. Theoretical predications and qualitative results for Burao by social capital type and armed conflict level

Compared to the other cities, field research from Burao indicated the city as being the safest and having the lowest degrees of violence. The armed conflict variables highlighted in previous research and focus group discussions by Saferworld still exist, albeit at much lower levels.

147

Importantly, mechanisms and processes are in place to handle the various conflict variables to avoid violence erupting. Issues related to grievance and greed, horizontal inequalities, [30] and transnational dynamics were not mentioned either.

As the results of the fieldwork show, Burao demonstrates a positive relationship between non-state and state actors. Political tension within Burao was seen as having decreased following the government's increased capacity to administer, with its role seen as "forcing peace on parties"[31]. Increased administrative capacity was not limited to simply achieving a monopoly of violence but may have included the important dynamic of building trust between the state and community. With public services in such areas as education, policing, justice, and public health being provided, the significance and role of the state had increased over time. This provided an opportunity for trust to be developed between the local authorities and community.

The role of the state and its effect on social capital is an area that needs further exploration. For example, what effect does increased governance by the state have on social capital? Do emerging governance structures lead to personal networks deteriorating as impersonal state services (such as modern state bureaucracy) improve? Does the state replace or supplement bridging social capital created by communities with impersonal bridging mechanisms? Can state bureaucracy manage to handle asymmetries that social capital is assumed to deal with so effectively? The analysis of the two other cities will attempt to provide further insight.

4.3 Mogadishu – A Qualitative Approach

This section is based on field research primarily conducted in 2011, with additional visits in 2012 and 2013, and consists of focus group discussions, interviews, and the small-n survey. It also includes research from my first visit to Mogadishu in September 2004, prior to the establishment of the TFG, when south central Somalia was literally "stateless". Regarding secondary research, it uses the results of the focus group discussions carried out by the Somali Youth Development Network (SOYDEN 2010a&2010b) to support the UNDP baseline study to establish an overview of the conflict variables in Mogadishu. Referring to the theoretical prediction, social capital levels and armed conflict for Mogadishu are summarized in the table below.

	Bridging (Prediction 1)	Bonding (Prediction 2)	Hard Linking (Prediction 3)	Soft Linking (Prediction 4)	Armed Conflict
Theoretical prediction	L	H	H	L	H

Table 36. Theoretical predictions for Mogadishu by type of social capital and assumed level of armed conflict

4.3.1 Mogadishu—Contextual Background

As the capital of Somalia, Mogadishu has been the center stage for political and economical power. Literature referring to Mogadishu has focused primarily on the various political and security developments and dynamics prior to and following state collapse where rival clan militias fought each other while civilians suffered the effects of the armed conflict. In addition to the chronic clan fighting in the early nineties, groups based on religious ideology, such as Al Itahad and Al Shabaab, emerged in 2000 contributing to the complex armed conflict dynamics in Mogadishu. Mogadishu has also seen United Nations peacekeepers from multiple countries in the early nineties, Ethiopian troops in 2006, and AMISOM troops consisting of Burundian, Ugandan, Ethiopian, Djiboutian and Kenyan forces.

Proxy wars have also been held in Mogadishu, with the United States supporting warlords against the Islamic Courts Union, Eritrea providing technical and military support to Al Shabaab, and the international community knowingly or unknowingly training security forces affiliated to specific clans or warlords. [32] With an array of different actors emerging and retracting, literature (and academic research) related to Mogadishu has struggled to keep up with the fluid dynamics on the ground and has mainly focused on analyzing events through an agent-oriented approach, a parsimonious approach, treating conflict variables based simply on actors at the macro-level such as: "central government versus anti-government elements", "TFG/FGS versus Al-Shabaab", "Hawiye versus Darod", "AMISOM versus Al Shabaab", and "warlords versus the TFG/FGS". While analyses related to the armed conflict in and surrounding Mogadishu have focused on the protagonists, actors at the community level and social dynamics have tended to be excluded.

While analyzing conflict dynamics at the macro-level based on political and security paradigms are essential for understanding the wider picture and acquiring a quick snapshot (especially for practitioners), conflict analysis at the micro-level within Mogadishu has tended to be neglected. For example, practitioners from the United

149

Nations, World Bank, and international donors have repeatedly highlighted the need for a political economy analysis for Mogadishu followed by a nationwide analysis. However this has yet to be done[33]. Security challenges to conduct research on the ground may have also contributed to the lack of micro-level research and with the majority of the diplomatic corps based in Nairobi, the tendency has been to outsource analysis to a handful of experts with access on the ground and produce reports that are not widely distributed.[34]

Despite the constraints of conducting field research in Mogadishu, several detailed reports specifically focusing on Mogadishu have been produced. These reports attempt to go beyond an agent-oriented approach and have not received wide attention. Hansen (2007) and Marchal (2002, 2011) provide the most comprehensive overview regarding the role of the Mogadishu business community in peacemaking and the Mogadishu economy respectively. Although not widely available, Amir (2009) provides a detailed profile of Mogadishu which includes a SWOT analysis (strengths, weaknesses, opportunities, and threats) of all the 16 districts. Safeworld (2012) carried out a large-n survey (n=800) in 2012 to map conflict and governance dynamics in Mogadishu with a focus on security dynamics, migration, food and resources, and opinions on regional and international stakeholders in Somalia.[35] In regard to an overview of governance structures for Mogadishu city, Bryld and Kamau (2012) carried out a study in three districts for implementing development programs. For the mapping of key stakeholders in Mogadishu, UNPOS and AMISOM jointly conducted a profiling in September 2012 however the results were never made public.[36]

Known to the residents as Xamar, Mogadishu consists of 16 districts which make up the Benadir region. The population is estimated between one to two million with numbers fluctuating largely due to the IDPs and diaspora who come and go.[37] Mogadishu is the political center for the FGS (and the previous TFG) and hosts the military headquarters of AMISOM, numerous United Nations entities, and an increasing number of diplomatic missions. The city boasts the largest seaport in Somalia and has a fully functioning airport that caters to international and domestic flights.

The governance structures for Mogadishu are legally unclear as a city charter was never finalized for the city[38] (Bryld and Kamau 2012:20). In addition to being the capital of the country, Mogadishu is also the regional capital for the Benadir region. The mayor of Mogadishu is also, by de factor, the governor of the Benadir region although how the roles of the mayor and the governor differ is unclear. Each of the 16 districts has a District Commissioner and District Council. The districts themselves are split into waah, laan, and tabelle which is the lowest administrative level consisting of 50 to 200 households each (Bryld and Kamau 2012:20). In reality, however, the de facto governance structure depends on each district with the District Commissioner having authority in most cases and the mayor having little control or oversight over daily affairs within the districts.

Economic assets and security arrangements vary by district with some District Commissioners having their own militia outside of the command and control of the central government or mayor. With their own security forces, they are able to have a large influence on the security situation on the ground and can either be a contributor to security or insecurity. For districts of little economic value, the District Commissioners may have very little influence and usually lack their own security arrangements.

Considered by many Somalis as a cosmopolitan city in terms of clan makeup, Mogadishu has a history of being inhabited and controlled by different actors and clans. Outside of the Somali traditional (main family) clans, historically it has been inhabited by Arabs, Persians, and Cushitic groups, whose descendents can still be seen in certain parts of Mogadishu. As a multi-ethnic city, discussing the issue of "original" inhabitants is a sensitive issue with Hawiye and Darod clan members seeing themselves as the original residents of Mogadishu. Interestingly, however, both Hawiye and Darod clan members agree that the "original-original" occupants of Mogadishu are the light skinned minority group with Arab descent referred to as the Benadiri or Reer Xamari who are politically marginalized and are not seen as a credible group to take political power in Mogadishu. These minority groups have been victimized by the larger clan groups and have tended to seclude themselves in the Hamarweyne district near the old seaport area.

Prior to state collapse, districts were fairly mixed in terms of clan composition. Following the collapse of the Barre regime, which was mainly dominated by Darod clan members, the Hawiye clans came to control Mogadishu both politically and economically after the exodus of the Darod clan. Control of Mogadishu was further divided amongst the different Hawiye sub-clans and Somalis frequently refer to the divide as one of Abgal versus Haber Gedir. As the fighting increased between different sub-clans of the Hawiye, the spatial division within Mogadishu also changed and was determined by clan affiliation.

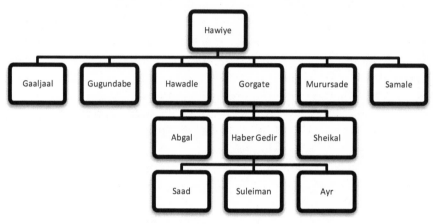

Figure 10. Hawiye clan family with selected sub-clans

Looking at the 16 districts[39], the intensity and type of armed conflict has tended to vary between districts and time. Prior to state collapse, anti-government forces of the USC[40] attacked all parts of Mogadishu that represented the state apparatus, regardless of clan affiliation. With the expulsion of the Barre state, many residents who belonged to the Darod clan also left fearing retaliation from the approaching USC who consisted of mainly Hawiye militias. Those Darod members who stayed were either killed or forced to leave (Marchal 2002:11).

As mentioned above briefly, Mogadishu was then divided between the Habar Gedir clan and Abgal clan warlords following the split of the USC who had previously fought together to oust Barre. The infamous "green line" split Mogadishu into two from north-west to south-east, with Mohamed Farah Aidid's Habar Gedir clan controlling the southern-side and Ali Mahdi Mohamed's Abgal clan controlling the north. [41] Following the split of Mogadishu into two, further fragmentation along clan lines emerged with different sub-clans of the Hawiye family fighting each other. Hansen provides details of the different "rounds of fighting" from 1991 to 2007 noting that "at times Mogadishu was relatively peaceful, at times there were large scale clashes and combat operations involving heavy artillery and airpower" (2007:35). During this period the USC, which started as one cross-clan affiliation, "fragmented into more than ten different factions, all following sub-clan divides, and with little or nothing in common with the USC of 1990" (Hansen 2007:36).

The risk of armed conflict was particularly high in areas close to the green line. Residents living adjacent to the green line left and rival militia groups guarded their respective territories. In hotly contested areas, such as the new seaport area and airport, no one-group was able to take control and these areas were left abandoned.[42] The green line itself could move, sometimes daily, as accidental skirmishes could unexpectedly turn into full-blown battles moving the line. The line provided a useful reference point of where fighting might be expected and the areas the line crossed were usually heavily destroyed by years of fighting, such as Shibis district, which is probably the most destroyed district in Mogadishu.[43]

Following the arrival of Ethiopian troops and AMISOM, the green line was replaced with a frontline as Al Shabaab attempted to take over Mogadishu from the central government. From 2006 onwards, every district controlled by the TFG and AMISOM was a possible target for attack and a clear frontline emerged separating areas controlled by Al Shabaab and the TFG/AMISOM. In particular the following districts experienced some of the heaviest fighting between Al Shabaab and TFG/AMISOM forces: Abdiaziz (known as the "district of ghosts" because of its emptiness of inhabitants), Hawalwadag (where the country's largest market, Bakara market, is located), Karan (a residential area on the outskirts of Mogadishu), Shangani (a historic district inhabited by the Reer Xamar), Shibis (located close to the Presidential Palace), and Yaqshid (on the periphery of Mogadishu with an approach to the Presidential Palace).

From mid-2009 to August 2011, the frontline moved gradually towards the outskirts of Mogadishu as TFG and AMISOM troops slowly retook areas house-by-house and street-by-street.[44] On 6 August Al Shabaab withdrew from Mogadishu, announcing a "tactical retreat", and the frontline ceased to exist as fighting switched from symmetrical to asymmetrical warfare. Mogadishu highlights how green lines were replaced by front lines, and front lines then disappeared to be taken over by asymmetric insurgent type combat between conventional military forces (AMISOM) and a designated terrorist group (Al Shabaab). In terms of spatial divisions following the collapse of the state, "most of the districts in Mogadishu would seem to be either dominated by a single clan or divided in various clusters, but still dominated by a single clan" (Marchal 2002:13).

Applying an agent-oriented approach, overall the armed conflict in Mogadishu can be split into five periods over the course of 25 years: fighting between the USC and the Barre government (1987 to 1991); fighting between the Hawiye sub-clans (1991); various Hawiye sub-clans fighting each other and the United Nations peacekeepers (1991 to 1995); Hawiye sub-clans clans fighting each other following the withdraw of the United Nations peacekeepers (1995 to 2006); and Ethiopia, TFG, and AMISOM versus Al Shabaab (2006 to 2011). Within these different periods, the intensity and location of the armed conflict varied, with various pockets of peace and violence emerging and retracting. While the agents varied for each period, the conflict drivers and precipitating causes also changed for each period with some remaining and others emerging and subsiding.[45] For example, a precipitating cause that is widely mentioned during the first United Nations peacekeeping mission (UNOSOM) was the introduction of new resources, which included humanitarian aid and employment opportunities with international aid agencies.

What makes the conflict analysis challenging is trying to categorize the conflict variables for each period as the objectives behind the fighting differ for each period. At the time of writing, this had not been attempted, most likely due to the complexity of analyzing the various agents and dynamics. In addition, as conflict variables between periods are intricately connected, identifying the direction of causality would be extremely challenging and most likely see equifinality emerging. As mentioned in chapter one, an alternative approach is to look at cases where peace has been maintained while surrounding areas were broiled in armed conflict. This allows the analysis to move beyond agents and structures and focus on norms.

Several districts, such as Wadajir and Dharkenley, provide interesting case studies as they were relatively peaceful and are also coincidentally part of the UNDP baseline study while the remaining four out of the six districts (Hamarjajab, Hamarweyne, Shangani, and Waberi) have experienced various levels of armed conflict. The social capital analytical framework is applied to address the research inquiry qualitatively for the six districts in Mogadishu to look beyond agents and structures.

4.3.2 Conflict Setting and Fieldwork Results on Armed Conflict in Mogadishu

This section summarizes the main findings of four focus group discussions conducted by SOYDEN in Mogadishu over four days in October 2010 and compares the findings with my own fieldwork and the 2011 UNSOA opinion poll. Each group discussion organized by SOYDEN had about 20 participants from each district and consisted of government workers, traditional elders, youth groups, business community representatives, and civil society organizations. This section attempts to provide a general profile of the armed conflict and security issues, and underlying causes of violence in Mogadishu. It also reviews armed conflict management systems briefly. The SOYDEN focus group discussions were conducted with representatives from Wadajir, Dharkenley, and Waberi, which were part of the UNDP baseline study, and also included Hodan which was not part of the UNDP quantitative study.

Focus group participants noted the oligarch nature of the District Commissioners and how the authority of the mayor was not recognized. However they highlighted improvements to the security situation in Wadajir and Dharkenley districts due to the strength of the District Commissioners. Contradictorily they also viewed the "perpetrators of violence are still too often holding power in Mogadishu districts" (SOYDEN 2010b:7).

The following conflict variables were highlighted by focus group participants in relation to specific types of violence (SOYDEN 2010b:8-10).

> ➤ Clan conflicts—Conflict between clans was the most common type of violence in the districts and clans were seen as being used for personal interests and financial gain by individuals who were able to manipulate clan identity to mobilize clan militia. "Clan solidarity and sense of honor is such that no clan member will dare question such self-serving motives and refuse

155

to participate to fight" (SOYDEN 2010b:8).

➤ Political violence/war—Transcending clan lines, this was violence between the TFG and anti-government elements such as Al Shabaab.

➤ Forced recruitment/child soldiers—Jihadist groups, such as Al Shabaab, were seen as recruiting youth through persuasion and psychological manipulation.

➤ Illegal checkpoints—Clan-based and warlord checkpoints for revenue generation were seen as more permanent features versus checkpoints manned by freelance militia which were seen as more temporary.

➤ Forced displacement and violence against IDPs—Viewed as clan-based conflict, this involved violence between host communities and IDPs in urban centers. In addition, insecurity within IDP camps was seen as a problem and clan elders were not able to manage security issues in the camps.

➤ Violence against women—This included sexual and psychological violence perpetrated by warring militiamen and different ethnic groups experienced gender based violence differently.

➤ Land disputes/looting of property—Forgery of documents related to land ownership led to conflict between parties. Land disputes were an issue also for IDPs in refugee camps where land was limited.

➤ Kidnapping and torture—This was seen occurring at the height of the clan conflict between clans in the past, with kidnapping from 2009 onwards focused on foreigners.

Following discussions on the above types and contributors of violence, focus group participants were asked to look at the causes and risk factors (SOYDEN 2010b:11-13). For organizational discussion purposes, causes of insecurity were split into social, economic, political, and security-related causes.

➤ Social causes: clan identity being manipulated "often in the economic or power interest of a leading individual" (SOYDEN 2010b:11); tribal aggressiveness; misinterpretation of religious teachings; injustice based on a weak justice system; lack of future opportunities for the youth; ignorance based on illiteracy and lack of education; trauma from the past; misinformation and rumors creating tension and contributing to violence.

➢ Economic causes: poverty and unemployment lead youth to join armed groups and makes recruiting for militant groups easier; limited resources create disputes, especially amongst IDPs regarding land and basic services.

➢ Political and governance causes: lack of a functional government contributing to lawlessness; lack of adequate communication between government authorities and conflict-affected groups; narrow political interests based on clan representation for individual or clan interests; lack of tolerance for alternative political or ideological views and a belief that only armed opposition is a solution; nepotism and corruption; meddling by neighboring states.

➢ Security-related causes: easy availability of firearms; warlordism seen as a cause in the past.

In terms of armed conflict management, traditional elders supported by religious leaders were seen as the only actors involved in conflict prevention and reduction of disputes and crimes. Religious leaders were seen as passing impartial judgments and being "very rigid, giving little consideration to the practical nature of the conflict, or the perceptions of the people involved in the conflict" (2010b:14). Women and youth groups were also seen as key to making and maintaining peace between communities. Participants noted the importance of xeer in conflict resolution but also highlighted its weakness. "Compensation monies do not always reach the aggrieved when unscrupulous clan elders appropriate the money for their personal benefit, thereby undermining the credibility of elders and sometimes leading to a continuation of hostilities between clans" (2010b:17). The application of xeer was seen as being applied unevenly, as minority clans were forced to adhere to the decisions of stronger and larger clans.

The above causes of conflict from the SOYDEN focus group discussions were compared with the fieldwork data based on the small-n survey and data from the UNSOA 2011 opinion poll that covered the same six districts. The small-n survey asked "How often do the following cause violence in your community? (Q7.5)" Based on the four causes highlighted above (social, economic, political, and security), the small-n survey causes were allocated respectively as shown in the table below.

	1. A lot	2. A little bit	3. Not at all
A. Differences in clan (Social cause)	27	42	30
B. Differences in landholdings (Economic cause)	19	47	34
C. Economic differences (Economic cause)	26	40	34
E. Differences in political party affiliations (Political cause)	41	31	28
F. Differences in religious views (Social cause)	47	41	13

Table 37. How often do the following cause violence in your community? (in percentage terms)

The small-n survey showed that roughly one-third of respondents did not see differences in clan, landholdings, and wealth being a cause of conflict while differences in political party affiliations and religious views were seen as major causes of conflict, in line with the SOYDEN results.

The UNSOA opinion poll asked: "What do you think is the main cause of the current conflict in Somalia? (Q33)" The most common causes, as highlighted in the table below, were social (disagreements, tribalism, etc), political (mistrust, political rivalry, etc), and economical (desire for money and power). Security-related causes were also highlighted in the form of "armed opposition and Al Shabaab".

	Frequency	Valid Percent
Disagreements / Conflicts / tribalism / Tribal beliefs / Injustices / Discrimination / nepotism	98	24.0
Mistrust / Lack of understanding / Political rivalry /disunity	91	22.3
Desire for power and / or money	80	19.6
Opposition /armed opposition / shabaab	31	7.6
Foreign interference	30	7.4
Anarchy /insecurity / all people are armed /bandits	20	4.9
Weak government forces / lack of support for the government /lack of support for government leaders	17	4.2
Religion / not interfere our religion affairs / religious wars	9	2.2
Other	8	7.8
Total	408	100.0

Table 38. What are the main causes of the current conflict in Somalia? (in percentage terms)

Besides the survey data, the focus group discussions and individual interviews I conducted in Mogadishu over a one-year period displayed a variety of causes, with answers ranging widely depending on profession, gender, location of residence, and age. Interviewees also pointed out how the armed conflict in Mogadishu had changed over time, shifting from clan conflict to warlordism, followed by religious conflict to the recent conflict against the TFG.[46]

With robbery, violence, and insecurity relatively widespread in Mogadishu, the research inquiry focuses on the results of the small-n survey for the qualitative approach. Nearly 80% of respondents saw their neighborhood as peaceful (Q7.6) while nearly 90% saw the level of violence in the neighborhood as having decreased "a little" or "a lot" (Q7.7). In terms of walking alone at night, 40% felt unsafe while 87% felt safe from crime and violence at home (Q7.8). Mogadishu had the highest number of respondents in percentage terms (42%) that had experienced violent crime in the past twelve months (Q7.9) and also the highest level out of the five cities that had personally experienced some sort of political violence (77% had experienced political violence "often" or "several times" (Q8.2)). The difference between perception (questions 7.6 to 7.8) and actual incidents widely differed (questions 7.9 and 8.2) with Mogadishu having the highest number of incidents related to crime and political violence compared to the four other cities.

Based on the small-n survey, we can conclude that Mogadishu has the highest levels of armed conflict compared to the other four cities and the causes mentioned in the SOYDEN focus group discussions support the results of the primary fieldwork and UNSOA opinion poll.

4.3.3 Fieldwork Results on Social Capital in Mogadishu

Based on the six social capital proxies, the findings of the fieldwork in Mogadishu indicate high levels of both bonding and bridging social capital, contradictory to the theoretical prediction of low levels of bridging social capital. As previous, the section reviews each social capital proxy individually.

Identity

Mogadishu is considered a cosmopolitan city in terms of clan composition with the Hawiye perceived as the majority followed by the Digil-Mirifle and Bantu clans. However, focus group discussions highlighted tension primarily between the Hawiye and Darod clan, who held political and economical strength during Barre's reign, in the areas of politics and business. Whether this is a simply a spillover effect from Villa Somalia politics[47] or engrained from historical rivalry is difficult to determine. However, in interviews and focus group discussions, clan tensions focused primarily on this Darod-Hawiye cleavage especially in the areas of high-value businesses and economic activities, such as control of the seaport, contracts for large construction projects, and logistic services for humanitarian aid.[48] Despite the Digil-Mirifle and Bantu having a large presence in the city, their politically marginalized status and weak security forces (clan militia) in Mogadishu seems to have (fortunately) excluded them from armed conflict between the other clans.

The issue of clan indicated a mixture of strong and weak bonding social capital. Compared to other cities, clan identity was seen as the best way to differentiate people (total 56%) and know more about that person (total 79%) (Q2.5). On the other hand, nearly 70% did not see clan as providing a social safety net or a basis for social life (Q2.5).

Outside of the economic realm, community relations seemed benign between clans. One reason could be because nearly all the participants in the focus group discussions were from the Hawiye family clan (90% (n=31) of the small-n respondents said they belonged to the Hawiye clan (Q2.1)), therefore presenting a clan bias. The small-n survey, focus group discussions, and interviews show a mixed picture of whether clannism is a source of cleavage in the community and whether bonding social capital is abundant based on clannism.

Groups and Group Networks

Despite the armed conflict having been the most severe in Mogadishu, CSOs have been able to proliferate ever since the state collapsed. Prior to state collapse, CSOs were tightly regulated and controlled by the Barre regime. Following state collapse, CSOs emerged initially in the areas of humanitarian aid delivery (health and food) followed by service delivery (education) and advocacy (human rights, reconciliation). [49] During focus group discussions in Mogadishu, animosity towards CSOs based in the capital was not mentioned. High levels of trust were expressed towards local CSOs which were seen as providing much needed services that the state failed to delivery. However Nairobi based CSOs, including the United Nations (especially UNDP), were widely viewed with mistrust.

Somali CSOs based in Mogadishu were not seen as competing in delivery services with the state because of the weakness of the local authorities. TFG bureaucrats I spoke to did not see CSOs either as competitors and instead highlighted their competencies in helping the local population.[50] An important caveat to add is that the CSOs, in the Somali context and focus group discussions, do not include the business community. Based on my own personal working experience in the area of private sector development and discussions with two United Nations officials familiar with the Mogadishu business community, the Somali business community has a number of "oligarchs" who may be benefiting from the armed conflict in Somalia and could be considered as spoilers.[51] However the issue of spoilers was not raised in any of the focus group discussions and business people who participated, representing 60% (n=22) of the group, did not raise the issue of animosity towards them.

Importantly, interviews with businessmen in Mogadishu highlighted the lack of formal institutions that consisted of different clans[52] and I could not find a functioning chamber of commerce in 2011 that represented the wider Mogadishu business community. Instead I identified several "chairmen" representing various chambers of commerce, usually based on clan, for the Mogadishu area.[53]

Similar to Burao, nearly 40% (n=15) of small-n survey respondents in Mogadishu belonged to some form of a group with the main beneficiary being the community (Q3.1,Q3.3). Over 90% (n=19) said they belonged to groups that consisted of different clan members and 76% (n=29) said the neighborhood they lived in consisted of an equal mixture of different clans (Q3.6,Q3.7). The results of the small-n survey display bridging social capital levels similar to Burao in the area of groups and group networks. Participants of the focus group discussions said CSOs were broadly trusted and benefitted the broader community across clan lines. However results of the research are probably biased due to the large number of Hawiye participants in the focus group discussions (close to 90%).

Personal networks

The utilization of personnel connections was only highlighted in the context of conducting business, mainly related to credit issues between business partners and customers. The issue of personal trust seemed like the bedrock for individual networks in regards to conducting business based on credit. [54] Interestingly, the small-n survey results related to personnel networks (political connections, interacting with different clan members, and borrowing money) did not highlight any major variances from the Burao results despite state institutions being relatively absent in Mogadishu.

Community leadership

Focus group discussions and interviews painted a mixed picture regarding who community leaders were in Mogadishu. In terms of district administrations, each district has a District Commissioner however primary and secondary research (Bryld and Kamau 2012:11) both showed that the power and actual roles of the Commissioners varied by district. [55] Fieldwork showed that depending on the district, community leaders could be "clan elders/leaders" by residents, while for outsiders these same clan elders could be viewed as warlords. [56] Throughout the fieldwork, it became clear that asking people to identify their "community leader" provided a wide range of answers.

While clan elders were commonly referred to in Burao, the District Commissioners in Mogadishu were highlighted as community leaders for participants who lived in districts where security and basic services were more widely available (relative to other Mogadishu districts), such as the district of Wadajir. [57] For example in the district of Wadajir, considered as one of the "safer" districts, the District Commissioner effectively established an independent administration from the TFG and was seen by residents as a charismatic leader who delivered while the mayor of Mogadishu considered him a warlord. On the other hand, the district of Waberi (which is adjacent to Wadajir) was considered as the one of the least safe districts in Mogadishu and lacked any clear community leader, while the District Commissioner there was seen as notoriously corrupt. [58]

In the small-n survey, 37% (n=14) of respondents noted their community leaders as clan elders followed by 21% (n=8) who said there were no community leaders in their community (Q5.1). NGOs, CSOs, and working professionals came in next at 16% (n=6) followed by government officials at 11% (n=4). Importantly, Mogadishu had the highest number of responses that said there was no community leaders versus the other four cities.

Community leaders were seen as having the power to mobilize the community with 84% of respondents in total answering "always", "often", or "sometimes" (Q5.2). In times of emergency, community leaders were seen as important (a total of 84% answered "always" or "often") and kept the community organized (a total of 92% answered "always", "often", or "sometimes"). Respondents saw community leaders as providing guidance to the community and as providers of security (a total of 84% and 64% answered "always", "often", or "sometimes" respectively (Q5.3)). In terms of "command and control" by the community leadership on the local populace, interviewees highlighted that the local "people are very poor so they will be obedient to anyone and will serve who[ever] gives them money".[59]

The fieldwork from Mogadishu shows a mixture of hard and soft linking social capital with clan elders, warlords, District Commissioners/administrations, and NGOs/CSOs as community leaders. The presence of notable community leaders was usually in districts with relative security. Importantly, in some districts that experienced large amounts of insecurity (armed conflict), community leaders were absent suggesting low levels or complete absence of hard and soft linking social capital. Instead warlords, militias, and gangs would be abundant in these areas while the local community simply kept a low profile, such as in the districts of Abdiaziz, Shibis, and Yaqshid.[60] This suggests that the direction of causality may indicate insecurity having an effect on linking social capital rather than linking social capital having an effect on armed conflict. This also suggests a negative correlation between armed conflict and hard/soft linking social capital: when armed conflict is high, both hard and soft linking social capital diminishes. Linking social capital, both hard and soft, seem to also flourish in secure settings, suggesting that improved security also has some sort of effect on linking social capital.

Trust

Relative to the other four cities, the small-n survey suggests that Mogadishu had the lowest levels of trust. Based on the question: "Generally speaking, would you say that most people can be trusted, or that you cannot be too careful in your dealings with other people" (Q6.3), only about one-third (38%, n=12) answered that "most people can be trusted" while 63% (n=20) chose "you cannot be too careful". Relative to the other four cities, Mogadishu participants indicated the lowest level of trust towards people from the same clan, clan elders, businessmen, and religious leaders (Q6.4).

		1. A lot	2. A little	3. Not at all
A	People from your clan	19	60	22
B	People from other clans	11	89	0
C	Teachers	76	18	6
D	Clan elders	22	50	28
E	Businessmen/businesswomen	19	48	32
F	Politicians, government officials	3	44	53
G	Military persons	4	50	46
H	Religious leaders (Ullaama U Ddin/Culuma)	53	33	14
I	Police	19	47	33
J	NGOs run by Somalis	22	47	31

Table 39. How much do you trust the following people? (in percentage terms)

Interestingly, focus group respondents and interviewees highlighted that they had more trust in people from different clans versus people from the same clan. When inquiring the reason, some respondents noted that people from the same clan expected help and assistance based on their clan affiliation while people from different clans were less likely to demand support. In addition, interviewees highlighted the issue of mistrust even within their own clan and that having the same clan affiliation did not lead to increased trust.

Focus group discussions did not highlight the abundance or lack of trust in the wider community. Interviews and discussions on trust focused on clan elders, religious leaders, and government officials. The influence of clan leaders was seen as having diminished over time.[61]

At the community level, the main role of the clan elders was to mediate local disputes (Bryld and Kamau 2012:25) however their role in governance and security matters depended on their relationship with the district administration. Some districts administrations would see clan elders having a role in governance while in other districts they would marginalize clan elders.[62]

Trust towards clan elders were mixed depending on the interlocutors. While most students referred to clan elders as wise and trustworthy, some government officials questioned their legitimacy and saw them as simply looking out for their own personal interests and financial enrichment. In addition, the proliferation of self-declared clan elders was a point raised and that this led to the diminishing of trust and legitimacy towards clan elders.[63] From a state perspective, clan elders were also seen as contributing and promoting tribalism and creating cleavages between communities while undermining the authority of the local administrations.

Trust towards religious leaders again depended on the interviewee. On the one side religious leaders can suffer from low trust for being related to radical Islam and being suspected of having links with Al Shabaab (Bryld and Kamau 2012:25). On the other hand, they can enjoy high levels of trust for being related to humanitarian aid delivery and community development. In both cases, the religious actors are considered off-shoots of the Muslim Brotherhood, with groups like Alhu Sheikh seen as a highly politicized clique with personal agendas ranging from power and money.[64] Membership in Alhu Sheikh includes the former TFG president Sheikh Sharif and members of the previous parliament. As highlighted in the focus group discussions, Al-Islah,[65] another religious group, has a large following in urban areas by students and is considered a religious-social movement, managing schools and community development projects and allegedly enjoys the trust of the communities it works in.

Other religious groups and religious leaders in Mogadishu also vary in terms of trust levels by the community.[66] Al-Itisam is the remake of Al Itahad, which was a violent religious movement in the 1990s and saw some of its former members join Al Shabaab. Upon denouncing violence, Al-Itisam has attempted to regain its reputation but suspicions remain due to its links with the business "oligarchs". The Council of Religious Scholars, established to counter Al-Shabaab's radical ideology, is considered nationally as having moral authority but is viewed with suspicion by non-Somalis due to some of its key members' violent past (UNPOS 2012: Nairobi). Unlike Burao, trust levels towards religious leaders varied widely in Mogadishu with suspicions prevalent due to the intentional or unintentional politicization of religious leaders and groups.

As mentioned previously, trust towards government officials, such as the District Commissioner and district administration, varied primarily on whether the interviewee was benefitting from the government officials. However the small-n survey showed that most respondents saw government officials as being corrupt, with 45% (n=14) believing that most were involved in corruption and 42% (n=13) as having some involvement in corruption (Q6.2). In numerous discussions with government officials in Mogadishu, many saw their own colleagues as being corrupt[67], indicating low levels of trust towards government officials.[68] Lack or no pay of salaries for civil servants, compounded by financial desperation, was seen as contributing to corruption.[69] However, compared to the issue of the state not being able to provide security for its citizens, corruption was seen as a minor issue. Contradictory, CSOs saw the role of the state as minimal and viewed privatization as optimal with the state simply needing to provide basic health and carrying out a watchdog function.[70]

Overall the fieldwork pointed to low levels of bridging social capital. Trust levels were high within selected groups, such as religious groups, or communities who had "strongmen" providing security and basic services. Trust levels were high towards clan elders and religious leaders when one was directly affiliated or had access to these parties. Trust levels were low towards the business community, which was seen as also promoting corruption amongst government officials. Government officials lacked trust from the community, more likely because the local administration was not able or willing to provide basic services that were impartial. Lack of resources, funding, and weak legal frameworks may have contributed to the low levels of trust towards the state suggesting that financial resources to fund the state may be a requisite for the community to trust the state in conflict or post-conflict settings. In addition, the unclear "role of the state" may have contributed to low levels of trust and lack of recognition of state institutions.[71]

Social Cohesion

As previously noted in table 4.2 (Q7.4), the small-n survey showed the feeling of togetherness or closeness in the neighborhood for Mogadishu (61%, n=23) to be similar with levels of Burao (56%, n=15). Compared to Burao (48%, n=13), Mogadishu had more responses (66%, n=21) agreeing that "everybody should be free to pursue what is best for themselves as individuals" versus "each person should put the well being of the community ahead of their own interests" (Q7.1). Most likely due to the cosmopolitan clan makeup of Mogadishu, 65% (n=20) of respondents chose "we must learn to accept differences of opinion within the community" versus "in order to make decisions in our community, we should talk until everyone agrees" (Q7.2). The above answers indicate a possible preference for individualism versus a group approach.

Mogadishu importantly recorded the highest number of responses (45%, n=17) that chose "in this country, it is sometimes necessary to use violence in support of a just cause" (Q8.1). This response may be related to the high levels of armed conflict that Mogadishu has historically experienced, causing residents to become used to witnessing violence and war. The issue of crime and personal security was mentioned on numerous occasions during focus group discussions while land disputes and deegan between permanent residents were not highlighted, most likely because of the urban setting. On the other hand, land disputes amongst IDPs were highlighted, with local administrations seen as dealing with this matter. These security issues were not referred to as destroying communal relations. Diya payments were not flagged in focus group discussions for settling disputes even though 46% (n=17) said they belonged to a diya paying group (Q2.8).

Cooperation between local CSOs and the local administration were at best informal and ad hoc, with formal institutions or frameworks absent for engagement between the two entities. Interestingly, a number of government officials belonged to or had set up CSOs themselves, further blurring the lines between public and private organizations.[72] Despite membership consisting of government officials, CSOs were viewed with suspicion by the central government and seen as a rival, an issue also highlighted by Menkhaus et al (2010:346).

Based on the numerous CSOs I interviewed in Mogadishu, I came to suspect that the CSOs consisted of members from the same clan, although where the clan divide emerged was not clear due to the flexible nature of clan identity. Tim Randall[73], a United Nations consultant who has probably spent the most amount of time working in Mogadishu with CSOs since 2011, also highlighted this point: "Most [CSOs] seem to be based on clan, or clan groupings, but some are not. However, the few I have come across that purport to be open to all clans tend to be made up from minorities who might not otherwise get recognition from majorities/elite".[74] In agreement with Randall, this is not to say that all CSOs in Mogadishu simply serve vested interests or one particular group, as there are several NGOs who clearly were trying to cross clan lines and help the wider community.

In the context of Mogadishu, exclusive membership in CSOs may be unintentional and simply be a surviving mechanism for operating in a high risk security environment. Furthermore, social cohesion in Mogadishu seemed to be compartalized within groups, indicating

167

bonding social capital prevailing over bridging social capital. Whether social cohesion extended to different groups was not clear. Exclusive social cohesion may be unintentional and instead could also be a survival tactic for getting by in Mogadishu. Low levels of bridging social capital could be noticed as focus group participants highlighted that they would not venture around the city unnecessarily, which would therefore limit the opportunities for bridging social capital to be developed.

4.3.4 Summary of Armed Conflict and Social Capital in Mogadishu

As shown above, both primary and secondary qualitative fieldwork indicates high levels of armed conflict in Mogadishu. Criminal activities, organized crime, warlordism, Al Shabaab, lack of rule of law, unemployment, idle youth, and economic disparities were seen as contributing to insecurity. Mogadishu displayed high levels of bonding social capital and low levels of bridging social capital. The proliferation of CSOs, albeit of an exclusive type, indicated high levels of soft linking social capital. Hard social capital was also abundant due to the large number of "strong men" and District Commissioners who had questionable pasts related to warlordism and violence. The qualitative fieldwork results can be summarized in the following table against the theoretical predictions.

	Bridging (Prediction 1)	Bonding (Prediction 2)	Hard Linking (Prediction 3)	Soft Linking (Prediction 4)	Armed Conflict
Theoretical Prediction	L	H	H	L	H
Qualitative results	L	H	H	H	H

Table 40. Theoretical predications and qualitative results for Mogadishu by social capital type and armed conflict level

Inclusive bridging networks were limited and cleavages seemed to prevail between different groups such as CSOs, the business community, and even the diaspora returnees despite the security situation improving in certain neighborhoods. As argued by Paffenholz (2010:396) and Menkhaus et al (2010:341), and described in detailed in section 2.6.2, CSOs in Somalia tend to be clan-based organizations which in the majority of cases unintentionally reinforce social cleavages. This is very much the case in Mogadishu, where CSOs seem to rarely transcend major clan divides and be based on charismatic personalities as also seen in other parts of Somalia (Menkhaus et al 2010:334).

Analyzing bonding social capital proved to be challenging due to the issue of scalability as respondents seemed to be regularly expanding and decreasing their social networks based on the context and their needs (whether related to security or economical needs). Clan identities were used conveniently to either include or exclude others as necessary based on the context and there were no clear set criteria (or divides) within the clan for distinguishing between "them" and "us". Marginalized clans, such as the Bantus and Digil-Mirifle, were widely excluded from political issues and experienced higher levels of violence and victimization, indicating a relationship of low levels of bridging social capital and high levels of armed conflict. Attaching oneself to a "strong" clan could lead to improved security but this would require inclusive social networks and dynamics to extend from the stronger clan to the weaker clan.

Importantly, Mogadishu highlights the crucial role of the state in regard to its effect on social capital. Results indicate that districts with strong administrations, such as Wadajir, were creating and sustaining exclusive networks and therefore had low levels of bridging social capital. On the other hand, fieldwork showed tensions emerging between district administrations and the central government as the Ministry of Interior slowly attempted to exercise its monopoly of violence in the capital city. The central government's weakness to exert influence on the district administrations and provide basic services may have contributed to strengthening bonding social capital within communities. The emergence of bonding social capital would be expected during times of armed conflict where defensive mechanisms of a bonding type would come before bridging social capital. As security in Mogadishu improves, how bonding social capital is "dismantled" by the state and replaced with impersonal bridging mechanisms will be a point of interest. Will emerging central governance by the FGS lead to increased bridging social capital and less bonding social capital, or will it have the opposite effect and strengthen bonding social capital?

In the meantime, mechanisms and processes to handle conflicts between different clans do not seem to be in place to systematically address the conflict variables highlighted earlier (section 4.3.2). With an abundance of bonding social capital and a zero-sum game mentality prevailing in Mogadishu, the central government may actually be best placed to create bridging social capital and the necessary networks between communities for mitigating conflict. The results indicate that whether armed conflict contributes to a zero-sum game mentality and exclusive networks is difficult to judge. However, what is clear is that district administrations are keen to maintain the "equilibrium" of power (economic, political, and security) they hold, being reluctant to allow the central government to exercise its role and disturb the current setup. Bonding social capital may therefore continue to prevail in Mogadishu for the time being.

4.4 Galkayo—A Qualitative Approach

This section is based on field research conducted in April 2013.[75] Numerous attempts since 2010 to visit Galkayo were made however arranging logistics and meetings on the ground with interlocutors proved extremely difficult. Securing arrangements for the necessary security procedures were complex and political instability also prevented me from visiting on several occasions due to my status as an UNPOS staff member. Finally, in early April 2013, I was able to visit Galkayo with the generous logistical support of UNICEF and WFP colleagues[76] who have guest houses located in northern Galkayo.

From a security perspective, conducting fieldwork in Galkayo was extremely difficult due to the constant risk of being kidnapped. Galkayo is notorious for kidnappings and is infamously known as the country's "kidnap capital". When moving about in northern Galkayo, I would have at least two or more police vehicles. Moving around southern Galkayo was even more complicated (due to higher levels of insecurity) and required at least three police vehicles.[77] Even when travelling between the airport and the city, the Somali police escorts always chose different routes to decrease the risk of possible attacks and kidnappings. To conduct independent research as a non-Somali in Galkayo is extremely challenging and incidents of foreign aid workers and researchers being kidnapped seemed to be more frequent in Galkayo than Mogadishu.[78] Despite the security risks, Galkayo provides an extremely interesting case study for analyzing social capital due to the city being politically divided into two.

The analysis focuses primarily on the armed conflict between north and south Galkayo and examines bridging social capital between the two, while also looking at the bonding social capital dynamics within the two communities. Research processes follow previous sections, using results of the Saferworld[79] (2011) focus group discussions in Galkayo and other secondary data to establish a baseline of the conflict variables (Quero 2011b). This is then followed by an analysis of my own qualitative work to review the conflict variables and the four theoretical predictions related to social capital. Based on the four theoretical predictions, social capital levels and armed conflict for both north *and* south Galkayo would be as follows:

	Bridging (Prediction 1)	Bonding (Prediction 2)	Hard Linking (Prediction 3)	Soft Linking (Prediction 4)	Armed Conflict
Theoretical prediction	L	H	L	L	H

Table 41. Theoretical predictions for Galkayo by type of social capital and assumed level of armed conflict

The theoretical prediction states that both north and south Galkayo suffer from low levels of bridging social capital between each other and instead both have high levels of bonding social capital in their respective regions. In terms of armed conflict, this is seen as relatively high. The qualitative results based on my fieldwork paint a rather complicated picture regarding bridging social capital, with efforts having been made to make bridges at the administrative level but not at the community level.

4.4.1 Galkayo – Contextual Background

Known as the "bellybutton/stomach" of Somalia, Galkayo is a strategic trading city bordering both Puntland and south central Somalia with inroads to neighbouring Ethiopia. It is politically and economically divided into two. North Galkayo is primarily inhabited by the Darod clan (Majeerteen sub-clan) and south Galkayo by the Hawiye clan (Haber Gedir sub-clan). Politically, north Galkayo is part of the Puntland State (established in 1998) while south Galkayo is the capital of the self-declared Galmudug administration which was formed on 14 August 2006. Economically, the north is more developed than the south and the north's population is estimated to make up around 70 percent of the total urban population of Galkayo.[80]

Physically, the city is divided by a series of road check points and this division is referred to as the "green line", an imaginary line, and at times a real physical divide and border which cuts the city into two from east to west. Where roads cross the green line, passing traffic is checked by security forces from both sides, similar to an international border crossing. High profile individuals such as powerful businessmen, politicians, community and CSO leaders, and clan elders may have their movement restricted when trying to cross sides while other people are usually free to cross sides.

In terms of clan composition, the Omar Mohamud sub-clan of the Majeerteen (part of Darod clan) is the main clan residing in north Galkayo while the Sa'ad sub-clan of the Haber Gedir (part of the Hawiye clan) is the major clan in south Galkayo. South Galkayo is the administrative capital of the Galmudug "State", which is seen as a "Sa'ad project", driven politically and financially by diaspora and "strongmen" from the Sa'ad clan. [81] As an administration, it has developed over time by slowly building alliances with other Haber Gedir sub-clans, such as the Sarur and Cayr, and sub-sub clans within the Sa'ad while at the same time experiencing armed conflict with the Suleiman rival sub-clan who have their own ambitions of a state (and are also part of the Haber Gedir).

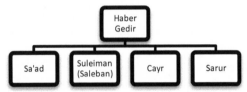

Figure 11. Haber Gedir clan family with selected sub-clans

Importantly, Galmudug State consists of only certain parts of Galguduud and Mudug regions and *not* the entire two regions which under the previous Transitional Charter [82] was the minimum requirement to establish a federal state. Despite not achieving the legal requirement for statehood, as stipulated in the Charter or having effective control on the ground, the Galmudug State was a significant political player during the end of the transition in 2012. Similar to other parts of Somalia, at the time of research, the administration had limited control, if any, of the areas it claimed to represent with local clan dynamics superseding state control. It has seen several presidents emerge since it was established and consists of an executive, judiciary, and parliament.

Historically, the city of Galkayo was established in 1903 and colonized by the Italians from 1924 to 1939 followed by British rule in 1941. Major confrontations between the Hawiye and Darod in the region were recorded from 1943 to 1964, even after Somalia's independence in 1960 (Quero 2011b:14). Saferworld notes "Italian colonial practices initially reinforced and established clan-based lines in the area… Colonial practices of establishing clan-based borders to decrease conflict, along with the 'divide and rule' practices of the Barre regime, reinforced clan divides" (2011:7).

In the 1980s, with civil war erupting, the Barre administration used its alliance with the Darod sub-clans and exploited the tensions between the Darod and Hawiye clans in Galkayo. Following the collapse of the Barre administration in 1991, which itself was seen as a Darod clan-based alliance, the Hawiye backed USC party (dominated mainly by the Sa'ad sub-clan of the Hawiye) attacked the Majeerteen-Darod clan in northern Galkayo. These attacks between 1991 and 1992, referred by the Darod northerners as a massacre, are still seen as the major reason for mistrust between the two clans.[83]

In 1993 a cessation of hostilities was agreed upon by Abdulahi Yusuf (who would become the first president of the TFG) on behalf of the Darod and General Mohamed Farah Aidid for the Hawiye (interestingly both shared a prison cell under the Barre regime). But not all sub-clans of the Hawiye and Darod supported this initiative (Quero 2011b:14). Known as the 1993 Mudug Peace Agreement, Yusuf and Aidid were able to develop the basic framework for ending the armed conflict allowing their respective clans to consolidate power in their traditional power bases and also create a secure environment for business to flourish in Galkayo. Importantly this also helped Aidid free up his military forces from south Galkayo and concentrate on the war in Mogadishu against his Abgal rival (also part of the Hawiye clan family) Ali Mahdi Mohamed. Formulated in Mogadishu, the Mudug Peace Agreement was seen as a Somali owned and financed process however its objective was not to address the root causes of the conflict and deal with reconciliation ("positive peace"[84]) but focused instead more on a cease fire ("negative peace") (Saferworld 2011:8). Since then, at the time of research, the two administrations have avoided major war between each other but clashes between clan militias and the two communities have prevailed.

Economically, Galkayo primarily relies on trade due to its central location between the north and south parts of Somalia and Ethiopia. In the rural areas, pastoralism is practiced. The city has an airport located on the northern side, several universities (both in the north and south),

173

hospitals, and a main market place located just north of the green line which both southerners and northerners use. Revenue sharing between the two administrations is limited to the airport which is managed by north Galkayo.

4.4.2 Conflict Setting and Fieldwork Results on Armed Conflict in Galkayo

Saferworld conducted six focus group discussions in April 2010 with community elders and religious leaders, the district council, women, youth (male and female), police and judiciary actors, and IDPs. Focus group discussions were only with participants from northern Galkayo and excluded individuals from rural areas (Quero 2011b:13). Even though the discussions have a northern bias, they still provide an interesting analysis of the armed conflict between the north and south by allowing participants to discuss this specific issue.

The discussions identified the following types of violence in Galkayo against men: clan violence; political violence; assassinations and unknown killings; and clan revenge. Women highlighted rape as a type of violence against them. The main safety concerns and threats of the participants were piracy, Al Shabaab, land disputes, clan and political issues, gangs, theft, rape, and drug use (Quero 2011b:22). It was not clear whether the types of violence and safety concerns were related to inter-clan issues between the Darod and Hawiye.

Similar to the analysis for Mogadishu, causes of insecurity were split into social, economic, political, and security-related causes (Saferworld 2011:19-24, Quero 2011b:30-32).

> ➤ Social causes: clan; restricted social interactions; absence of strong initiatives supported by community and political leaders to reconcile the two communities; poor social-economic opportunities; population movements; social norms towards domestic violence; marginalization of youth in social decision-making processes; weakening of traditional justice systems; qat consumption; perceived bias of the United Nations and international NGOs operating in north Galkayo.

> ➤ Economic causes: lack of social services and social-economic opportunities; economic disparities between north and south Galkayo; disputes over grazing areas during times of drought.

> ➤ Political and governance causes: two-state structure of Galkayo

city where the existence of two administrations within one city creates challenges for governance.

➢ Security-related causes: failure of formal security and justice systems; history of violence; lack of formal collaboration between the police forces of the north and south; availability of firearms; Al Shabaab.

The above causes of insecurity clearly highlight the divide between the two administrations and communities. Some of the same causes of insecurity were also highlighted during interviews I had conducted in northern Galkayo, such as: restricted social interactions between the north and south; absence of strong initiatives supported by community and political leaders to reconcile the two communities; and lack of formal collaboration between the police forces of the north and south.

In terms of armed conflict management, the Saferworld discussions noted local traditional elders supported by government security institutions dealt with clan-based killings. Clan elders also dealt with community-wide conflicts and political settlements between the north and south (Saferworld 2010). Religious leaders were not mentioned in handling north-south conflicts.

Comparing the causes of conflict from the Saferworld focus group discussions and the results of the small-n survey conducted in south Galkayo, the prevalence of social, economic, and political causes was also highlighted. (The small-n survey (Q7.5) asked "How often do the following cause violence in your community?")

	1. A lot	2. A little bit	3. Not at all
A. Differences in clan (Social cause)	62	19	19
B. Differences in landholdings (Economic cause)	25	55	20
C. Economic differences (Economic cause)	47	16	37
E. Differences in political party affiliations (Political cause)	55	18	27
F. Differences in religious views (Social cause)	57	19	24

Table 42. How often do the following cause violence in your community? (in percentage terms)

The small-n survey highlighted differences in clan, wealth (economic differences), political affiliation, and religious views as causes of violence in the community, similar to the Saferworld results.

Focus group discussions and individual interviews conducted in north Galkayo during my visit highlighted tit-for-tat kidnapping between the north and south, assassinations by Al Shabaab, and spillover of rural conflicts between the Darod and Hawiye clans into the city.[85] Compared to three years ago, Al Shabaab's presence and strength had weakened but was still seen as a risk.[86] Differing from the Saferworld findings, pirates were no longer seen as a problem in Galkayo and this had improved the security situation in the city. No major collusions had happened over the past few years between the north and south and it was noted that "animosity is there but there isn't a lot of fear... Both have arms [weapons], there is no fear of war with them".[87]

North and south relationships had also seen an improvement, including political relations between the Galmudug and Puntland states. Criminals had a harder time using the north-south divide to escape from being captured but revenge killings could always trigger conflict.[88] All interviewees highlighted how the security situation in Galkayo had improved since 2010 when the Saferworld focus group discussions had taken place but highlighted the fragility and volatility of the security situation in Galkayo: "Security situation in 2013 is better than 2010 but still volatile, anytime anything can happen".[89]

In regards to perception of violence and armed conflict experienced by small-n survey respondents in south Galkayo, all respondents saw their neighborhood as peaceful (Q7.6) while 44% saw the level of violence in the neighborhood as having decreased "a little" or "a lot" (Q7.7). In terms of walking alone at night, 74% felt safe to do so while 96% felt safe from crime and violence at home (Q7.8). Only 13% had experienced violent crime in the past twelve months (Q7.9) while 54% had personally experienced some sort of political violence (Q8.2).

A follow-up survey to the UNDP baseline study was conducted by OCVP in north Galkayo from 13 to 16 April 2013 with 80 samples focusing on the state of conflict, safety and security in Galkayo (OCVP 2013). When asked about incidents related to clan conflict, 78% said there had been none in the past 12 months. In terms of reasons for the clan conflict, 91% said family disputes were the cause and 9% were resource-based. Nearly two-thirds (68%) felt unsafe after dark in their area of residence, significantly different to south Galkayo where 74% felt safe to walk alone at night (OCVP 2013:20).

OCVP focus group discussions highlighted "suicide attacks, organized killings, clan-based kidnapping, revenge killings, and mobile phone mugging were among the principle issues causing safety concerns in the district" (OCVP 2013:22). In terms of causes, "Women and youth participants considered the division of the district into two rivalry political administrations as one of the issues that triggered disputes between clans/communities" (OCVP 2013:22). The administrative split was also raised in key informant interviews such as the prosecutor, mayor, and a religious leader (OCVP 2013:23-25).

Based on the primary and secondary research, armed conflict between the north and south communities/clans were a concern. The existence of two administrations was seen as contributing to insecurity and conflict between the two communities. At the local level Al Shabaab and piracy, to lesser extent in 2013 than 2010, were seen as conflict variables in the north. Relative to the north, the small-n survey suggested the south to be more secure in terms of violence and crime despite having an administration that was comparingly new. Focusing on the issue of armed conflict between the north and south, the research data indicates a high level of potential armed conflict between the two communities and a high level of armed conflict in the past.[90] Although the current situation in Galkayo remains stable, and has seen an improvement over time, the armed conflict level is considered as high for the purpose of this research inquiry.

4.4.3 Fieldwork Results on Social Capital in Galkayo

This section focuses on bridging social capital between north and south Galkayo and bonding social capital within the two communities. Based on the fieldwork results, Galkayo displays high levels of bonding social capital and low levels of bridging social capital, supporting the theoretical prediction. The section reviews each social capital proxy of the analytical framework individually, with a focus on north-south relations.

Identity

The small-n survey supported the findings of the UNDP baseline survey showing that around 89% of habitants in the south were related to the Hawiye clan (Quero 2011a:16). The majority of inhabitants in the north, based on the UNDP baseline survey, belonged to the Darod clan (at 63%) with Digil-Mirifle, Bantu, and Dir also being present. All

177

interviewees and focus group participants from my fieldwork in north Galkayo belonged to the Darod clan. Focus group discussions in the north and south highlighted how intermarriage between individuals from the two communities had decreased compared to the past and was seen as a rare occurrence.[91]

Groups and group networks

References toward inter-clan group networks between the north and the south were not mentioned. OCVP reported a "peace school" was established in north Galkayo to accommodate children from the north and south but had been closed down (2011b:11). According to my own fieldwork, the school remained closed and had been converted into a police station.[92] No groups or chambers of commerce for the two business communities to interact were found.[93] Mosques located around the green line were identified as places where residents from the north and south mixed, however whether this led to improved relationships between the two sides was not clear.[94]

At the community level in the south, the small-n survey showed 53% (n=14) belonged to some sort of group (Q3.1). However only two respondents said the purpose of the group they belonged to was to unite communities or bring different clans together. Local NGOs were able to work in both locations however it was not clear whether the NGOs consisted of members from both the north and south.[95] The fieldwork indicated an abundance of groups and group networks within the respective communities in the north and south, however no formal groups consisting of the two sides were identified.

Personal networks

Interviewees highlighted that they had friends from the other respective sides of Galkayo however the north-south divide made it difficult for people to visit and interact on a regular basis as movement from one side to the other could be restricted and pose risk to one's personal safety: "Because of insecurity, they cannot come here and it is very difficult for us to go there".[96] Personal networks between clan elders from the north and south were limited to ad hoc interactions when problems arose.[97] The two business communities had no engagement with each other and businessmen in the north relied on their personal networks and trust for daily operations without reliance on written contracts or the government for enforcement.[98] Women were seen as having stronger personal networks than men between the two sides as it was easier for them to cross the green line. [99] Furthermore, as women were always the victims of armed conflict, they were seen as being able to easily build linkages between each other, despite clan affiliation, to overcome everyday hardships.[100]

Community leadership

The Mudug region, where north Galkayo is located, is administered by the Regional Governor for Mudug, appointed by the Puntland President. North Galkayo city itself is administered by the mayor, deputy mayor, and city council. The city council members are elected by clans and facilitate and communicate with the respective clan-based leadership in the area (Quero 2011b:18). South Galkayo is managed at the regional level by the Galmudug President. At the district level the city is administered by the District Council and mayor with the chieftaincy playing a key informal role in the governance of the district. All appointments in south Galkayo are made in consultations with sub-clans (Bryld and Addow 2011:6-7).

In the north, interviewees did not specifically highlight the linkage between the district administration and community, although trust towards the police was mentioned as low. Clan elders were not specifically referred to as community leaders. In the south, the small-n survey showed government and CSOs as the community leaders (both 31%, n=8), followed by religious leaders (23%, n=6) (Q5.1). Community leaders in the south were seen as having the power to mobilize the community, were important in times of emergency, kept the community organized, and provided guidance and security (Q5.3). Interestingly 48% (n=10) said their community was not from the same clan (Q5.4).

Primary and secondary research indicated de jure leadership as being with the state while de facto governance was an informal partnership between the administration and community clan elders based on sub-clan representation. District councils and city councils included representatives chosen by the community but interactions between the two administrations were limited during times of armed conflict to resolve issues.[101]

Trust

Interviewees in the north expressed strong trust for clan elders to resolve intra and inter-communal conflicts. In regard to inter-communal conflicts with the south, the role of the state was not mentioned in resolving issues with clan elders.[102] The small-n survey results from the south showed teachers having the most trust followed by religious leaders, while trust towards clan elders was relatively low.

		1. A lot	2. A little	3. Not at all
A	People from your clan	46	41	14
B	People from other clans	24	71	5
C	Teachers	88	12	0
D	Clan elders	22	50	28
E	Businessmen/businesswomen	14	76	10
F	Politicians, government officials	30	40	30
G	Military persons	5	47	47
H	Religious leaders (Ullaama U Ddin/Culuma)	67	24	10
I	Police	36	46	18
J	NGOs run by Somalis	24	29	48

Table 43. How much do you trust the following people? (in percentage terms)

Relative to the other four cities, south Galkayo had similar results with Burao regarding the issue of general trust: "Generally speaking, would you say that most people can be trusted, or that you cannot be too careful in your dealings with other people", 58% (n=15) answered that "most people can be trusted" while 42% chose "you cannot be too careful" (Q6.3).

During interviews in the north, mistrust and lack of trust between the Sa'ad and Majeerteen clans was highlighted repeatedly with neither administration taking action to address this issue between the two communities. The division of the city and war between the two communities in 1991 was blamed for the lack of trust for the north and south.[103] Although the lack of trust was blamed for insecurity between the two cities, this did not stop residents from both communities interacting with each other where necessary: "There is mistrust, but not [at a] level of not dealing with each other".[104]

Xeer and the practice of diya were seen as functioning only within each respective community and not between the north and south.[105] Interviewees highlighted that xeer arrangements between the Majeerteen and Sa'ad clans were "canceled" following the south invasion of 1991, thereby leaving no traditional systems to quickly handle compensation payments.[106]

Overall the fieldwork pointed to low levels of bridging social capital between the two communities and high levels of bonding social capital within north and south Galkayo. For the north, trust levels were high towards clan elders for resolving intra and inter-communal disputes versus the government. Similar to Burao, it was noted that, "Elders have to defend their tribe, every time, whether they [the clan] are right or wrong, even if they are wrong".[107] Religious leaders were relied on for handling marriage, divorce, and inheritance issues.[108] In south Galkayo, trust levels were higher towards religious leaders than clan elders, similar to the results of the UNDP baseline study. General trust within the community was similar to Burao and therefore displayed higher levels than Mogadishu (Q6.3).

Social cohesion

Before 1991, Galkayo was "one city" with everyone acknowledging the deegan of the various clans. Pasture sharing was practiced between nomads from the south and north. Although tribal problems used to occur before the state collapsed in 1991, they were manageable and only became unmanageable when cleavages between the communities became politicized following the collapse of the state.[109]

In April 2013 the central market place, located just north of the green line, was the only area in which daily interaction between the two communities occurred, leaving little room for any attempts at fostering social cohesion and peace. Other so-called "neutral spaces" included hospitals, mosques, and the airport. The airport, located in north Galkayo and several kilometers east from the city center, has been used on several occasions as a place for discussion between the north and south clan elders and the two administrations for resolving conflicts (Quero 2011b:38). Besides these ad hoc arrangements, which emerge during times of conflict, formal or informal mechanisms for regular interaction between the elders of both communities were lacking. Although Galmudug and Puntland signed an agreement in February 2011 to establish two committees to primarily handle security related issues, the committees seem to have not met (Joint Agreement 2011).[110]

At a quotidian level, interactions between the two communities were limited to hospitals, the central market place, mosques, and some schools. The hospitals saw patients from both sides and allegedly did not differentiate patients by clan or residence. Patients were free to seek medical care from both sides, depending on the service needed.[111] Although not common, secondary schools and higher education institutions saw a limited number of students from the other side of the community, such as the Puntland State University, located in north Galkayo, with approximately five percent of the enrolled students originating from the south.[112] A technical school for women located in the north saw enrolment rates from the south as high as 40 percent, highlighting the relative ease for women to cross the green line.[113]

Cleavages between the north and south are not only an urban phenomenon. Interviewees highlighted that the majority of clan conflicts originated in the rural areas between nomads, who are seen as "wild", and then spill over to the city and contribute to insecurity.[114]

In the city, insecurity and mistrust is blamed for the lack of interaction between the two communities. Several initiatives to improve social cohesion between the two communities were undertaken by CSOs in the past. In 2003 women from both sides demonstrated for the abolishment of the green line. This initiative helped students cross the green line to attend schools on different sides. Youth groups have organized some sporting events involving both sides. For example, in December 2012, north Galkayo held a marathon for the first time in support of women's rights and included participants from south Galkayo. Despite these initiatives, quotidian relations between the two communities are difficult to maintain and require effort and come with more risks for men who are seen as legitimate targets for revenge regardless of their age while women were not targeted.[115]

Based on my fieldwork, at the state level relations between the Galmudug State and Puntland State are seen as relatively good, following the process for ending the transition of the Transitional Federal Institutions in 2012. Galmudug State was one of the signatories of the process for ending the political transition, granting it political recognition by default from the Puntland State, and a consultative meeting was even held in Galkayo in March 2012 (Communiqué 2012). However, interactions between both administrations have tended to be sporadic and have decreased following the end of the transition in September 2012.[116]

Furthermore, the two administrations continue to lack any formal functioning structures for engagement despite external support from

CSOs. In October and November 2010 a local CSO funded by UNDP initiated a project to bring the north and south administrations together (DIAL 2011). A meeting was held at the airport and the mayors from the two administrations met for the first time in 18 months. Following this meeting, Local Peace Committees and District Peace Working Committees were established to handle governance and security issues affecting both communities. However, both committees have struggled to carry out their mandates due to the lack of capacity and financial incentives for the its members (DIAL 2011:10).

A DIAL representative opines that the committees have not prevented conflict "but rather respond to problems when they escalate to crisis level. For them [Local Peace Committees and District Peace Working Committees] to prevent conflict there are many issues to be sorted out and there are outstanding difference[s] that are deep rooted and need extensive work... the Committee is doing to halt conflict whenever it happens and ensure it does not escalate to full blown war".[117]

Initiatives to improve social cohesion at the community and administrative level have to overcome mistrust and a complex security environment with a history of violence vividly remaining in the minds of many longtime residents from both sides. Insecurity and a history of mistrust make it easy to maintain the status quo and low levels of bridging social capital between the two communities.

4.4.4 Summary of Armed Conflict and Social Capital in Galkayo

As predicted, the analysis shows Galkayo displaying low levels of bridging social capital between north and south Galkayo amid the lack of relations at the community and administrative level. Bonding social capital, based on intra-clan relations, is relatively high in the north and south with some CSOs attempting to bridge the two communities together. Hard linking social capital is low due to the lack of trust and expectations for the state to resolve conflicts and build relations with the other side. Countering the theoretical prediction, soft linking social capital within each community is relatively high with strong trust towards religious leaders and clan elders in resolving inter and intra-communal conflicts.

	Bridging (Prediction 1)	Bonding (Prediction 2)	Hard Linking (Prediction 3)	Soft Linking (Prediction 4)	Armed Conflict
Theoretical Prediction	L	H	L	L	H
Qualitative results	L	H	L	H	H

Table 44. Theoretical predications and qualitative results for Galkayo by social capital type and armed conflict level

As mentioned earlier, for the purpose of this study, armed conflict levels in Galkayo are seen as relatively high based on the past history and risks of conflict relapsing in the future. The fieldwork indicates that armed conflict between the north and south has decreased compared to three years ago but there continues to be a high risk for violence to relapse spontaneously. A lack of formal and informal relations between the two communities and administrations are seen as contributing to the increased likelihood of armed conflict erupting due to the lack of mitigation mechanisms that one would usually expect to find in a structured or semi-structured arrangement between two communities or administrations.[118]

Primary and secondary data suggest that relationships between the two have improved, albeit at a gradual pace. Despite various external shocks—such as pirates, Al Shabaab, and droughts—over the past three to five years, one can argue on the one hand that Galkayo has done relatively well in mitigating armed conflict and minimizing violence between the two communities. On the other hand, one can argue that Galkayo has simply resisted further integration between the two communities and that a security equilibrium has been maintained. Linkages between the two administrations and clan elders of the north and south tend to focus on *reacting* to issues and incidents of insecurity versus *preventing* them from occurring.

The 1993 Mudug Peace Agreement's prime objective was to establish negative peace without addressing the root causes of the conflict, as one interviewee explained, "an agreement was only to come together and live together side-by-side... and did not address the [root] problems".[119] The fieldwork showed that both communities were fully aware of the risks and triggers for armed conflict erupting spontaneously between the two communities. They also both highlighted their faith in their clan elders, versus the state, to resolve these inter-communal conflicts while acknowledging that the root causes would not be addressed in these resolution processes.

The situation in Galkayo begs the question, why isn't there more violence? Is it because a state of equilibrium exists to deal with the current conflict setting and conflict variables or is bridging social capital, albeit at low levels, extending its reach passively to mitigate armed conflict? Galkayo may provide a possible example of weak bridging social capital being able to mitigate violence in a protracted conflict setting.

As mentioned earlier, at the government level initiatives have been implemented to promote bridging social capital between the two sides. However transforming ideas and strategies into daily operations on the ground to deal with preventing conflict between the two communities remains a challenge. At the community level, such as clan elders and religious leaders, joint initiatives are still at an infancy and hesitation might be present because of the political and security complications related to creating bridges. Youth, clan elders, and businessmen maybe targeted or stigmatized by their own communities for trying to create such bridges. CSOs and other non-state actors may therefore be cautiously watching the results of the bridging initiatives between the north and south administrations before taking a leap of faith to further establish linkages between the two communities.

The administrations should therefore take the initiative to create bridging social capital between the north and south to decrease transaction costs for interaction between the two communities. Primary and secondary qualitative research indicates that with increased bridging social capital between the two administrations and communities, armed conflict has the strong potential of decreasing as the actors will be able to jointly handle cross-border issues such as security and governance. As mentioned numerous times during my fieldwork in Somalia: the conflict in Galkayo represents the national conflict of Somalia; if the conflict in Galkayo can be fixed, then the conflict in Somalia will be fixed!

4.5 Conclusions of the Qualitative Approach

The following table summarizes the findings of the qualitative analyses for the three cities against the four theoretical predictions. The gray cells contradict the theoretical predictions.

		Bridging (Prediction 1)	Bonding (Prediction 2)	Hard Linking (Prediction 3)	Soft Linking (Prediction 4)	Armed Conflict Level
Burao	Theoretical Prediction	H	L	L	H	L
	Qualitative results	H	H	H	H	L
Galkayo	Theoretical Prediction	L	H	L	L	H
	Qualitative results	L	H	L	H	H
Mogadishu	Theoretical Prediction	L	H	H	L	H
	Qualitative results	L	H	H	H	H

Table 45. Theoretical predictions against the qualitative results for the three selected cities

The findings support the first theoretical prediction with Burao having high levels of bridging social capital versus Galkayo and Mogadishu. For theoretical prediction two, Burao displayed high levels of bonding social capital similar to Galkayo and Mogadishu, therefore rejecting the prediction. Regarding hard linking social capital, prediction three, Burao had high levels instead of the low levels, thereby rejecting the prediction. Mogadishu and Galkayo displayed high levels of soft linking social capital instead of the low levels as expected by theoretical prediction four. Armed conflict levels were as predicted. In conclusion, the qualitative analyses only support theoretical prediction one with the case of Burao rejecting predictions two and three, and Galkayo and Mogadishu rejecting prediction four.

An important finding that emerged from the qualitative analyses is the role of the state on social capital. Burao highlighted the importance of communities possessing a conducive relationship between state and non-state actors in dealing with security and governance issues, which in the case of Burao indicated high levels of hard linking social capital (thereby rejecting theoretical prediction three). The hard linking social capital seen in Burao suggests a benign type of hard linking social capital where the entities possessing hard power exercise this for the greater public good in the community versus supporting narrow interests as seen in Mogadishu.

Mogadishu highlighted the important role of the state and insecurity in regard to social capital. Districts with strong administrations created and sustained exclusive networks that led to low levels of bridging social capital and high levels of bonding social capital. On the other hand, districts with weak or non-existent administrations showed low levels of bonding, bridging, and linking (hard and soft) social capital and had higher levels of armed conflict.

North and south Galkayo showed the importance of having bridging social capital between the two administrations to mitigate violence and also for bridging social capital to be developed at the communal level. Galkayo also showed the limitations of CSOs in establishing bridging social capital. Although CSOs had attempted to create neutral spaces for both communities to interact, without state support these initiatives are prone to failure. However my own research suggests that the state will lack interest to support such initiatives when government resources are scarce and the benefits from doing so are not straightforward. This is ever so more the case when the state feels threatened by such initiatives. Therefore, projects to promote bridging social capital amongst non-state actors need to demonstrate clear benefits for the state in order to get government buy in.

The case studies clearly highlight the relevance of the government to build social capital within the community and in a protracted conflict like Somalia the state may be best placed to do so versus CSOs, who are usually seen as the main actors for developing social capital. Furthermore, the state can lower transaction costs for developing and sustaining bridging social capital by utilizing the hard linking social capital it possess for the greater good, as seen in the case of Burao. This could be implemented by having the state establish inter-communal platforms for conflict resolution, such as peace committees, and providing enforcement mechanisms to implement agreements and decisions taken to resolve conflicts. Other policy options include the state developing district security committees that bring together non-state and state actors to manage security arrangements within the community.

In conclusion, the three case studies have further highlighted the complex relationship between the different types of social capital and armed conflict. The possibility of reverse causality remains even at the city level and indications of equifinality can also be seen at the district level in Mogadishu where armed conflict diminishes bridging social capital and strengthens bonding social capital and thereby increases armed conflict.

The next chapter pulls together the qualitative and quantitative findings of this research inquiry to provide an overview of the results and highlight outstanding issues.

Notes

1   For more details on the "birth" of Somaliland, Renders (2012) and Bradbury

(2008) provide a comprehensive history.

2 For ease of reading, the "%" mark is used interchangeably with "percent".

3 Fieldwork: 1 to 3 April 2013, Burao.

4 The exact number of inhabitants is unclear as no accurate census figures have been recorded. The number of 400,000 was mentioned by NGO and university officials and also by Ramadhan and Rynn (2010:2).

5 Interview: SOYDAVO 2 April 2013, Burao.

6 Interestingly, in Galkayo it was the victim who had to provide food for the perpetrator and payment to the police for custody (Interview: Haji 7 April 2013, north Galkayo).

7 Fieldwork: 1 to 3 April 2013, Burao.

8 The reference is made to the question number in the small-n survey which can be found in the Appendix.

9 On 15 August 2013, an oil exploration company had to stop operations in some parts of Togdheer region as a sub-clan of the Haber Yonis complained that the company was sharing revenues with the local community (DSS 2013a).

10 Interview: Warsame 3 April 2013, Burao.

11 Interview: SOYDAVO 2 April 2013, Burao.

12 Interview: SOYDAVO 2 April 2013, Burao.

13 Interview: SOYDAVO 2 April 2013, Burao.

14 Interview: SOYDAVO 2 April 2013, Burao.

15 Interview: SOYDAVO 2 April 2013, Burao.

16 Interview: Focus group discussion in Burao 2 April 2013.

17 Interview: SOYDAVO 2 April 2013, Burao.

18 Interview: SOYDAVO 2 April 2013, Burao.

19 Interview: Focus group discussion in Burao 2 April 2013.

20 Interview: SOYDAVO 2 April 2013, Burao.

21 Interview: SOYDAVO 2 April 2013, Burao.

22 Interview: SOYDAVO 2 April 2013, Burao; Focus group discussion in Burao 2 April 2013.

23 In April 2013, the price of one camel was around 700 US dollars. Prices had seen a declining trend as rural to urban migration by nomads had led to a surplus of camels being sold.

24 Interview: SOYDAVO 2 April 2013, Burao.

25 Interview: Warsame 3 April 2013, Burao.

26 Interview: SOYDAVO 2 April 2013, Burao; Focus group discussion in Burao 2 April 2013.

27 Farah et al (2002) provide an overview of how deegan is significant to understand the armed conflict in south central Somalia.

28 Interview: Warsame 3 April 2013, Burao.

29 Interview: Warsame 3 April 2013, Burao.

30 Stewart (2008) highlights horizontal inequalities as "inequalities in economic, social or political dimensions or cultural status between culturally defined groups" (2008:3). Furthermore he argues "mobilization along group identity lines has become the single most important source of violent conflict" (2008:7).

31 Interview: Warsame 3 April 2013, Burao.

32 In 2009, Germany provided police training to militia troops belonging to the Darod clan, who were affiliated to the then President Abdullahi Yusuf Ahmed. Initiatives to vet and train a multi-clan police force were met with reluctance by the Germans despite analysts and experts highlighting the need to create a security force that cut across the different clans. From 2008 onwards, the French also provided several training courses in Djibouti to security forces belonging primarily to one main clan family.

33 The objective of the 2012 DRC report (Bryld and Kamau 2012) titled *Political Economy Analysis in Mogadishu* was to identify districts for development in Mogadishu and entry points for program implementation.

34 During my time as a Program Planning Officer at UNPOS from March 2010 to April 2013, I would hear of numerous "conflict studies" being conducted on Mogadishu by donors. However the results of these conflict studies were rarely shared, if ever.

35 I would like to thank Saferworld for sharing the large-n survey raw data.

36 I was personally involved in reviewing the final report and provided inputs based on my own research.

37 EIU puts the population of Mogadishu, based on 2012 World Gazetteer estimates, at 1.6 million inhabitants (EIU 2012:4). UNHCR estimates the IDPs in Mogadishu at 369,000 (2013b).

38 Interview: McAuslan 2012, email.

39 The 16 districts are: Abdiaziz, Bondhere, Daynille, Dharkenley, Hamarjajab, Hamarweyne, Huriwa (Heliwa), Hodan, Hawalwadag, Karan, Shangani, Shibis, Waberi, Wadajir, Wardhigley, and Yaqshid.

40 The United Somali Congress (USC) consisted of, inter alia, the Haber Gedir clan and Abgal clan and had both fought together to oust Barre.

41 The Abgal clan-controlled Karan, Yaqshid, Shangani, Shibis, and Bondhere (Marchal 2002:13).

42 Fieldwork: 19 September 2004.

43 Fieldwork: 8 September 2011, Mogadishu; 20 November 2012, Mogadishu.

44 Personal communication: Bancroft mentors 23 May 2011, Mogadishu; AMISOM troop commander 24 May 2011, Mogadishu.

45 I borrow Menkhaus' approach to differentiate between underlying causes of war (root causes) and precipitating causes of war. "In Somalia as elsewhere, underlying of structural factors which render a country vulnerable to armed conflict are relatively easy to identify. But identification of the specific precipitating causes (or combinations of causes) that can suddenly trigger armed violence on a large scale is far more difficult to achieve" (Menkhaus 2011:9).

46 Interview: Focus group discussions in Mogadishu 29, 30 January and 2, 5 February 2012.

47 Villa Somalia is the location for the offices and residences of the President, Speaker, and Prime Minister, located approximately eight kilometers from Mogadishu International Airport.

48 Interview: Haber Gedir business community representatives 2 February 2012, Mogadishu; Somali Ports Authority representatives 10 July, 29 November 2011, Mogadishu.

49 Fieldwork: 13 to 20 September 2004, Mogadishu. Interview: Jamalle 20 May 2011, Mogadishu; SCODA 12 July 2011, Mogadishu; SOYDEN 12 July 2011, Mogadishu; SWDC 9 July 2011, Mogadishu.

50 Interview: Benadir Regional Administration representatives 9 July 2011, Mogadishu; Ministry of Finance representatives 3 February 2012, Mogadishu; SAHDO 3 February 2012, Mogadishu.

51 In 2010 I was involved in preparing for the "Istanbul Political, Security and Reconstruction Conference for Somalia" and in 2012 the "Second Istanbul Conference on Somalia: Preparing Somalia's Future: Goals for 2015". Both conferences focused on economic development, private sector development, and public-private partnerships.

52 Interview: Focus group discussions in Mogadishu 29, 30 January and 2, 5 February 2012.

53 Interview: Chamber of commerce representatives 22 November 2012, Mogadishu; "Egal" 23 May 2011, Mogadishu; Djibouti based Somali business community 20 October, 22 November 2011, Djibouti.

54 Interview: Focus group discussions in Mogadishu 29, 30 January and 2, 5 February 2012.

55 Interview: District Commissioners of the Benadir Regional Administration 24 November 2012, Mogadishu; Randall 24 November 2012, Mogadishu.

56 Fieldwork: 2 to 9 September 2011, Mogadishu.

57 Interview: Focus group discussions in Mogadishu 29, 30 January and 2, 5 February 2012.

58 Interview: United Nations employee 8 September 2011, Mogadishu.

59 Interview: Mogadishu focus group respondent number "thirteen" 30 January 2011, Mogadishu.

60 Fieldwork: 13 to 20 September 2004, Mogadishu; 8 September 2011, Mogadishu; 20 November 2012, Mogadishu.

61 Interview: Jamalle 20 May 2011, Mogadishu.

62 Interview: United Nations employee 8 September 2011, Mogadishu.

63 Interview: Mahdi 25 June 2012, Nairobi.

64 United Nations staff member 2013, email.

65 Abdullahi (2008) provides a comprehensive background on the Al-Islah movement.

66 Interview: Academics based in Mogadishu 5 August 2011, Mogadishu.

67 Whether government officials in Somalia are corrupt is debatable in my view. Although the mainstream view is to treat the issue of corruption as a dichotomy, corruption in Somalia has various "shades" based on my professional experience dealing with this issue. With an outdated penal code and lacking regulatory frameworks, accusing someone of outright corruption proves to be a challenge. Alternatively, Somali officials may be seen as utilizing the lack of regulations and loopholes for their personal gain.

68 Interview: Somali Ports Authority representatives 10 July, 29 November 2011, Mogadishu; Ministry of Finance representatives 3 February 2012, Mogadishu.

69 Interview: Jamalle 20 May 2011, Mogadishu.

70 Interview: CSOs 5 July 2011, Mogadishu.

71 Interview: Akhtar 11 December 2011, Dubai.

72 Interview: Ministry of Finance representatives 3 February 2012, Mogadishu.

73 I am indebted to Tim Randall for sharing his knowledge on Mogadishu for the purpose of this research.

74 Interview: Randall 2013, email.

75 I am deeply grateful to Abdirizak Mohamed Haji who was instrumental in helping me conduct field research in north Galkayo.

76 I am grateful towards Sikander Khan, the head of UNICEF Somalia, who kindly provided me support. Yasuyuki Misawa of WFP also extended his kindness.

77 The number of police officers would vary on the time and location of places visited. Details are intentionally omitted for the sake of maintaining security confidentiality.

78 Michael Scott Moore, a journalist who came to research piracy was kidnapped on his way to Galkayo airport in January 2012. He was released in September 2014. Two humanitarian aid workers from Danish Deming Group were abducted in October 2011 also on their way to the airport and were released after three months following a United States military rescue operation.

79 The Saferworld (2011) report on Galkayo was used as basis for the OCVP report on Galkayo (2011b).

80 Population estimates for permanent residents range from 150,000 to 300,000 with large numbers of nomads frequenting the city on a seasonal basis.

81 Fieldwork: 2 to 9 September 2011, Mogadishu.

82 The Transitional Charter was the guiding document, "the basis for the federal constitution", for the transition period following the Mbagathi Agreement which established the Transitional Federal Institutions (Transitional Charter 2004: Article 11). The Charter provided the overall framework for the transition period and also referred to the 1960 Somali constitution. Legally, it has contradictions and from a political perspective was difficult to apply in the Somali setting (Fieldwork: 25 January to 1 February 2009, Djibouti).

83 During my stay in north Galkayo, numerous interlocutors referred to this attack as a "massacre".

84 I borrow Johan Galtung's terms related to peace and conflict.

85 Interview: Focus group discussion in north Galkayo 9 April 2013.

86 Interview: Health worker 8 April 2013, north Galkayo.

87 Interview: Haji 7 April 2013, north Galkayo.

88 Interview: PSU 8 April 2013, north Galkayo.

89 Interview: Health worker 8 April 2013, north Galkayo.

90 For example immediately following my visit to Galkayo, the Puntland State issued a press release highlighting that "During the past months criminal attacks planned and carried out in Puntland jurisdiction [north Galkayo] by residents of Galmudug [south Galkayo] have been increasing... antiaircraft launched from Galmudug in southern Galkayo, targeted a plane attempting to land at Galkayo Airport... Puntland Police have recorded 6 kidnappings and car hijackings in the past 6 months and several targeted killings stemming from south Galkayo" (Puntland Ministry of Security 22 April 2013).

91 Interview: Focus group discussion in north and south Galkayo 8, 9 April 2013.

92   Interview: PSU 8 April 2013, north Galkayo.
93   Interview: Businessman 8 April 2013, north Galkayo.
94   Interview: PSU 8 April 2013, north Galkayo.
95   Interview: Health worker 8 April 2013, north Galkayo.
96   Interview: PSU 8 April 2013, north Galkayo.
97   Interview: Focus group discussion in north and south Galkayo 8, 9 April 2013.
98   Interview: Businessman 8 April 2013, north Galkayo.
99   Interview: PSU 8 April 2013, north Galkayo.
100 Interview: NGO 9 April 2013, north Galkayo.
101 Interview: Haji 7 April 2013, north Galkayo.
102 Interview: Focus group discussion in north and south Galkayo 8, 9 April 2013.
103 Interview: PSU 8 April 2013, north Galkayo.
104 Interview: NGO 9 April 2013, north Galkayo.
105 Interview: PSU 8 April 2013, north Galkayo; Businessman 8 April 2013, north Galkayo.
106 Interview: Haji 7 April 2013, north Galkayo.
107 Interview: PSU 8 April 2013, north Galkayo.
108 Interview: PSU 8 April 2013, north Galkayo.
109 Interview: Health worker 8 April 2013, north Galkayo.
110 During my visit in April 2013, I was not able to verify whether the Committees were operating. Following my visit, interlocutors in Galkayo were also not able to verify the status of the agreement.
111 Interview: Health worker 8 April 2013, north Galkayo.
112 Interview: PSU 8 April 2013, north Galkayo.
113 Interview: NGO 9 April 2013, north Galkayo.
114 Interview: PSU 8 April 2013, north Galkayo.
115 Interview: NGO 9 April 2013, north Galkayo.
116 Fieldwork: 18 to 21 February 2013, Mogadishu; 14 March to 24 March 2013, Mogadishu.
117 Interview: Sheikh 2013, email.
118 On 20 August 2013, traditional elders from the Sa'ad and Majeerteen met at Galkayo airport to discuss a series of clan revenge killings in Godod (DSS 2013b), supporting the fieldwork findings that clan elders usually come together after an incident, lacking any formal or informal mechanisms for mitigating armed conflict.
119 Interview: Health worker 8 April 2013, north Galkayo.

CHAPTER 5. COMPARISON OF QUANTITATIVE AND QUALITATIVE ANALYSES

5.1 Introduction

This final chapter compares the findings of the quantitative and qualitative analyses. The chapter is structured as follows: a summary of the qualitative and quantitative results is provided; the four hypotheses are reviewed based on the qualitative and quantitative findings; the four theoretical predictions for the three selected cities used as case studies are reviewed; a conclusion is provided including scholarly and policy implications. The chapter concludes with areas for further research regarding social capital and armed conflict.

To recall, the objective of the research inquiry has been to identify relationships between social capital and armed conflict based on primary and secondary data; and to find explanations for the variances in armed conflict and social capital in the five cities studied. The research inquiry investigates if differences in social capital can be used to explain for variances in armed conflict or whether armed conflict affects social capital.

5.2 Summary of Results

As stated in the conclusion of chapter three, table 5.1 compares the four hypotheses against the results of the quantitative analyses at the national level. The next section reviews the four hypotheses by comparing the relationship between social capital and armed conflict using the qualitative results of the three cities from chapter four.

	Armed conflict vs. Bridging	Armed conflict vs. Bonding	Armed conflict vs. Hard Linking	Armed conflict vs. Soft Linking
Hypothesis	-ve	+ve	+ve	-ve
Quantitative results	-ve/+ve	-ve	+ve	-ve

Table 46. Hypotheses against the quantitative results based on the aggregated UNDP baseline data for the relationship between social capital and armed conflict

Table 5.2 consolidates the results of the quantitative and qualitative approaches for the four theoretical predictions. These quantitative and qualitative results for the four theoretical predictions are compared descriptively later on. The cells in gray highlight the results that contradict the hypotheses or theoretical predictions and are of particular interest.

		Bridging (Prediction 1)	Bonding (Prediction 2)	Hard Linking (Prediction 3)	Soft Linking (Prediction 4)	Armed Conflict Level
Burao	Theoretical Prediction	H	L	L	H	L
	Quantitative results	H	H	H	L	L
	Qualitative results	H	H	H	H	L
Galkayo	Theoretical Prediction	L	H	L	L	H
	Quantitative results	L	H	L	H	H
	Qualitative results	L	H	L	H	H
Mogadishu	Theoretical Prediction	L	H	H	L	H
	Quantitative results	L	L	L	L	H
	Qualitative results	L	H	H	H	H
Las Anod	Theoretical Prediction	L	H	L	L	H
	Quantitative results	H	H	L	H	H
Bosaso	Theoretical Prediction	H	L	L	H	L
	Quantitative results	H	H	H	H	L

Table 47. Theoretical predictions against the quantitative and qualitative results based on the UNDP baseline data

5.3 Review of the Hypotheses Qualitatively

In chapter three, logistic regression using the aggregated data at the national level was used to verify the four hypotheses. As seen, only two out of the four hypotheses were supported by the quantitative results (table 5.1). This section attempts to look at the relationships between the four types of social capital and armed conflict at the city level for the three cases studies of Burao, Mogadishu, and Galkayo. It thereby compares the quantitative results at the national level with qualitative results at the city level. The issue of reverse causality remains, whereby armed conflict impacts social capital.

Based on the qualitative findings in chapter four for the three cities, table 5.3 summarizes the individual relationships between the four types of social capital and armed conflict. It also includes the aggregate results. Individual descriptions of the relationships, based on the four types of social capital, are described in the sub-sections below with a focus on the findings that contradict the hypotheses, as highlighted in the gray cells. Contradictions between the quantitative and the qualitative results by city are expected as the quantitative results are based on the aggregated data which dilute the individual effects of the cities.[1] By separately analyzing the cities qualitatively, we are able to uncover the local dynamics related to armed conflict and social capital.

		Armed conflict vs. Bridging	Armed conflict vs. Bonding	Armed conflict vs. Hard Linking	Armed conflict vs. Soft Linking
	Hypothesis	-ve	+ve	+ve	-ve
Quantitative results (aggregated)		-ve/+ve	-ve	+ve	-ve
Qualitative	Burao	-ve	-ve	-ve	-ve
	Galkayo	-ve	+ve	+ve	+ve
	Mogadishu	-ve	+ve	+ve	+ve

Table 48. Armed conflict and social capital relationships for the hypotheses, aggregated UNDP baseline data, and qualitative results for the three case studies

5.3.1 Bridging Social Capital

In line with hypothesis one, the qualitative results for the three cities all show bridging social capital having a negative impact on armed conflict (the first column of table 5.3 summarizes this point). The qualitative results suggest that inclusive networks between adversary groups have low levels of armed conflict.

As highlighted in the conclusion of chapter three (section 3.7), the quantitative results at the aggregate level paint a mixed picture (as seen above in table 5.3, first column). Bridging social capital displayed a *negative* impact on armed conflict based on the bridging social capital proxies related to Group Networks and Trust in religious leaders thereby supporting the hypothesis. However Community Leadership and an increased Trust in police showed a *positive* impact on armed conflict contradicting the hypothesis.

To recall, Trust in police was treated as a bridging social capital proxy based on the premise that the police were an entity that crossed clan lines and would have an effect in mitigating armed conflict. However the contradictory results could suggest a reverse causality where a decreased perception of safety creates a sense of insecurity within the community, thereby increasing reliance and trust towards the police to provide security. Another possible explanation for the positive impact on armed conflict could be that Trust in the police is actually a proxy for bonding social capital and that the police are actually a monolithic entity dominated by one clan biasing specific groups. The quantitative analysis by city for both models suggests this possibility as the Trust in police variable is only statistically significant for Bosaso in the logistic regression and shows a positive impact on armed conflict in Bosaso (table 3.19).

Although Bosaso was not undertaken as a case study in the qualitative analysis, the results of my fieldwork (small-n survey and interviews) also indicate high levels of trust towards the police which are in line with the UNDP baseline data (table 3.15). The high levels of armed conflict in Bosaso, as stipulated in the UNDP baseline data, could be explained by the proliferation of assassinations and unexplained killings in Bosaso during the time of the UNDP survey. During my fieldwork in 2012 and 2013 interlocutors highlighted how in 2010 there was a continuous spree of killings and assassinations that the police were not able to prevent, and that Al Shabaab was seen as responsible. This could have led to respondents feeling a decreased perception of safety and increased threat from a fanatic group.

Alternatively, the results from Burao show a relationship of increased trust in the police and low levels of armed conflict. Overall, with the exception of using Trust in police and Community Leadership as a bridging social capital proxy quantitatively, we can conclude from the research inquiry the presence of bridging social capital having a negative impact on armed conflict, thereby partially supporting hypotheses one. Furthermore, because the status of the police in Somalia is ambiguous as it portrays state and non-state characteristics, the results suggest the predictive power tends to be weaker for this proxy.

In regard to the direction of causality, further analysis is required to identify whether low risk areas, such as Burao, have high levels of bridging social capital and if high risk areas, for example as Mogadishu, have low bridging social capital from the onset. As the qualitative and quantitative results have shown, the issue of equifinality (reverse causality) remains and the protracted conflict in Mogadishu and Galkayo has created a vicious cycle where insecurity has eroded bridging social capital which has led to an increase in violence and vice versa.

5.3.2 Bonding Social Capital

The quantitative analysis highlights the issue of scalability related to bonding social capital and the complicated intrinsic mechanisms of defining group networks and exclusive social networks. Limitations in interpreting and identifying clear proxies from the UNDP baseline data related to bonding social capital were seen when trying to find category sets to differentiate variables that could represent the mindset of "them" versus "us".

Another challenge was clearly differentiating whether the armed conflict proxies used from the UNDP data represented intra-clan or inter-clan conflict. Although the data collected by UNDP asked for the "most common reason of dispute between other clan/communities" (table 3.6), the answers did not differentiate between intra and inter-clan conflict. The issue of scalability also comes into play when analyzing the relationship between bonding social capital and armed conflict using Putnam's maxims: one would expect low levels of *intra*-clan conflict when bonding social capital is strong within a community. The difficultly of analyzing this proposition, based on Putnam's logic, is that the issue of scalability emerges for both determining what is "intra" and what is "within the community". With these quandaries in mind, the quantitative analysis therefore deliberately neglects intra-clan disputes and treats the armed conflict proxy as an "inter" clan affair. However, the limitations and deficiencies to this approach may contribute to the mixed results seen when attempting to quantitatively analyze the relationship between bonding social capital and armed conflict.

Socially and culturally, the dynamism of scalability related to bonding social capital and armed conflict can be illustrated in the following Somali proverb:

Me and my clan against the world;
Me and my family against my clan;
Me and my brother against my family;
Me against my brother.

The above proverb emphasis the strong emphasis on context and the moving and flexible alliances related to armed conflict in Somali culture.

Of the three cities, the qualitative analysis shows only Burao contradicting hypothesis two. Although this contradiction compared to the other cities may be expected due to the problems of scalability, the qualitative results support the important logic that before bridging social capital can be established, bonding social capital needs to be present (Larsen et al 2004:65, Nan 2009, Putnam 1994, Warren et al 2001:9). As Putnam (2000) has pointed out, trust and social cohesion within groups are a priori to bridging social capital being formulated. This may explain the high levels of bonding social capital in Burao found qualitatively with high levels of bridging social capital. Interestingly, the quantitative results for Las Anod and Bosaso also saw high levels of bonding social capital present with high levels of bridging social capital (table 3.27) supporting the logic that bonding social capital needs to precede bridging social capital.

The research inquiry clearly demonstrates the importance of determining the scale of "boundaries" for bonding social capital: the boundaries of where bonding social capital begins and ends in terms of social networks and groups. By establishing accurate scales and division lines between groups, in Sacks' term category sets, one can attempt to differentiate between bonding and bridging social capital and address the lack of clarity between the two. The scalable properties of bonding social capital therefore need to be taken into careful consideration when using bonding social capital theory. As expected in terms of interpretation, the results from the research inquiry show bonding social capital having a positive and negative impact on armed conflict due to the issue of scalability. In sum, the qualitative and quantitative results emphasize both the limitations and essence of using bonding social capital.

5.3.3 Hard Linking Social Capital

The aggregated quantitative results based on the UNDP baseline data and qualitative results for Galkayo and Mogadishu support hypothesis three. The exception was the qualitative results for Burao, which saw hard linking social capital having low levels of armed conflict. As highlighted in chapter four, Burao saw high levels of trust between the community and the city administrations, such as the police and mayor's office. For Burao, high levels of hard linking social capital stemmed from the presence of functioning *benign* state institutions which in effect may have led to lower levels of armed conflict, thereby contradicting the hypothesis.

Clan elders and political/government officials were considered as community leaders and both actors worked together to resolve conflicts. These working arrangements, based on mutual trust between clan elders and government officials, may have also contributed to the community having increased trust in their elders and police, thereby creating a virtuous cycle where the community was able to entrust the police and elders to resolve and mitigate conflict within the community.

Within Burao benign state institutions, that are to a certain degree functioning, may have dampened the positive impact of hard linking social capital on armed conflict. Alternatively, Burao could be a case which possesses excessive amounts of hard linking social capital—to the degree of having command and control of the local population—and therefore instead creates a situation of low armed conflict. Burao importantly highlights that not all hard linking social contributes to armed conflict and that in some instances excessive amounts of hard linking social capital may have a negative impact on armed conflict. Whether conflict was successfully mitigated outside of the xeer and deegan framework is unclear, but when focusing on hard linking social capital to resolve conflict within Burao, the qualitative results indicate low levels of armed conflict with the community. In sum, excluding Burao, both the qualitative and quantitative results support hypothesis three.

5.3.4 Soft Linking Social Capital

With the exception of the qualitative results for Galkayo and Mogadishu, the aggregated quantitative and qualitative results for Burao support hypothesis four. Galkayo and Mogadishu, which were both considered as having high levels of armed conflict, indicated soft linking social capital having a positive impact on armed conflict. Both Mogadishu and Galkayo had significant cleavages within the cities between the various communities. Even though Galkayo had only one major cleavage between the Sa'ad and Majeerteen clans, the relationship between soft linking social capital and armed conflict was similar to Mogadishu which had multiple cleavages between the various clans and districts.

In both Galkayo and Mogadishu qualitative research showed trust levels to be high towards clan leaders and CSOs, representing high levels of soft linking social capital. Although soft linking social capital initially seems to be benign in mitigating conflict, as seen in the case of Burao, the two cities of Galkayo and Mogadishu may show otherwise with context and conflict setting being important factors to consider when analyzing the effects of soft linking social capital in a protracted conflict setting. For example, both cities displayed limited inter-clan linkages between clan elders and this may have enforced exclusive social networks within the community. Due to the high levels of trust in clan elders, exclusive networks would therefore have been easily sustained within the community if these elders chose to maintain cleavages between communities, which may simply have been the status quo over many years. Alternatively clan elders could have addressed these cleavages, which unfortunately in the case of Galkayo and Mogadishu has not been the case for a variety of reasons. Clan elders therefore may have strengthened or enforced bonding social capital and exclusive networks in the community while not reaching out to their own counterparts across clan divisions. Similar dynamics were present with CSOs which intentionally or unintentionally reinforced cleavages between groups, clans, and government administrations.

As already shown, clan elders in Burao had the unique role of enforcing decisions made during conflict resolution processes to mitigate armed conflict. Peace processes were led and supported by clan elders and CSOs, who were expected by the community to find solutions and prevent armed conflict from escalating. Why CSOs and clan elders in Burao were seen as actively resolving conflicts may have to do with the important role of the state in also supporting these peace processes. Burao highlights a situation where CSOs, clan elders, and state institutions all worked together in resolving conflicts within the city.

When considering the qualitative and quantitative results for hypothesis four, the results are mixed and are inclusive in supporting or rejecting the hypothesis.

5.4 Review of the Theoretical Predictions

This section reviews the quantitative and qualitative findings for each of the three case studies relative to the four theoretical predictions as stipulated in table 5.2. It provides an overall summary of social capital in the three cities.

5.4.1 Burao

The qualitative results for Burao showed high levels for all four types of social capital used in the research inquiry. The theoretical prediction had predicted low levels of bonding and hard linking social capital in an environment of low armed conflict. As predicted, armed conflict levels were low relative to the other four cities based on both quantitative and qualitative data. The research inquiry shows how high levels of bonding and hard linking social capital can support conflict resolution however it was not possible to analyze the relationship between hard linking social capital and bonding social capital.

As mentioned earlier, hard linking social capital, in terms of benign state presence, may actually positively contribute to peace within the community, albeit certain conditions may be required to avoid the opposite effect. Unlike the predatory state seen during the Barre regime, where cleavages between groups were exacerbated by the state leading to increased tension and conflict, Burao shows that the state can take on and facilitate bridging social capital characteristics to mitigate armed conflict. One may see "modern" state bureaucracy as exerting bridging social capital and benign bonding social capital in Burao. The city highlights the mixed results in regard to bonding social capital and the difficulties of interpreting bonding social capital due to the issue of scalability.

5.4.2 Mogadishu

The quantitative results for Mogadishu showed low levels of bonding and hard linking social capital, contrary to the predictions. The statistical analysis of the six districts in Mogadishu had only three significant variables based on the two models, thereby limiting the interpretation of quantitative results. The qualitative results for Mogadishu supported the theoretical predictions with the exception of soft linking social capital.

The quantitative results showed low levels of trust towards clan elders and religious leaders (proxies for hard and soft linking social capital respectively) while qualitative results showed high levels of trust towards these two entities. An explanation for this discrepancy could be that the majority of the participants in the qualitative

research hailed from the Hawiye clan while the quantitative approach had a broader representation of the different clans residing in Mogadishu.

5.4.3 Galkayo

Overall the results from both approaches supported the theoretical predications related to Galkayo with the exception of soft linking social capital which was found to be high both quantitatively and qualitatively. Both north and south Galkayo had high levels of trust towards clan elders and CSOs which were however exclusive in clan membership and thereby intentionally or unintentionally failed to bridge the two communities from both sides.

5.5 Conclusion

Incorporating the quantitative and qualitative results, the findings from both approaches in general support hypotheses one and three: *bridging social capital has a negative impact on armed conflict; hard linking social capital has a positive impact on armed conflict.* In terms of the four theoretical predictions, the research inquiry findings support only the first proposition: *Bosaso and Burao have relatively higher levels of bridging social capital versus Mogadishu, Galkayo, and Las Anod.*

As the analyses demonstrated, each city displayed various dynamics of social capital at play in relationship to armed conflict. In Burao, high levels of all types of social capital highlighted the positive role in mitigating and resolving armed conflict. In Mogadishu, cleavages between clans and communities led to increased levels of armed conflict which in turn also sustained or increased divisions between groups, thereby promoting exclusive social networks and mistrust between communities. Galkayo clearly highlighted how the lack of bridging social capital made mitigating armed conflict a challenge between the north and south parts of the city.

For both Galkayo and Mogadishu, bonding social capital was seen as creating a conducive environment for armed conflict to reoccur while at the same time armed conflict was seen as hindering bridging social capital from developing and allowing bonding social capital to flourish. Both cities highlighted the issue of equifinality, highlighting the difficulty of identifying the direction of causality between social capital and armed conflict.

As expected, the results of the research inquiry at the national level were not able to explain the overall effect of social capital on armed conflict at the city level. However, the dynamism and relationships between social capital and armed conflict were clearly seen at the city level when analyzed locally and allowed the various types of social capital to be used as a tool for the research inquiry.

Finally, the analytical framework used for this research inquiry proved to be a useful tool in analyzing the relationship between social capital and armed conflict. The framework successfully allowed the research inquiry to analyze the four types of social capital, both qualitatively and quantitatively at all levels. The framework showed clear results for bridging social capital and mixed results for bonding social capital as expected. Both types of linking social capital were analyzed for the quantitative and qualitative approach as well, highlighting the usefulness of looking at vertical relationships in the context of armed conflict. In terms of conducting fieldwork in a conflict and post-conflict setting, the analytical framework provided a pragmatic and effective approach for carrying out research under challenging security circumstances.

5.5.1 Scholarly Implications

The research inquiry has frequently used the clan paradigm as incited by Lewis. Clan identity was used as a category set for the Identity social capital proxy and for studying bonding social capital in detail. At the national level, clan was statistically significant while at the city level the results were less so. Qualitative results showed how interviewees and focus group participants repeatedly referred to clannism to explain armed conflict or the conflict setting in their city. While the clan paradigm was an important explanatory variable for predicting armed conflict, the research inquiry showed the importance of social capital in the areas of trust, group networks, and the role of the state.

Based on the results, the research inquiry highlighted how context and conflict setting determined if clan was the primary unit of analysis and foundation for understanding armed conflict and social and political organizations in Somalia or whether other factors and variables were at play in addition to clan. The five cities clearly show when and how clan can be used for analysis and the analytical framework uses Lewis' approach and theories conveniently depending on the context and results of the statistical analysis.

In critiquing Lewis' approach, in addition to the points already highlighted by other scholars, the research inquiry would suggest that Lewis may have overseen the importance and significance of trust in Somali society that went beyond one's own clan and xeer arrangements. Trust in state institutions, CSOs, and entities and initiatives that cut across clan lines without reference to xeer and deegan are areas that Lewis overlooked in explaining how armed conflict was mitigated and resolved. Furthermore, what the three case studies have importantly shown, both parties must earnestly want to have peace and avoid bloodshed for conflict prevention and resolution to succeed. Understanding when and how groups and individuals reach that point is something that is not clear using Lewis' paradigm.

5.5.2 Policy Implications

For practitioners, strengthening civil society is an obvious choice to bolster social capital but for academics other options exist and need to also be considered by practitioners. Although implementing projects in places like Somalia is challenging, simply focusing only on promoting CSOs in the short term is a narrow approach that leads to limited and uneven results. The research inquiry has shown that practitioners need to focus on multi-pronged approaches that are long term instead of piecemeal approaches that focus only on simply building CSOs that achieve short term programmatic objectives. In short, promoting CSOs are a quick fix and do not address the long term processes related to statebuilding in protracted conflict situations.

Furthermore, the analysis shows that simply strengthening CSOs does not automatically mitigate armed conflict. This supports Forster and Mattner findings that argue "strengthening civil society does not automatically contribute to peacebuilding... civil society is not a panacea" (2006: v). The research inquiry suggests that certain conditions may have to be present for social capital to successfully mitigate armed conflict.

Burao and Galkayo show that when there are only two major parties to bridge between (such as the Sa'ad and Majeerteen or Habar Yonis and Habar Jeclo), mitigating armed conflict is relatively more manageable versus bridging amongst several parties, such as the case of

Mogadishu. This could be because of the higher transaction costs involved in bridging multiple parties versus simply linking two parties.

The DIAL project in Galkayo highlights the difficulties and challenges of simply trying to just bring together two parties, such as north and south Galkayo, to establish committees to handle security issues (DIAL 2011).[2] Having worked in Mogadishu on planning and coordination issues with Somali interlocutors (state and non-state actors), I can easily relate to the complexities and challenges to bring different groups in Mogadishu from the various district administrations, clan leaders, and CSOs. Besides the difficulties (mainly political and logistical) of bringing the different parties together, facilitating discussions are a huge challenge with so many different actors bringing their vested interests to the table. For example, even after one has brought all the 16 District Commissioners in Mogadishu together, the challenges of having constructive and meaningful discussions to establish linkages between the districts was a huge challenge because of historical and existing rivalries and suspicions.[3] Practitioners may therefore want to consider initiatives that promote bridging social capital to focus on narrowing cleavages between two adversary groups (as seen in Galkayo) versus trying to bring several groups together at one time.

The research inquiry has highlighted the important role of the state for producing and promoting bridging social capital. This is something that tends to be omitted in the social capital literature where CSOs are seen as the primarily caretakers for developing bridging social capital.[4] The interesting case of Galkayo has highlighted the limitations of CSOs' attempts in building bridging social capital. One can argue that a political settlement, a track one conflict resolution process, needs to be in place for track three processes that lead to conflict transformation and bridging social capital being developed. Contrary to conventional literature, the research inquiry has shown how the state can have an important role in building bridging social capital as the capacities and effectiveness of CSOs may simply be limited for political, financial, personal, and historical reasons. In the extreme case, which some may argue is the norm in functioning bureaucracies, state institutions and "modern faceless" bureaucracies may even be a replacement for bridging social capital altogether! Policies establishing functioning bureaucracies should therefore be mindful of the effects in creating bridging social capital but also of the risks and advantages of replacing existing bridging social capital between communities.

As seen in Burao, carefully planned polices and arrangements implemented between the state and non-state actors can nurture bridging social capital and mitigate armed conflict. On the other hand, policies and programs that intentionally or unintentionally bridge only selective groups, while marginalizing others, may have the opposite effect and create cleavages which lead to armed conflict. Put succinctly, the case of Somalia has shown that the state can at times be the best actor to support the development of bridging social capital for nurturing peace in situations undergoing protracted armed conflict or it can deepen bonding social capital.

From a programmatic perspective, the SOYDEN focus group discussions in Mogadishu touched upon capacities for peace and reducing armed violence, which included recommendations regarding norms and mechanisms contributing to peace within the community. The results of the research inquiry support these recommendations and capacities for peace, with the caveats highlighted below that focus on establishing bridging social capital.

> Poems and songs by women on peace were seen as contributing to peace (SOYDEN 2010b:17). *Caveat:* Poems and songs need to focus on reconciliation and establishing peace at an inter-clan level instead of highlighting historical clan animosities and war stories that boast of conquer and victory.

> Establishing locally-based trust and traditional peace processes (SOYDEN 2010a:11). *Caveat:* Local peace processes may be driven by clan elders and religious leaders but need to involve the local administrations, even if it is participation as an observer.

> Conducting sports events and traditional dances that bring the youth together to create friendships and help to resolve inter-clan conflicts (SOYDEN 2010a:13). *Caveat:* The planning and organization of such events are more important in creating bridging social capital than the actual events themselves. Meeting venues that are seen as "neutral spaces" by all parties need to be identified and agreed in order to convene preparatory meetings and allow unhindered access.

> Establishing "school-based peace clubs" to reinforce messages

of peace towards the community (SOYDEN 2010a:13). *Caveat:* In addition to soliciting the community, peace clubs need to have the support of clan elders and local administration to have an impact in transforming conflict.

The project managed by DIAL (2011) in Galkayo showed the challenges of consistently bringing the two administrations and clan elders from both communities to prevent and manage conflicts through discussions. Despite political agreements at the highest level between the two administrations, the results in bringing together the two parties to mitigate armed conflicts were minimal. Furthermore, my own research identified only limited initiatives and spaces that brought the two communities together (schools, hospitals, the market place, and the marathon event) and I was limited to only finding one additional option under the current setting to promote bridging social capital between the north and south. Future research in Galkayo could attempt to identify other options to build social capital between the two communities.

The additional option to be considered in Galkayo is creating a "joint security police force" consisting of police personnel from both the north and south to patrol and provide security in border areas which are prone to violence. By establishing a security force that works together on a daily basis at the operational and tactical-level, this would potentially have a spillover effect leading to increased interaction and networking between the two administrations at the political and leadership level, including the community. In short, a joint security police force would be a way of "operationalizing" bridging social capital beyond political agreements and projects managed by CSOs.

From a policy perspective, the findings of the research inquiry suggest that Somalia could follow in many ways the orthodox recipes for statebuilding and that Somalia is actually not an anomaly. Although practitioners are tempted to sometimes provide creative solutions to perceived anomalies like Somalia, to probably deal with short timelines and immediate needs, academically the solutions are sometimes actually quite basic and applicable to other cases when looked at in the long term.[5]

5.5.3 Areas for Further Research Regarding Social Capital and Armed Conflict

The relationship between the political economy and armed conflict is an area requiring urgent research in Somalia. Although practitioners have repeatedly highlighted the need for such analysis for programmatic and strategic purposes, unfortunately no academic research has been undertaken to look at the relationship of these two issues in Somalia. As social capital theory has been used widely in analyzing the effect on economic development and growth, it could provide a useable framework for analyzing the relationship between the political economy and armed conflict in Somalia. For example, anecdotal evidence from Somalia paradoxically shows how areas with high levels of economic activity have higher levels of armed conflict as various groups compete for control of money-making assets (as seen in Mogadishu and Kismayo which both have seaports). However, there are other parts of Somalia also having significant economic activity but with low levels of armed conflict, such as Berbera and Bosaso in northern Somalia which also both have seaports. With minor adjustments, the analytical framework used in this research inquiry could be applied conveniently for both qualitative and quantitative approaches.

Another area requiring further research is on the Somali youth: "over 70 percent of Somalia are under the age of 30; most face blocked transitions to adulthood due to multiple social, economic and political exclusions" (UNDP 2012: xix). Youth participation and empowerment, or a lack of, are areas that are likely to have effects on armed conflict. With an increasing amount of research conducted on youth, such as the 2012 UNDP Somalia Human Development Report focusing on youth empowerment, the analytical framework could be used for studying youth networks and groups against armed conflict (UNDP 2012).

The need to systematically research the Somali political economy and youth are issues that came to my attention in 2004 when I first visited Mogadishu. Back then interviewees, who had never left Mogadishu during the civil war, highlighted the emergence of economic and social class cleavages between the "rich" and "poor".[6] Research shows that even in a stateless society, class divisions between the rich and poor exist and are a serious problem (Matsukawa 2006). As the protracted conflict in Somalia has shown, after years of anarchy a small group of Somalis have been able to create tremendous amounts of wealth, while the majority struggle to make ends meet (Bryden 2013, Grosse-Kettler 2004, Menkhaus 2007, Webersik 2006).[7]

The business community has rightly fully or wrongfully taken advantage of unregulated markets to make quick profits while economic cleavages also emerged between educated returning diaspora and those who never left Somalia. One can argue that economic cleavages and economic marginalization supported the establishment of Al Shabaab, whose many recruits and foot soldiers are marginalized Somali youth.

Today's Somali youth also present an interesting case of a generation with no concept of government. In 2004 when I first met Somali university students and interviewed them about what kind of future government they wanted, I soon realized that very few of them had ever experienced living in a society with a functioning government. I wondered if they knew what a policeman did, understood what the role of the government was, and would be able to understand why people paid taxes or concepts related to the rule of the law. Understanding the views of the youth, who face exclusion from many parts of Somali society, will be crucial in establishing a future political social contract[8] that has the buy in and legitimacy from the largest group of the Somali population. Social capital theory can be used comprehensively to analyze the new data related to youth and study the effects of economic and social marginalization of a group that has never experienced a functioning government.

Finally, two further areas of research for consideration. First, in terms of social capital theory and armed conflict, the issue of causality still remains. With relevant data available, future quantitative research may want to address the issue of causality by using structural equation modeling, machine learning, or undertaking randomized controlled trials. Second, as highlighted by Rothstein and Stolle (2003:207), the role of the state in developing or hindering social capital requires further research as well.[9] As the case of Burao showed, the ability of the state to provide basic services may have contributed to bridging social capital being developed, supporting Widner's point that the ability of governments to deliver basic services plays a larger role than anticipated in shaping social capital (2004:235). Improving government performance, such as the delivery of basic services, may be the simple solution to increase bridging social capital. Paradoxically, impersonal

209

state delivery of services may bring about social cohesion and mitigate armed conflict in complex conflict settings such as Somalia.

Notes

1   Durlauf and Fafchamps argue that "aggregate social capital studies have not been successful in providing compelling empirical evidence on the effects of social capital... [instead] efforts should be directed towards micro-level studies as the problems with country-wide studies seem too intractable to overcome" (2004:55). This research inquiry attempts to take such a micro-level approach.
2   Interview: Sheikh 2013, email.
3   Interview: Randall 2013b, email.
4   Rothstein and Stolle (2003) highlight the importance of an impartial state implementing public policy and how "impartial and fair procedures practiced by government institutions have a positive effect on trust in a society... if we want political institutions to have a positive effect on social capital levels, the character of bureaucracies and welfare state institutions would have to be our primary areas of interest" (Hooghe and Stolle 2003:15).
5   Personal communication: Thesis Committee 13 December 2013, Tokyo.
6   Interview: Kimiko 17 September 2004, Mogadishu.
7   Although slightly outdated, Mubarak (1997) argues that "as far as economic welfare is concerned, absence of government has proven to be better than the repressive institutions and improper polices of Barre's government (2028). In short he argues that statelessness maybe preferred for economic development under certain conditions. I disagree with Mubarak as he omits any reference to "oligarchs" and "monopolists" who I see as dominating the Somali (political) economy and resisting the transition from statelessness to state structures.
8   Leonard and Samantar (2011) argue "that the legitimacy of a post-conflict state in contemporary Africa relies on two social contracts – one within the community and another between it and the larger state" (2013:44).
9   For example Gellner argues that "it is precisely anarchy which engenders trust or... which engenders social cohesion. It is effective government which destroys trust." (1988:143). Gellner (1988) points out that modern state administrations, especially in urban settings, eroded trust and social cohesion that existed in tribal groups and villages. However the case of Burao indicates that the local administration may engender social cohesion, therefore contradicting Gellner's argument.

ANNEX

Annex I. Questionnaire on Social Networks and Identity

I would like to ask you questions about your identity, social groups you belong to, your personnel networks, and experience with armed conflict/violence. The answers you provide will be analyzed and used for my Doctorial thesis at the University of Tokyo in Japan.

Instructions: Please mark with a clear "v" and where required, please write clearly your answers in Somali or English script. If you have any questions, please do not hesitate to ask during the survey.

Date: _____

I. YOUR PROFILE
Please tell me about yourself.

1.1 Age: _____

1.2 Gender: 1. Male ( ) 2. Female ( )

1.3 What is your marital status?
   1. Single ( )   2. Married ( )   3. Divorced ( ) 4. Widowed ( )

1.4 Occupation: 1. Student ( )   2. Business person ( )
   If business person, what type of
business:_____

1.5 What foreign languages do you speak?
    1. Arabic ( )   2. English ( )   3. Italian ( )   4. French ( )
    5. Other language _____

1.6 What level of education have you completed?
    1. Primary school completed ( )   2. Intermediate completed ( )
    3. Secondary / high school completed ( ) 4. University/college completed ( )
    5. Religious school ( ) 6. Other (specify)
_____

1.7 Which region are you from? (Please write number from below)
_____

1.8 Which region is your father from? (Please write number from below) _____

1.9 Which region is your mother from?(Please write number from below)_____
      1. Awdal 2. Bakool 3. Banaadir   4. Bari   5. Bay
      6. Galguduud   7.Gedo   8.Hiiraan 9.Jubbada Dhexe
      10.Jubbada Hoose   11. Mudug 12. Nugaal 13. Sanaag
      14.Shabeellaha Dhexe   15.Shabeellaha Hoose 16. Sool
    17.Togdheer 18. Woqooyi Galbeed

II. BELONGING
I would like to first ask you questions about your identity and belonging in society.

What clan are the following people? (Please check as many as necessary)

		Darod	Hawiye	Dir	Isaq	Mirifile	Digil	Other
2.1	Yourself							
2.2	Mother							
2.3	Father							
2.4	Wife/husband (if married)							

2.5 Please answer each of the following statements. (Please answer A to E)

	Agree Strongly	Agree Somewhat	Neither agree nor disagree	Disagree somewhat	Disagree strongly
A. Clan is the best way to differentiate people					
B. Clan helps me to know more about that person					
C. Clan helps me to know who I can trust					
D. Clan provides a social safety net					
E. Clan provides the basis of my social life					

2.6 When thinking about *marriage*, is clan identity a concern?
1. Yes, it matters ( )   2. Yes, but only a bit ( )   3. Does not matter ( )

2.7 In general, how do you rate your living conditions compared to those of other Somalis?   1. Much better ( ) 2. Somewhat better ( )
    3. About the same ( )   4. Somewhat worse ( )
        5. Much worse ( )   777. Don't know ( )
2.8 Do you belong to a *diya* paying group?   1. No ( )   2. Yes ( )

2.9 Would you say you are able to have multiple clan identities?
1. Agree strongly ( )   2. Agree somewhat ( ) 3. Neither agree nor disagree ( )
    4. Disagree somewhat ( )   5. Disagree strongly ( )

III. GROUPS AND GROUP NETWORKS

3.1 I would like to ask you about the groups or organizations, networks, associations to which you belong. These could be formally organized groups or just informal groups of people who get together regularly to do an activity or talk about things.   **Of how many such groups are you a member?**

_____

If you do not belong to a group, please go to Question 3.7.

3.2 Of all these groups to which you belong, which group is the most important?

_____

3.3 What is the main benefit from joining this group? (Choose one)
   1. Improves my household's current livelihood or access to services ( )
   2. Important in times of emergency in future ( )
   3. Benefits the community ( )
   4. Enjoyment/recreation ( )
   5. Spiritual, social status, self-esteem ( )

3.4 Are some members richer or poorer than others, or do they all have mostly the same income level? (Choose one)
1. Mostly same income level ( )   2. Mixture of rich/poor ( )   3. Don't know ( )

3.5 Would you say that there is strong pressure in the group for members to obey the group's decisions? (Choose one)
1. Agree strongly ( )   2. Agree somewhat ( )   3. Neither agree nor disagree ( )   4. Disagree somewhat ( ) 5. Disagree strongly ( )

3.6 Do you belong to any groups that _consist of different_ clan members?
   1. No ( )   2. Yes ( )
3.7 Would you say, the neighborhood you live in consists of people from:
   1. Mainly the same clan ( )
   2. An equal mixture of different clans ( )
   3. One major clan and one/several minor clans ( )

3.8 Would you mind if your next door neighbor is from a different clan?

    1. No ( )   2. Yes ( )

IV. YOUR PERSONAL NETWORKS

I would like to ask you about your social networks and associations.

4.1 If you suddenly needed to borrow a small amount of money (equal to about one week's wages), are there people *beyond your immediate household and close relatives* to whom you could turn and who would be willing to provide this money? (Check one)

    1. Definitely ( )   2. Probably ( )   3. Unsure ( )

      4. Probably not ( )   5. Definitely not ( )

4.2 How comfortable do you feel about interacting with members of *different* clans? (Please choose one) 1. I feel very comfortable ( )

        2. I feel somewhat comfortable ( )

        3. Neither ( )

        4. I feel somewhat uncomfortable ( )

        5. I feel very uncomfortable( )

4.3 Does your family or do you have connections with people in *political authority from the same clan*?

    1. No ( )   2. Yes ( )   3. Don't know ( )

    1.4.4 Does your family or do you have connections with people in *political authority from different clans*?

    1. No ( )   2. Yes ( )   3. Don't know ( )

V. COMMUNITY LEADERSHIP

I would like to ask some questions about your community leaders.

5.1 In your community, who are the community leaders? (Please choose one)

1. Clan elders ( )

2. Businessmen/women ( )

3. Political people/government officials ( )

4. Warlords/military persons ( )

5. Religious people/group ( )

6. NGO related, civil society group leaders, or working professionals (doctors, lawyers, engineers, journalists, etc) ( )

7. No community leaders ( ) →If no community leaders, please go to question 6.1

8. I don't know ( ) → Please go to question 6.1

5.2 Do your community leaders have the power to mobilize the community?
1. Always ( )   2. Often ( )   3. Sometimes ( )   4. Rarely ( ) 5. Never ( )

5.3 Please tell me about your community leaders. Please select one for each statement.

	Always	Often	Sometimes	Rarely	Never
A. Improves my family's current livelihood or access to services					
B. Important in times of emergency, such as settling conflicts					
C. Keeps the community organized					
D. Finances recreation and festivals					
E. Provides guidance					
F. Provides security					

5.4 Are the community leaders from the same clan as the community?
1. No ( )   2. Yes ( )   777. Don't know ( )

VI TRUST
I would now like to ask you questions about trust and solidarity.

6.1 How well or badly would you say the current government is handling the following matters: resolving conflicts between communities?
1. Very well ( )2. Fairly well ( )   3. Fairly badly ( )   4. Very badly ( )
6.2 How many government officials do you believe are involved in corruption?
1. All of them ( )   2. Most of them ( )   3. Some of them ( ) 4. None ( )

6.3 Generally speaking, would you say that most people can be trusted, or that you cannot be too careful in your dealings with other people?

    1. Most people can be trusted ( )   2. You cannot be too careful ( )

6.4 How much do you trust the following people: (Please answer for each category)

		1. A lot	2. A little	3. Not at all
A	People from your clan			
B	People from other clans			
C	Teachers			
D	Clan elders			
E	Businessmen/businesswomen			
F	Politicians, government officials			
G	Military persons			
H	Religious leaders			
I	Police			
J	NGOs run by Somalis			

6.5 In a government election, would you vote for a candidate from a different clan if they were better qualified than the candidate from your own clan?

    1. No ( )   2. Yes ( )

6.6 Should political parties be divided on a political/ideological basis or clan basis?

    1. Political ideological basis ( )   2. Clan basis ( )

6.7 One can only trust politicians from *your own* clan?

1. Agree strongly ( )   2. Agree somewhat ( ) 3. Neither agree nor disagree ( )

    4. Disagree somewhat ( )   5. Disagree strongly ( )

VII. Social Cohesion and Inclusion

I would like to ask you about three topics: inclusion, sociability, and conflict and violence in your community.

7.1 Which do you agree with?

A Each person should put the well being of the community ahead of their own interests.
B Everybody should be free to pursue what is best for themselves as individuals. (Choose one)

      1. Agree with A ( )   2. Agree with B ( )

7.2 Which do you agree with?
A In order to make decisions in our community, we should talk until everyone agrees.
B Since we will never agree on anything, we must learn to accept differences of opinion within the community.

      1. Agree with A ( )   2. Agree with B ( )

7.3 Which do you agree with?
A Even if there are conflicts between groups, Somalia should remain united as one country.
B The differences among Somalis are too strong; for the sake of peace, the country should be broken apart.

      1. Agree with A ( )   2. Agree with B ( )

7.4 How strong is the feeling of togetherness or closeness in your neighborhood?
1. Very distant ( ) 2. Somewhat distant ( )   3. Neither distant nor close ( )

    4. Somewhat close ( )   5. Very close ( )

7.5 How often do the following cause violence in your community?

	1. A lot	2. A little bit	3. Not at all
A. Differences in clan			
B. Differences in landholdings			
C. Economic differences			
D. Differences between diaspora and non-diaspora			
E. Differences in political party affiliations			
F. Differences in religious views (eg fundamentalism, liberalism)			

7.6 In your opinion, is the neighborhood you live in generally peaceful or marked by violence?
   1. Very peaceful ( )   2. Moderately peaceful ( ) 3. Neither ( )
   4. Moderately violent ( )   5. Very violent ( )

7.7 Compared to one year ago, has the level of violence in the neighborhood increased, decreased, or stayed the same?
1. Increased a lot ( )   2. Increased a little ( ) 3. Stayed about the same ( )   4. Decreased a little ( )   5. Decreased a lot ( )

7.8 Please answer the following statements with one answer for each statement.

	Very safe	Moderately safe	Neither safe nor unsafe	Moderately unsafe	Very unsafe
A. In general, how safe from crime and violence do you feel when you are alone at home?					
B. How safe do you feel when walking down your street alone after dark?					

7.9 In the past 12 months, have you or anyone in your household been the victim of a violent crime, such as assault or mugging?   1. No ( )
   2. Yes ( )

7.10 If YES, how many times?

VIII. ARMED CONFLICT
Finally, I would like to ask you about your experience with conflict.

8.1 Which do you agree with?
A The use of violence is never justified in Somali *politics*

B In this country, it is sometimes necessary to use violence in support of a just cause.

      1. Agree with A ( )   2. Agree with B ( )

8.2 In the past year, have you personally experienced some sort of **political violence, outside of your family?**

1. Yes, often ( )   2. Yes, several times ( )   3. Not at all ( )

8.3 Have you participated in demonstrations in the past year?

1. Yes, often ( )   2. Yes, several times ( )   3. Yes, once or twice ( )

4. No, but would do it if I had the chance ( ) 5. No, would never do this ( )

8.4 Scholars argue that the clan system is the cause of conflict. Would you agree with this view?

1. Agree strongly ( )   2. Agree somewhat ( ) 3. Neither agree nor disagree ( )

    4. Disagree somewhat ( ) 5. Disagree strongly ( )

Please write any comments you would like to make:

Thank you very much for your cooperation! If you would like to receive information on the research results, please send me an email to:

Annex II. Suaalo la xiriira xiriirka bulshada iyo aqoonsiga

Waxaan doonayaa in aan ku waydiiyo suaalo la xiriira aqoonsiga iyo kooxda bulsho ee aad xubin ka tahay, xiriirkaaga shaqo, iyo khibradda aad u leedahay dagaallada iyo rabshadaha. Jawaabaha aad bixiso waan dersi doonaa, waxaana aan u isticmaalayaa qoraalkayga heerka jaamacadeed ee *Doctorate* ee Jaamacadda Tokyo oo ku taal Japan.

Tilmaan-bixin: Fadlan ku calaamadee "v" meesha loo baneeyey kuna qor jawaabahaaga afka Soomaaliga ama afka Ingiriiska. Haddaad su'aalo qabtid, ha ka laba-labeyn inaad i waydiiso waqtiga tira-koobka.

I. Taariiq nololeedkaaga
Fadlan isu kay sheeg.
1.1 Da'da: _____   1.2 Jinsi: 1.Lab ( )   2. Dheddig ( )

1.3 Waa maxay xaaladaada nololeed ?
  1. Kali nool ( )   2. Xaas ah ( ) 3. Kala tagay ( )   4. Garoob/Iskaabulo ( )

1.4 Shaqo: 1. Arday ( )   2. Ganacsatada ( )
 Hadii aad tahay Ganacsade, Waa maxay ganacsiga aad hada ku hawlan tahay?_____

1.5 Afka labaad: 1. Carabi ( )   2. Ingiriis ( )   3. Talyaani ( )   4. Faransiis ( )
                    5. Af kale: _____
1.6 Heer wax barasho intee le,eg ayey/ayuu dhamaystay / dhamaysatay?
    1 . Dugsi hoose dhamaystay ( )   2. Dugsi dhexe dhamaystay ( )
    3. Dugsi sare dhamaystay ( )   4. Jamacad/Macad dhamaystay ( )
    5. Dugsi quran ( )   6. Kuwa kale
(cadee)_____

1.7 Gobolkee ka timid? (Fadlan ka dooro mid ka mid ah nambarada hoose ee u taagan Gobolka)_____
1.8 Gobolkee buu aabahaa ka yimid?
_____

1.9 Gobolkee beey hooyadaa ka timid?

---

1. Awdal   2. Bakool   3. Banaadir   4. Bari
5. Bay   6. Galgaduud
7. Gedo   8. Hiiraan   9. Jubada Dhexe   10. Jubada
Hoose   11. Mudug   12. Nugaal
13. Sanaag   14. Shabeelaha Dhexe   15. Shabeelaha Hoose
16. Sool   17. Togdheer
18. Waqooyi Galbeed

II. Xubinnimadaada

Waxa aan doonayaa in aan wax kaa weydiiyo aqoonsigaaga iyo bulshada halka aad kaga jirto.

Waa qabiiladee dadka hoos ku qoran? (Fadlan calaamadee inta loo baahan yahay)

		Daaorod	Hawiye	Dir	Isaaq	Mirifile	Digil	Mid kale
2.1	Adiga							
2.2	Hooyadaa							
2.3	Aabahaa							
2.4	Xaaskaaga /saygaaga							

2.5 Fadlan ka jawaab qoraalada hoos ku qoran mid walba. (Fadlan ka jawaab A ilaa iyo E)

	Si aad ah ayaan u raacsanahay	Wax ayaan ku raacsanahay	Kuma raacsani kamana horjeedo	Wax baan ku diidanahay	Kuma raacsani gebi ahaan
A. Qabiilka ayaa ugu fudud sida dadka loo kala sooco					
B. Qabiilka wuxuu igu					

caawiyaa aqoonsashada qofka					
C. Qabiilka wuxuu igu caawiyaa qofka aan aamini karo					
D. Qabiilka wuxuu caawiyaa badbaadada bulshada					
E. Qabiilka waa saldhigga noloshayda bulsho					

2.6 Marka aad ka fakareysid guur, ma ku khuseeyaa qabiilkooda? (mid dooro)

1. Haa, waa I khuseeyaa ( )   2. Haa, xogaa ayuu I khuseeyaa ( )   3. Maya, ima khuseeyo ( )

2.7 Caadiyan waa si dee xaaladaada nololeed marka loo fiiriyo heerka nololeed ee dadka kale?

1. Aad u wanaagsan ( )   2. Si uun uga wanaagsan ( )
3. Igu dhawaan la mid ah ( )
                    4. Si uun uga liidata ( )   5. Aad uga liidata ( )
777. Ma garanayo ( )

2.8 Ma ka mid tahay koox bixisa diyada?   1. Maya ( )   2. Haa ( )

2.9 Ma oran laheed waxaan ku abtirsadaa qabiilo kala duwan? (mid dooro)
1. Si aad ah ayaan u raacsanahay ( )   2. Wax ayaan ku raacsanahay ( )
        3. Kuma raacsani kamana soo horjeedo ( )   4. Wax baan ku diidanahay ( )
                5. Kuma raacsani gebi ahaan ( )

223

III.Kooxaha iyo Xiriirka Kooxaha

3.1 Waxaan doonayaa in aan ku waydiiyo kooxaha, ururada, xiriirka, iyo ururada danwadaagta ah ee aad xubin ka tahay. Waxa ay noqon karaan kuwo aad si rasmi ah xubin uga tahay ama kuwo aan rasmi ahayn oo isu yimaadda si ay wax u wada qabtaan ama arrimo uga hadlaan.

Meeqo kooxo noocyadaan ah ayaad xubin ka tahay?

_____

Hadii aadan ka mid ahayn koox,fadlan aad su'aasha 3.7

3.2 Kooxahaan aad xubin ka tahay, midee baa ku ugu muhiimsan?

_____

3.3 Waa maxay faa'iidada ugu muhiimsan ku darsamida kooxdan? (mid dooro)

    1. Dhaqaalaha nolosha qoyskayga hagaajisaa ama waxaan ka helaa agab ( )
    2.Waxay muhiim tahay waqtiyada xaalad deg-deg timaaddo ee aayaha ( )
    3.Waxay faa'iido u tahay bulshada ( )
    4.Raaxo/madadaalo ( )
    5. Diini, heerka bulsho, niyad-sami ( )

3.4 Xubnaha qaarkood ma ka dhaqaale badan yihiin ama ma ka faqiirsan yihiin kuwa kale mise waa isku wada dakhli? (mid dooro)

1. Waa isku dakhli badankoodu ( )   2. Isku jir taajir/faqri ( )
   3. Magaranayo ( )

3.5 Ma oran lahayd waxaa jira cadaadis lagu hayo xubnaha kooxda si ay u fuliyaan ammarada hogaamiyaha? (mid dooro)
1. Si aad ah ayaan u raacsanahay ( )
2. Wax ayaan ku raacsanahay ( )
3. Kuma raacsani kamana soo horjeedo ( )
4. Wax baan ku diidanahay ( )
5. Kuma raacsani gebi ahaan ( )

3.6 Ma ka mid tahay kooxo ka kooban qabiilo kala duwan?
    1. Maya ( )   2. Haa ( )

3.7 Ma oran lahayd, xaafadda aad ku nooshahay waxay ka kooban tahay dad ka mid ah:
    1. Ugu badnaan isku qabiil ( )
    2. Isuga jira qabiilo kala duwan ( )
    3. Ugu badnaan hal qabiil iyo hal ama qabiilo kale oo yar yar ( )

3.8 Ma ka soo horjeedi lahayd haddii dariskaaga uu ka mid yahay qabiil mid kaada ka duwan?
    1. Maya ( )   2 Haa ( )

IV Xiriirkayga Shaqsi
Waxaan rabi lahaa in aan ku weydiiyo xiriirkaaga bulsho iyo kooxeed.

4.1 Hadii aad u baahatid si kadis ah inaad lacag yar deensatid (oo la mid ah mushaarka hal todobaad), ma jiraan dad ka baxsan qoyskaaga iyo ehelkaaga oo ku deymin kara lacagtan?
1. Shaki la'aan way jiraan ( )   2. Laga yaabaa ( )   3. Lama hubo ( )   4. Lagama yaabo ( )   5. Shaki la'aan ma jiraan ( )

4.2 Kalsooni intee le'eg ayaad ku qabtaa dhexgalka daka aan qaabiilkaaga ahayn?
(mid dooro)
1. Waan ku kalsoonahay aad iyo aad ( ) 2. Xoogaa ayaan ku kalsoonahay ( ) 3. Midna ( )   4. Xoogaa ayaanan ku kalsoonayn ( )   5. Aad uguma kalsooni ( )

4.3 Qoyskaaga ama adiga xiriir ma la leedihiin dad ka mid ah xukuumadda isla markaana aad isku qabiil tihiin.
1. Maya ( )   2. Haa ( )   3. Ma garanayo ( )

4.4 Qoyskaaga ama adiga xiriir ma la leedihiin dad ka mid ah xukuumadda isla markaana aadan isku qabiil ahayn. (Fadlan ku calaamadee calaamada saxda sanduuqa gudihiis)
1. Maya ( )   2. Haa ( )   3. Ma garanayo ( )

V. Hogaanka bulshada

Waxaan rabi lahaa inaan suaalo kaa weeydiiyo dhinaca hogaamiyaha bulshada.

5.1 Bulshadaada, yaa ah hogaamiyaha bulshada? (mid dooro)
1. Odayaasha qabiilka ( )
2. Ganacsatada ( )
3 Dadka siyaasada/saraakiisha dowlada ( )
4. Hoggaamiyaha dagaalka/ama ciidanka ( )
5. Dadka diineedka/Koox ( )
6. Hay'adaha gargaarka, hogaamiyeyaasha hay'adaha mujtamaca, ama dadka aqoonta leh (dhaqtar, qareen, muhandas, suxuufi, iwm) ( )
7. Ma jiro hogaamiye Bulsho ( ) → Haddii aadan laheyn hogaamiye Bulsho, Fadlan aad

su'aasha 6.1
8. Kuwa kale ( ) → Haddii aadan laheyn hogaamiye Bulsho, Fadlan aad su'aasha 6.1

5.2 Hogaamiyaha bulshadaada ma leeyahay awood uu ku ururiyo bulshada? (mid dooro)
      1. Mar kasta ( )   2. Inta badan ( )   3. Mararka qaarkood ( )
      4. Mar dhif ah ( )   5. Marnaba ( )

5.3 Fadlan wax iiga sheeg hogaamiyaha bulshadaada. Fadlan qoraalkiiba mid dooro.

	Mar kasta	Inta badan	Marka qaarkood	Mar dhif ah	Abidkaa
A. Wuxuu horumariyaa nolol-maalmeedka qoyskayga iyo adeegga					
B. Wuxuu muhiim yahay waqtiyada xaaladaha deg-dega, sida, khilaafka la					

xallinayo					
C. Wuxuu abaabul ku hayaa bulshada					
D. Wuxuu maalgeliyaa munaasabadaha iyo madaddaalada					
E. Wuxuu bixiyaa talada					
F. Wuxuu kaalmeeyaa amaanka					

5.4 Hogaamiyeyaasha bulshada ma waxay isku qabiilyihiin bulshada?
     1. Maya ( )   2. Haa ( )   777. Ma garanayo ( )

VI. Kalsoonaan

Waxaan rabi lahaa inaan su'aalo kaa weeydiiyo kalsoonida iyo isku xirnaanta.

6.1 Ma waxeey kula tahay in dawlada hada jirtaa aay si fiican ama six un aay ax uga qabato arrimahan: xallinta khilaafaadka u dhaxeeya beelaha?
     1. Si aad u fiican ( )   2. Si yare fiican ( )
          3. Si yare xun ( )   4. Si aad u xun ( )

6.2 Imisa sarkaal dowladeed baad rumeysan tahay ineey ku dhex jiraan musuqmaasuq
  1. Kuligood ( ) 2. Intooda badan ( ) 3. Qaarkood ( )   4. Midna ( )

6.3 Guud ahaan, ma oran laheyd dadka intooda badan waa la aamini karaa, ama ma aamini kartid, lamana macaamili kartid?
     1. Dadka intooda badan waa la aamini karaa ( )
     2. Ma aamini kartid dadka intooda badan ( )

6.4 Immisa **kalsooni** ahna ayaad adigu shakhsiyan ku qabtaa mid kasta oo kooxahaan dadka ah ka tirsan?: (Fadlan ka jawaab qeyb walba)

1. In badan		
	2. In yar	3. Sinaba

A	Dadka aad isku qabill tahiin			
B	Dadka qabiillada kale ah			
C	Macalimiinta			
D	Madaxa qabiilka			
E	Ganacsatada			
F	Siyaasiyiinta/saraakiisha dowladda			
G	Dadka ciidamada ku lug leh			
H	Hogaamiyeyaasha diinta			
I	Booliiska			
J	Ururada aan dawliga ahayn ee Soomaalida (NGOs)			

6.5 Markii ay dhacayso doorashada dowladda, codkaada ma siin lahayd qof kaa qabiil duwan haddii xataa uu uga haboon yahay jagada musharraxa qabiilkaaga?

    1. Maya ( )   2. Haa ( )

6.6 Ma waxay tahay in Xisbiyada siyaasadda loo kala sooco Aragti siyaasadeed ama mid ku dhisan siyaasad qabiil ama mid diineed?
1. Siyaasad ku dhisan fikir ama argti/caqiido ( )   2. Mid ku dhisan qabiil ( )

6.7 Dadku kaliya ma waxay ku kalsoon yihiin siyaasiga aay isku qabiilka yihiin?
       1. Si aad ah ayaan u raacsanahay ( ) 2. Wax ayaan ku raacsanahay ( )
       3. Ma racsaani kamana horjeedo ( )   4. Wax baan ku diidanahay ( )
          5. Kuma raacsani gebi ahaan ( )

VII Isku xirnaanta iyo isku darida bulshada

Waxaan rabi lahaa inaan ku weydiiyo seddex mawduux: ka mid ahaanshaha, bulshaynta, iyo khilaafaadka iyo rabshadaha beeshaada.

7.1 Midkee raacsan tahay?

A Qof walba waan inuu danaha beesha ka hormariyaa dantiisa?
B Qof walba waa u xor inuu danahiisa ilaashado.

(Mid dooro)
1. Waxaan raacsanahay A ( )   2. Waxaan raacsanahy B ( )

7.2 Midkee raacsan tahay?
A Si go'aan loogu gaaro bulshadeena, waa in aan wada hadalnaa ilaa iyo inta arrin la isku raaco.
B Maadaama aan waligeen wax isku raaceyn, waa inaan baranaa sida loo aqbalo fikradaha kala duwan ee dhexyaal bulshada gudaheeda.

(Mid dooro)
1. Waxaan raacsanahay A ( )   2. Waxaan raacsanahy B ( )

7.3 Midkee raacsan tahay?
A Haddii xataa kooxo kala duwan is khilaafaan, Soomaaliya waa in ay wali ahaataa hal waddan.
B Kala duwanaashaha Soomaalida aad buu u xooggan yahay, nabadda darteed waa in Soomaaliya la kala qeybiyaa.

(Mid dooro)
1. Waxaan raacsanahay A ( )   2. Waxaan raacsanahy B ( )

7.4 Sidee buu u xoogan yahay dareenka wadajirka ama isu dhowaanta ee xaafaddaada?

 1. Si aad u kala fog ( )   2. Si dhexdhexaad u fog ( )   3. Ma foga mana dhowa ( )
        4. Si dhexdhexaad u dhow ( )   5. Si aad u dhow ( )
7.5 Sida badan arrimahan hoos ku qoran miyaa keena dhibaatooyinka bulshada ?

	1.In badan	2. In yar	3. Sinaba
A. Kala duwanaanshaha qabiilka			
B. Kala duwanaanshaha deegaanka			
C. Kala duwanaanshaha dhaqaalaha			
D.Kala duwanaanshaha u			

dhexeeya degenaanshaha dhow iyo kan dheer			
E. Kala duwanaanshaha u dhexeeya kuna xiran xisbiyada siyaasiga			
F. Kala duwanaanshaha u dhexeeya aragtida diinta (sida asal raaca diinta, fikradaha balaaran)			

7.6 Ra'yigaaga ma kula tahay in xaafadda aad ku nooshahay ay tahay nabad ama meel rabsho?

   1. Nabad aad ah ( ) 2. Nabad dhexdhexaad ( )3. Midna ( )

    4. Rabsho dhexdhexaad ( )   5. Rabsho aad ah ( )

7.7 Hadii loo bar-bar dhigo sannad ka hor, heerka rabshada xaafadaada ma kor bey u kacday, hoos beey u aaday, mise waa isku heer?

   1. Aad bey u badatay ( )   2. Wax yar bey badatay ( )3. Isku meel beey tahay ( )   4. Wax yar bey yaraatay ( )   5. Wax badan bey yaraatay ( )

7.8 Fadlan ka jawaab qoraalaha hoos ku qoran, halkii qoraalba bixi hal jawaab.

	Nabad aad ah	Nabad dhexdhexaad ah	Nabad ma ahan Nabad la'aan ma ahan	Nabad la'aan dhexdhexaad ah	Nabad la'aan aad ah
A. Guud ahaan, ma dareentaa inaad ka nabadgashay rabshad, iyo dembi marka aad keligaa guriga joogto?					
B. Ma dareentaa nabadgelyo marka aad waddada socoto habeenkii?					

7.9   12kii bilood ee la soo dhaafay, adiga ama qof qoyskaaga ka mid ah dhib ma ka soo gaareen rabsho dambi ah, sida gardarro, weerar ama dhac oo kale

1. Maya ( )   2. Haa ( )

7.10 Hadii eey tahay Haa, Meeqa jeer?   [   ]

VIII Khilaafaadka ciidamada hubeysan

Ugu dambeeyntii, waxaan rabi lahaa in aan ku weeydiiyo khibradda aad u leedahay khilaafaadyada.

8.1 Ku wee baad raacsan tahay?

A̲ Adeegsashada rabshadaha waligeed laguma sababayn karo siyaasadaha Soomaaliya.

B̲ Waddankan, mar marka qaarkood waa lagama maarmaan in la isticmaalo rabshado si loo taageero cadaaladda.

(Mid dooro)
    1. Waxaan raacsanahay A ( )   2. Waxaan raacsanahy B ( )

8.2 Sanadka la soo dhaafay, ma dareentay, shaqsi ahaan, **rabshado siyaasadeed oo ka baxsan qoyskaaga?**

1. Haa, mar badan ( )   2. Haa, dhowr goor ( )   3. Marnaba ( )

8.3 Ma ka qeybqaadatay mudaaharaad sannadkii ugu dambeeyay?
        1. Haa , inta badan ( )
        2. Haa, marar badan ( )
        3. Haa, hal mar ama labo mar ( )
        4. Maya, laakiin waan sameen lahaa hadaan fursad u helo ( )
        5. Maya, waligeey ma sameeyeen ( )

8.4 Aqoonyahanada waxeey ku doodaan in nidaamka qabiilka uu sabab u yahay khilaafaadka. Aragtidan ma raacsan tahay?

1. Waan ku raacsanahay ( )
2. Dhexdhexaad ayaan ku raacsanahay ( )
3. Kuma raacsani kamana soo horjeedo ( )
4. Sidaa aad ah uguma raacsani ( )
5. Kuma raacsani gebi ahaan ( )
Fadlan waxii faallo ah halkaan ku qor:

Waad ku mahadsantahay waqtigaaga iyo la shaqayntaada! Hadii aad rabi laheed in aad hesho aqbaarta natiijada cilmi baaristaan, fadlan email iigu soo dir:

Annex C. Victimisation Survey Questionnaire
Form: VSQ-1
Victimisation Survey Questionnaire
Ver Burao

A. Enumerator's Profile		
A-1	Enumerator's Name:	
A-2	Enumerator's code:	
A-3	Date of interview (dd/mm/yyyy):	_ _ / _ _ / _ _ _ _
A-4	Report Number (daily starting from 1):	

B. Area Information:		
B-1	Region:	Togdheer Region
B-2	District Name:	Burao
B-3	Subdivision / Village Name (See area-code list):	
B-4	GPS coordinate:	N/A
B-5	Area Classification:	1 = Urban 2 = Rural Sedentary 3 = Rural Nomadic [ ]

C: Interview Session Outcome (*Fill in this part after completing each interview session*):		
C-1	Result of interview:	1 = Completed 2 = Incomplete: some questions not answered 3 = Refused to be interviewed 4 = Not at home [ ]
C-2	Supervisor's Name:	Khadar Ibrahim
Enumerator's memo (use to take note of any special observation etc):		

D: Date Management Information
Internal Use Only (by database entry team):

D-1	Date of data entry (dd/mm/yyyy)::	_ _ / _ _ / _ _ _ _
D-2	Name of Data Entry Staff:	
D-3	Supervisor's Name:	
Notes:		

Good morning/Good afternoon. My name is _____ from _____. We are conducting a survey to know people's views on community safety. It will help agencies better plan their activities in the future to make this area safer. Would you help us by answering the interview for about 40 minutes? This is purely for research and we are not going ask your name. All your answers will remain completely confidential.

--- Start interview ---

	Interview start time (12 hrs format)	_ _ _:_ _

1. Responder's Profile

(READ OUT) First I would like to ask a few questions about your life in general.			Code
RP-1	Gender of Responder:	1 = Male 2 = Female	
RP-2	How old are you? **(DO NOT READ OUT)** **(ONE ANSWER)**	ROW NUMBER _____ 77 = Don't know 88 = Refused to answer 99 = Not applicable	
RP-3	What is your marital status? **(DO NOT READ OUT)** **(ONE ANSWER)**	1 = Single 2 = Married 3 = Divorced 4 = Widowed 77 = Don't know 88 = Refused to answer 99 = Not applicable	
RP-4	How many male do you have		

	in your household?	ROW NUMBER _____	
	(DO NOT READ OUT) **(ONE ANSWER)**	77 = Don't know 88 = Refused to answer 99 = Not applicable	
RP-5	How many of them are under 15 years old? **(DO NOT READ OUT)** **(ONE ANSWER)**	ROW NUMBER _____ 77 = Don't know 88 = Refused to answer 99 = Not applicable	
RP-6	How many female do you have in your household? **(DO NOT READ OUT)** **(ONE ANSWER)**	ROW NUMBER _____ 77 = Don't know 88 = Refused to answer 99 = Not applicable	
RP-7	How many of them are under 15 years old? **(DO NOT READ OUT)** **(ONE ANSWER)**	ROW NUMBER _____ 77 = Don't know 88 = Refused to answer 99 = Not applicable	
RP-8	What is your relationship to head of household? **(DO NOT READ OUT)** **(ONE ANSWER)**	1 = Head 2 = Husband or Wife 3 = Son or Daughter 4 = Son-in-law / Daughter-in-law 5 = Grandchild 6 = Parent 7 = Parent-in-law 8 = Others 77 = Don't know 88 = Refused to answer 99 = Not applicable	
RP-9	In order to understand existing structures, we would also like to ask you which clan does head of your household belong to. If you do not mind I would appreciate your answer. **(DO NOT READ OUT)** **(ONE ANSWER)**	1 = Daarood 2 = Dir 3 = Hawiye 4 = Digil-Mirifle 5 = ISSAQ 6 = Indian 7 = Arab 8 = Bantu 9 = Others (specify) _____ 77 = Don't know 88 = Refused to answer 99 = Not applicable	
RP-10	Do you consider your household to be; **(READ OUT)**	1 = Permanent resident 2 = Refugee (from outside Somalia) 3 = IDP (from inside Somalia) 4 = Others	

	(ONE ANSWER)	77 = Don't know 88 = Refused to answer 99 = Not applicable	
RP-11	What is the occupation of the head of household? **(DO NOT READ OUT)** **(ONE ANSWER)**	1 = Unemployed 2 = Pastoralist 3 = Farmer 4 = Fisherman 5 = Labourer 6 = Private / non-governmental security force 7 = Government (incl. police, army etc) 8 = NGO / UN 9 = Entrepreneur / Trader 10 = Other (specify): _____ 77 = Don't know 88 = Refused to answer 99 = Not applicable	
RP-12	What is your household's annual income in SL shillings)? **(DO NOT READ OUT)** **(ONE ANSWER)**	ROW NUMBER _____ 77 = Don't know 88 = Refused to answer 99 = Not applicable	
RP-13	How much does your household spend per day on food in cash (in SL shillings)? **(DO NOT READ OUT)** **(ONE ANSWER)**	ROW NUMBER _____ 77 = Don't know 88 = Refused to answer 99 = Not applicable	
RP-14	Has your head of household ever completed any formal or informal education? **(DO NOT READ OUT)** **(ONE ANSWER)**	1 = No (Skip to RP-17) 2 = Yes, Informal 3 = Yes, Formal (Skip to RP-16) 77 = Don't know (Skip to RP-17) 88 = Refused to answer (Skip to RP-17) 99 = Not applicable (Skip to RP-17)	
RP-15	What level of informal education has he or she completed? **(DO NOT READ OUT)** **(ONE ANSWER)**	1 = Religious school (Dugsi) (Skip to RP-17) 2 = Life skill education / literacy class (Skip to RP-17) 3 = Other _____ (Skip to RP-17) 77 = Don't know (Skip to RP-17) 88 = Refused to answer (Skip to RP-17) 99 = Not applicable (Skip to RP-17)	

RP-16	What level of education has he or she completed? **(DO NOT READ OUT)** **(ONE ANSWER)**	1 = Primary school completed 2 = Intermediate completed 3 = Secondary / high school completed 4 = University / college completed 5 = Others 77 = Don't know 88 = Refused to answer 99 = Not applicable	
RP-17	What is the first source of information for your household to know about crimes or violent incidents? **(DO NOT READ OUT)** **(ONE ANSWER)**	1 = Community (friends, elders, family, colleagues etc) 2 = Private media (TV, radio, newspaper, satellite TV etc) 3 = Government media (TV, radio, newspaper) 4 = Internet 5 = Aid agency / foreign organisation (UN, NGOs etc) 6 = Other (specify) _____ 77 = Don't know 88 = Refused to answer 99 = Not applicable	
RP-18	Are female member(s) of household allowed to participate in village / town meeting? **(DO NOT READ OUT)** **(ONE ANSWER)**	1 = Yes (Skip to PV-1) 2 = No 77 = Don't know (Skip to PV-1) 88 = Refused to answer (Skip to PV-1) 99 = Not applicable (Skip to PV-1)	
RP-19	What is the main reason for that? **(DO NOT READ OUT)** **(ONE ANSWER)**	1 = Husband becomes jealous / lack of trust in loyalty 2 = Male household member dislikes female visibility in decision-making 3 = Family thinks women should focus on family issues 4 = Female household member feel uncomfortable of participation 5 = Other _____ 77 = Don't know 88 = Refused to answer 99 = Not applicable	

2. Perception of Violence / Safety

(READ OUT) I would like to ask your views on safety situation in your neighbourhood for the <u>LAST TWELVE MONTHS</u>.			
PV-1	Has your community become safe or unsafe compared to twelve months ago?	1 = Become very unsafe 2 = Become a little unsafe 3 = Become a little safer	

		4 = Become a lot safer	
	(READ OUT)	77 = Don't know	
	(ONE ANSWER)	88 = Refused to answer	
		99 = Not applicable	
PV-2	How safe do you feel walking alone in your area after the dark? **(READ OUT)** **(ONE ANSWER)**	1 = Very unsafe 2 = Rather unsafe 3 = Rather safe 4 = Very safe 77 = Don't know 88 = Refused to answer 99 = Not applicable	
PV-3	Do you avoid going to get daily supply such as food, firewood or water because of insecurity? **(DO NOT READ OUT)** **(ONE ANSWER)**	1 = Yes 2 = No 77 = Don't know 88 = Refused to answer 99 = Not applicable	
PV-4	Do you avoid going to open market, workplace or prayer due to insecurity? **(DO NOT READ OUT)** **(ONE ANSWER)**	1 = Yes 2 = No 77 = Don't know 88 = Refused to answer 99 = Not applicable	
PV-5	Do you avoid sending your child to school because of insecurity? **(DO NOT READ OUT)** **(ONE ANSWER)**	1 = Yes 2 = No 77 = Don't know 88 = Refused to answer 99 = Not applicable	
PV-6	Do you avoid using public transport or travelling outside community because of insecurity? **(DO NOT READ OUT)** **(ONE ANSWER)**	1 = Yes 2 = No 77 = Don't know 88 = Refused to answer 99 = Not applicable	
PV-7	Do you avoid keeping your livestock or property outside because of insecurity? **(DO NOT READ OUT)** **(ONE ANSWER)**	1 = Yes 2 = No 77 = Don't know 88 = Refused to answer 99 = Not applicable	
PV-8	How often do you feel a threat from fanatic group? **(READ OUT)** **(ONE ANSWER)**	1 = None 2 = Low 3 = High 77 = Don't know 88 = Refused to answer 99 = Not applicable	

3. Clan / Community Dispute

CD-1	How often does your clan / community experience disputes	1 = Never / almost none (Skip to WE-1)	

238

	with other clan / communities? **(READ OUT)** **(ONE ANSWER)**	2 = Yearly (every year / about once a year) 3 = Monthly (every month / about once a month) 4 = Weekly (every week / about once a week) 77 = Don't know 88 = Refused to answer 99 = Not applicable	
CD-2	How often does your clan / community experience disputes resulting in physical violence with other clan / communities? **(READ OUT)** **(ONE ANSWER)**	1 = Never / almost none (Skip to WE-1) 2 = Yearly (every year / about once a year) 3 = Monthly (every month / about once a month) 4 = Weekly (every week / about once a week) 77 = Don't know (Skip to WE-1) 88 = Refused to answer (Skip to WE-1) 99 = Not applicable (Skip to WE-1)	
CD-3	What is the most common reason of dispute between other clan / communities? **(DO NOT READ OUT)** **(ONE ANSWER)**	1 = Resources (land, water) 2 = Family disputes 3 = Crime (theft, robbery, rape, murder etc) 4 = Power / cultural struggle 5 = Revenge 6 = Other (Specify) _____ 77 = Don't know 88 = Refused to answer 99 = Not applicable	
CD-4	Is there a particular month you have more disputes with other clan / community? **(DO NOT READ OUT)** **(UP TO THREE ANSWER)**	1 = Beginning of Jiilaal (January) 2 = Middle of Jiilaal (February) 3 = End of Jiilaal (March) 4 = Beginning of Gu' (April) 5 = Middle of Gu'(May) 6 = End of Gu' (June) 7 = Beginning of Hagaa (July) 8 = Middle of Hagaa (August) 9 = End of Hagaa (September) 10 = Beggining of Dayr (October) 11 = Middle of Dayr (November) 12 = End of Dayr (December) 13 = No 77 = Don't know 88 = Refused to answer 99 = Not applicable	(3)

4. Weapons and Explosives

	(READ OUT) For research purpose, I would like to ask you about firearms in your community.		
WE-1	In your opinion, how has the availability of firearms changed in your village / township compared to twelve months ago? **(READ OUT)** **(ONE ANSWER)**	1 = Become far less available 2 = Become slightly unavailable 3 = Stayed the same 4 = Become slightly available 5 = Become far more available 77 = Don't know 88 = Refused to answer 99 = Not applicable	
WE-2	Do you or anyone in your household have any firearm? **(DO NOT READ OUT)** **(ONE ANSWER)**	1 = No (Skip to WE-7) 2 = Yes, one 3 = Yes, two 4 = Yes, three 5 = Yes, more than four 77 = Don't know (Skip to WE-7) 88 = Refused to answer (Skip to WE-7) 99 = Not applicable (Skip to WE-7)	
WE-3	What types of firearm(s) are they? **(DO NOT READ OUT)** **(UP TO THREEANSWERS)**	1 = Pistol / revolver 2 = Hunting rifle / shotgun 3 = AK-47 / automatic rifle 4 = Bombs, explosive, hand grenades, mines etc 5 = Others (specify) _____ 77 = Don't know 88 = Refused to answer 99 = Not applicable	
WE-4	What is the main reason you own them? **(DO NOT READ OUT)** **(ONE ANSWER)**	1 = Protection (from other clans, gangs etc) 2 = Work (police/soldier/watchman) 3 = Hunting 4 = Part of tradition 5 = Other (specify) _____ 77 = Don't know 88 = Refused to answer 99 = Not applicable	
WE-5	Would you be able to live without firearms in exchange for more Protection / Security? **(DO NOT READ OUT)**	1 = Yes 2 = No 77 = Don't know 88 = Refused to answer 99 = Not applicable	

	(ONE ANSWERS)		
WE-6	Would you be able to live without firearms if you have better Livelihood? **(DO NOT READ OUT)** **(ONE ANSWERS)**	1 = Yes 2 = No 77 = Don't know 88 = Refused to answer 99 = Not applicable	
WE-7	How often do you feel a threat from remote / time control bomb? **(READ OUT)** **(ONE ANSWER)**	1 = None 2 = Low 3 = High 77 = Don't know 88 = Refused to answer 99 = Not applicable	
WE-8	Are there any mines or UXOs (explosives) in this area? **(DO NOT READ OUT)** **(ONE ANSWER)**	1 = None 2 = Some 3 = A lot 77 = Don't know 88 = Refused to answer 99 = Not applicable	

5. Actors for Response (Clan/community Elders, Religious Leaders, Police, Court)

	(READ OUT) Now I would like to ask your opinions on roles of some actors in responding cases of violence and crime. [Community Elders] First let me ask you about Clan / community Elders.		
AR-1	What is the level of trust you have toward clan / community elders in responding violence and crime? **(READ OUT)** **(ONE ANSWER)**	1 = Very low 2 = Relatively low 3 = Relatively high 4 = Very high 77 = Don't know 88 = Refused to answer 99 = Not applicable	
AR-2	How accessible are they in terms of physical distance and easiness to find? **(READ OUT)** **(ONE ANSWER)**	1 = Very inaccessible 2 = Relatively inaccessible 3 = Relatively accessible 4 = Very accessible 77 = Don't know 88 = Refused to answer 99 = Not applicable	
AR-3	How rapidly do they respond to the cases? **(READ OUT)** **(ONE ANSWER)**	1 = Very slowly 2 = Relatively slowly 3 = Relatively rapidly 4 = Very rapidly 77 = Don't know 88 = Refused to answer 99 = Not applicable	

	[Religious leaders] Now let me ask you about religious leaders.		
AR-4	What is the level of trust you have toward religious leaders in responding violence and crime? **(READ OUT)** **(ONE ANSWER)**	1 = Very low 2 = Relatively low 3 = Relatively high 4 = Very high 77 = Don't know 88 = Refused to answer 99 = Not applicable	
AR-5	How accessible are they in terms of physical distance and easiness to find? **(READ OUT)** **(ONE ANSWER)**	1 = Very inaccessible 2 = Relatively inaccessible 3 = Relatively accessible 4 = Very accessible 77 = Don't know 88 = Refused to answer 99 = Not applicable	
AR-6	How rapidly do they respond to the cases? **(READ OUT)** **(ONE ANSWER)**	1 = Very slowly 2 = Relatively slowly 3 = Relatively rapidly 4 = Very rapidly 77 = Don't know 88 = Refused to answer 99 = Not applicable	
	[Police] Now I would like to ask you about police.		
AR-7	What is the level of trust you have toward police in responding violence and crime? **(READ OUT)** **(ONE ANSWER)**	1 = Very low 2 = Fairly low 3 = Fairly high 4 = Very high 77 = Don't know 88 = Refused to answer 99 = Not applicable	
AR-8	How accessible are they in terms of physical distance and easiness to find? **(READ OUT)** **(ONE ANSWER)**	1 = Very inaccessible 2 = Fairly inaccessible 3 = Fairly accessible 4 = Very accessible 77 = Don't know 88 = Refused to answer 99 = Not applicable	
AR-9	How rapidly do they respond to the cases? **(READ OUT)** **(ONE ANSWER)**	1 = Very slowly 2 = Fairly slowly 3 = Fairly rapidly 4 = Very rapidly 77 = Don't know 88 = Refused to answer 99 = Not applicable	
	[Court] Lastly I would like to ask about court.		
AR-10	What is the level of trust you have to court in responding	1 = Very low 2 = Fairly low	

	violence and crime? **(READ OUT)** **(ONE ANSWER)**	3 = Fairly high 4 = Very high 77 = Don't know 88 = Refused to answer 99 = Not applicable	
AR-11	How accessible are they in terms of physical distance and easiness to find? **(READ OUT)** **(ONE ANSWER)**	1 = Very inaccessible 2 = Fairly inaccessible 3 = Fairly accessible 4 = Very accessible 77 = Don't know 88 = Refused to answer 99 = Not applicable	
AR-12	How rapidly do they respond to the cases? **(READ OUT)** **(ONE ANSWER)**	1 = Very slowly 2 = Fairly slowly 3 = Fairly rapidly 4 = Very rapidly 77 = Don't know 88 = Refused to answer 99 = Not applicable	
AR-13	Would you go to criminal court if you become a victim of crime or violence? **(DO NOT READ OUT)** **(ONE ANSWER)**	1 = Yes (Skip to EV-1) 2 = No 77 = Don't know (Skip to EV-1) 88 = Refused to answer (Skip to EV-1) 99 = Not applicable (Skip to EV-1)	
AR-14	Why do you not go? **(DO NOT READ OUT)** **(ONE ANSWER)**	1 = Judgement is not fair 2 = Matter takes too long 3 = They don't take action 4 = They are far / not easy to access 5 = Fees are expensive 6 = Corrupt / Bribery 7 = Other (specify)_____ 77 = Don't know 88 = Refused to answer 99 = Not applicable	

6. Witness of Violence

	(READ OUT) Now I am going to ask about the crime or violence you witnessed WITHIN THE LAST TWELVE MONTHS.		
WV-1	Have you witnessed with your own eyes any crime or violence **against someone outside your household** for the last twelve months? **(DO NOT READ OUT)** **(ONE ANSWER)**	1 = Yes 2 = No (Skip to EV-4) 77 = Don't know (Skip to EV-4) 88 = Refused to answer (Skip to EV-4) 99 = Not applicable (Skip to EV-4)	

WV-2	How many property crimes have you witnessed within the last twelve months? **(DO NOT READ OUT)** **(ONE ANSWER)**	ROW NUMBER _____ 77 = Don't know 88 = Refused to answer 99 = Not applicable	
WV-3	How many physical violence have you witnessed within the last twelve months? **(DO NOT READ OUT)** **(ONE ANSWER)**	ROW NUMBER _____ 77 = Don't know 88 = Refused to answer 99 = Not applicable	

7-1. Victim Experience of Assault and Attack

AA-1	Has any member of your household experienced assault or physical attack within the last twelve months? **(DO NOT READ OUT)** **(ONE ANSWER)**	1 = Yes 2 = No (Skip to PC-1) 77 = Don't know (Skip to PC-1) 88 = Refused to answer (Skip to PC-1) 99 = Not applicable (Skip to PC-1)	
AA-2	How many times did it happen within the last twelve months? **(DO NOT READ OUT)** **(ONE ANSWER)**	ROW NUMBER _____ 77 = Don't know 88 = Refused to answer 99 = Not applicable	
(If respondent have several experiences within last twelve month) Please tell us details of the most recent case.			
AA-3	Which month did the incident happen? **(DO NOT READ OUT)** **(ONE ANSWER)**	1 = Beginning of Jiilaal (January) 2 = Middle of Jiilaal (February) 3 = End of Jiilaal (March) 4 = Beginning of Gu' (April) 5 = Middle of Gu'(May) 6 = End of Gu' (June) 7 = Beginning of Hagaa (July) 8 = Middle of Hagaa (August) 9 = End of Hagaa (September) 10 = Beggining of Dayr (October) 11 = Middle of Dayr (November) 12 = End of Dayr (December) 77 = Don't know 88 = Refused to answer 99 = Not applicable	
AA-4	Did it happen during; **(READ OUT)** **(ONE ANSWER)**	1 = Morning (between sunrise and midday prayers) 2 = Afternoon (between midday prayers and sunset) 3 = Night (after sunset) 77 = Don't know 88 = Refused to answer	

244

		99 = Not applicable	
AA-5	Where did it happen? **(DO NOT READ OUT)** **(ONE ANSWER)**	1 = At home 2 = On the street 3 = At a market / commercial area (shop, store, hotel, bar) 4 = At school 5 = In the work place 6 = In a field / bush / forest 7 = While traveling on public / private transport 8 = Other (specify) _____ 77 = Don't know 88 = Refused to answer 99 = Not applicable	
AA-6	What weapons were used to help commit the crime / violence? **(DO NOT READ OUT)** **(ONE ANSWER)**	1 = No weapon was used 2 = Stone / bottle / glass/ rope / stick / fire 3 = Knife / sward / panga / axe / club 4 = Pistol / revolver 5 = Hunting rifle / shotgun 6 = AK-47 / automatic rifle 7 = Bombs, explosive, hand grenade, mines etc 8 = Others (specify) _____ 77 = Don't know 88 = Refused to answer 99 = Not applicable	
AA-7	Who was / were the perpetrator of the incident? **(DO NOT READ OUT)** **(ONE ANSWER)**	1 = Family / Relative(s) 2 = Friend(s) / Neighbour 3 = Individual criminal 4 = Organised armed group (criminal group, militia group) 5 = Clan group 6 = Government (Including army, police) 7 = Foreigner troops 8 = Other (specify) _____ 77 = Don't know 88 = Refused to answer 99 = Not applicable	
AA-8	Was the perpetrator under the influence of drug, alcohol or khat?	1 = Yes 2 = No 77 = Don't know	

		88 = Refused to answer	
	(DO NOT READ OUT) **(ONE ANSWER)**	99 = Not applicable	
AA-9	How many member of your household became a victim due to the incident? **(DO NOT READ OUT)** **(ONE ANSWER)**	ROW NUMBER _____ 77 = Don't know 88 = Refused to answer 99 = Not applicable	
AA-10	What is the relationship of the victim to the head of household? If there are several victims, tell me about the oldest victim. **(DO NOT READ OUT)** **(ONE ANSWER)**	1 = Head 2 = Husband or Wife 3 = Son or Daughter 4 = Son-in-law / Daughter-in-law 5 = Grandchild 6 = Parent 7 = Parent-in-law 8 = Others 77 = Don't know 88 = Refused to answer 99 = Not applicable	
AA-11	Was the victim; **(READ OUT)** **(ONE ANSWER)**	1 = Male 2 = Female 77 = Don't know 88 = Refused to answer 99 = Not applicable	
AA-12	How old was the victim when the incident happened? **(DO NOT READ OUT)** **(ONE ANSWER)**	ROW NUMBER _____ 77 = Don't know 88 = Refused to answer 99 = Not applicable	
AA-13	What was the level of injuries of the victim? **(READ OUT)** **(ONE ANSWER)**	1 = Not injured 2 = Light injury (injured but no need for medical assistance) 3 = Medium injury (required medical assistance) 4 = Heavy injury (required admission to hospital) 5 = Death 77 = Don't know 88 = Refused to answer 99 = Not applicable	
AA-14	Was there any other victim(s)? **(DO NOT READ OUT)** **(ONE ANSWER)**	1 = Yes 2 = No (skip to AA-34) 77 = Don't know (skip to AA-34) 88 = Refused to answer (skip to AA-34) 99 = Not applicable (skip to AA-34)	
AA-15	What is the relationship of the	1 = Head	

246

	second oldest victim to the head of household? **(DO NOT READ OUT)** **(ONE ANSWER)**	2 = Husband or Wife 3 = Son or Daughter 4 = Son-in-law / Daughter-in-law 5 = Grandchild 6 = Parent 7 = Parent-in-law 8 = Others 77 = Don't know 88 = Refused to answer 99 = Not applicable	
AA-16	Was the victim; **(READ OUT)** **(ONE ANSWER)**	1 = Male 2 = Female 77 = Don't know 88 = Refused to answer 99 = Not applicable	
AA-17	How old was the victim when the incident happened? **(DO NOT READ OUT)** **(ONE ANSWER)**	ROW NUMBER _____ 77 = Don't know 88 = Refused to answer 99 = Not applicable	
AA-18	What was the level of injuries of the victim? **(DO NOT READ OUT)** **(ONE ANSWER)**	1 = Not injured 2 = Light injury (injured but no need for medical assistance) 3 = Medium injury (required medical assistance) 4 = Heavy injury (required admission to hospital) 5 = Death 77 = Don't know 88 = Refused to answer 99 = Not applicable	
AA-19	Was there any other victim(s)? **(DO NOT READ OUT)** **(ONE ANSWER)**	1 = Yes 2 = No (skip to AA-34) 77 = Don't know (skip to AA-34) 88 = Refused to answer (skip to AA-34) 99 = Not applicable (skip to AA-34)	
AA-20	What is the relationship of the third eldest victim to the head of household? **(DO NOT READ OUT)** **(ONE ANSWER)**	1 = Head 2 = Husband or Wife 3 = Son or Daughter 4 = Son-in-law / Daughter-in-law 5 = Grandchild 6 = Parent 7 = Parent-in-law 8 = Others 77 = Don't know 88 = Refused to answer	

		99 = Not applicable	
AA-21	Was the victim; **(READ OUT)** **(ONE ANSWER)**	1 = Male 2 = Female 77 = Don't know 88 = Refused to answer 99 = Not applicable	
AA-22	How old was the victim when the incident happened? **(DO NOT READ OUT)** **(ONE ANSWER)**	ROW NUMBER _____ 77 = Don't know 88 = Refused to answer 99 = Not applicable	
AA-23	What was the level of injuries of the victim? **(DO NOT READ OUT)** **(ONE ANSWER)**	1 = Not injured 2 = Light injury (injured but no need for medical assistance) 3 = Medium injury (required medical assistance) 4 = Heavy injury (required admission to hospital) 5 = Death 77 = Don't know 88 = Refused to answer 99 = Not applicable	
AA-24	Was there any other victim(s)? **(DO NOT READ OUT)** **(ONE ANSWER)**	1 = Yes 2 = No (skip to AA-34) 77 = Don't know (skip to AA-34) 88 = Refused to answer (skip to AA-34) 99 = Not applicable (skip to AA-34)	
AA-25	What is the relationship of the fourth eldest victim to the head of household? **(DO NOT READ OUT)** **(ONE ANSWER)**	1 = Head 2 = Husband or Wife 3 = Son or Daughter 4 = Son-in-law / Daughter-in-law 5 = Grandchild 6 = Parent 7 = Parent-in-law 8 = Others 77 = Don't know 88 = Refused to answer 99 = Not applicable	
AA-26	Was the victim; **(READ OUT)** **(ONE ANSWER)**	1 = Male 2 = Female 77 = Don't know 88 = Refused to answer 99 = Not applicable	
AA-27	How old was the victim when the incident happened? **(DO NOT READ OUT)**	ROW NUMBER _____ 77 = Don't know	

	(ONE ANSWER)	88 = Refused to answer 99 = Not applicable	
AA-28	What was the level of injuries of the victim? **(DO NOT READ OUT)** **(ONE ANSWER)**	1 = Not injured 2 = Light injury (injured but no need for medical assistance) 3 = Medium injury (required medical assistance) 4 = Heavy injury (required admission to hospital) 5 = Death 77 = Don't know 88 = Refused to answer 99 = Not applicable	
AA-29	Was there any other victim(s)? **(DO NOT READ OUT)** **(ONE ANSWER)**	1 = Yes 2 = No (skip to AA-34) 77 = Don't know (skip to AA-34) 88 = Refused to answer (skip to AA-34) 99 = Not applicable (skip to AA-34)	
AA-30	What is the relationship of the fifth eldest victim to the head of household? **(DO NOT READ OUT)** **(ONE ANSWER)**	1 = Head 2 = Husband or Wife 3 = Son or Daughter 4 = Son-in-law / Daughter-in-law 5 = Grandchild 6 = Parent 7 = Parent-in-law 8 = Others 77 = Don't know 88 = Refused to answer 99 = Not applicable	
AA-31	Was the victim; **(READ OUT)** **(ONE ANSWER)**	1 = Male 2 = Female 77 = Don't know 88 = Refused to answer 99 = Not applicable	
AA-32	How old was the victim when the incident happened? **(DO NOT READ OUT)** **(ONE ANSWER)**	ROW NUMBER _____ 77 = Don't know 88 = Refused to answer 99 = Not applicable	
AA-33	What was the level of injuries of the victim? **(DO NOT READ OUT)** **(ONE ANSWER)**	1 = Not injured 2 = Light injury (injured but no need for medical assistance) 3 = Medium injury (required medical assistance) 4 = Heavy injury (required admission	

		to hospital)	
		5 = Death	
		77 = Don't know	
		88 = Refused to answer	
		99 = Not applicable	
AA-34	Did you or your member of household report the incident to public? **(DO NOT READ OUT)** **(ONE ANSWER)**	1 = Yes (Skip to AA-36) 2 = No 77 = Don't know (Skip to AA-36) 88 = Refused to answer (Skip to AA-36) 99 = Not applicable (Skip to AA-36)	
AA-35	Why did you not report? **(DO NOT READ OUT)** **(ONE ANSWER)**	1 = Someone else reported (Skip to PC-1) 2 = Used other means to resolve (Skip to PC-1) 3 = Not available / accessible (Skip to PC-1) 4 = Physically unable to report (Skip to PC-1) 5 = Don't trust / No chance of recovery (Skip to PC-1) 6 = Persuaded by others not to report (Skip to PC-1) 7 = Fear of revenge (Skip to PC-1) 8 = Other(specify) _____(Skip to PC-1) 77 = Don't know (Skip to PC-1) 88 = Refused to answer (Skip to PC-1) 99 = Not applicable (Skip to PC-1)	
AA-36	To whom did you report first? **(DO NOT READ OUT)** **(ONE ANSWER)**	1 = Community Elders 2 = Religious leaders 3 = Non-state police / community based policing 4 = Government Police (Skip to AA-40) 5 = Armed group 6 = NGOs / UN 7 = Other (specify) _____ 77 = Don't know 88 = Refused to answer 99 = Not applicable	
AA-37	Were you satisfied with their response? **(READ OUT)**	1 = Very unsatisfied 2 = Rather unsatisfied 3 = Rather satisfied (Skip to AA-39) 4 = Very satisfied (Skip to AA-39) 77 = Don't know (Skip to AA-39)	

	(ONE ANSWER)	88 = Refused to answer (Skip to AA-39) 99 = Not applicable (Skip to AA-39)	
AA-38	Why were you not satisfied? **(DO NOT READ OUT)** **(ONE ANSWER)**	1 = Took time / waited long for first contact 2 = Took time for taking action after reporting 3 = They did not take action 4 = Treatment was not fair 5 = Harassed / Intimidated 6 = Other (specify) _____ 77 = Don't know 88 = Refused to answer 99 = Not applicable	
AA-39	Did you also report to the government police? **(DO NOT READ OUT)** **(ONE ANSWER)**	1 = Yes 2 = No (Skip to AA-42) 77 = Don't know (Skip to AA-42) 88 = Refused to answer (Skip to AA-42) 99 = Not applicable (Skip to AA-42)	
AA-40	Were you satisfied with their response? **(READ OUT)** **(ONE ANSWER)**	1 = Very unsatisfied 2 = Rather unsatisfied 3 = Rather satisfied (Skip to AA-42) 4 = Very satisfied (Skip to AA-42) 77 = Don't know (Skip to AA-42) 88 = Refused to answer (Skip to AA-42) 99 = Not applicable (Skip to AA-42)	
AA-41	Why were you not satisfied? **(DO NOT READ OUT)** **(ONE ANSWER)**	1 = Took time / waited long for first contact 2 = Took time for taking action after reporting 3 = They did not take action 4 = Treatment was not fair 5 = Harassed / Intimidated 6 = Other (specify) _____ 77 = Don't know 88 = Refused to answer 99 = Not applicable	
AA-42	Was there any criminal court decision made? **(DO NOT READ OUT)** **(ONE ANSWER)**	1 = Yes 2 = No (Skip to PC-1) 77 = Don't know (Skip to PC-1) 88 = Refused to answer (Skip to PC-1) 99 = Not applicable (Skip to PC-1)	
AA-43	Were you satisfied with their	1 = Very unsatisfied	

	response? **(READ OUT)** **(ONE ANSWER)**	2 = Rather unsatisfied 3 = Rather satisfied (Skip to PC-1) 4 = Very satisfied (Skip to PC-1) 77 = Don't know (Skip to PC-1) 88 = Refused to answer (Skip to PC-1) 99 = Not applicable (Skip to PC-1)	
AA-44	Why were you not satisfied? **(DO NOT READ OUT)** **(ONE ANSWER)**	1 = Judgement was not fair 2 = Matter took too long 3 = They didn't take action 4 = They were far / not easy to access 5 = Fees were expensive 6 = Corrupt / Bribery 7 = Other (specify)_____ 77 = Don't know 88 = Refused to answer 99 = Not applicable	

7-2. Property Crime

PC-1	Has any member of your household experienced property crime within the last twelve months? **(DO NOT READ OUT)** **(ONE ANSWER)**	1 = Yes 2 = No (Skip to SV-1) 77 = Don't know (Skip to SV-1) 88 = Refused to answer (Skip to SV-1) 99 = Not applicable (Skip to SV-1)	
PC-2	How many times did it happen within the last twelve months? **(DO NOT READ OUT)** **(ONE ANSWER)**	ROW NUMBER _____ 77 = Don't know 88 = Refused to answer 99 = Not applicable	
(If respondent have several experiences within last twelve month) Please tell us details of the most recent property crime.			
PC-3	What was the type of incident? **(READ OUT)** **(ONE ANSWER)**	1 = Street theft 2 = House burglary 3 = Theft of crops or livestock 4 = Theft of Land or water point 5 = Other 77 = Don't know 88 = Refused to answer 99 = Not applicable	
PC-4	Which month did the incident happen? **(DO NOT READ OUT)** **(ONE ANSWER)**	1 = Beginning of Jiilaal (January) 2 = Middle of Jiilaal (February) 3 = End of Jiilaal (March) 4 = Beginning of Gu' (April) 5 = Middle of Gu'(May) 6 = End of Gu' (June)	

		7 = Beginning of Hagaa (July) 8 = Middle of Hagaa (August) 9 = End of Hagaa (September) 10 = Beggining of Dayr (October) 11 = Middle of Dayr (November) 12 = End of Dayr (December) 77 = Don't know 88 = Refused to answer 99 = Not applicable	
PC-5	Did it happen during; **(READ OUT)** **(ONE ANSWER)**	1 = Morning (between sunrise and midday prayers) 2 = Afternoon (between midday prayers and sunset) 3 = Night (after sunset) 77 = Don't know 88 = Refused to answer 99 = Not applicable	
PC-6	Who was / were the perpetrator of the incident? **(DO NOT READ OUT)** **(ONE ANSWER)**	1 = Family / Relative(s) 2 = Friend(s) / Neighbour 3 = Individual criminal 4 = Organised armed group (criminal group, militia group) 5 = Clan group 6 = Government (Including army, police) 7 = Foreigner troops 8 = Other (specify) _____ 77 = Don't know 88 = Refused to answer 99 = Not applicable	
PC-7	Did he or she receive medication due to the incident? **(DO NOT READ OUT)** **(ONE ANSWER)**	1 = Yes 2 = No 77 = Don't know 88 = Refused to answer 99 = Not applicable	
PC-8	Did you or your member of household report the incident to public? **(DO NOT READ OUT)** **(ONE ANSWER)**	1 = Yes (Skip to PC-10) 2 = No 77 = Don't know (Skip to PC-10) 88 = Refused to answer (Skip to PC-10) 99 = Not applicable (Skip to PC-10)	
PC-9	Why did you not report? **(DO NOT READ OUT)**	1 = Someone else reported (Skip to SV-1) 2 = Used other means to resolve (Skip to SV-1) 3 = Not available / accessible (Skip to	

	(ONE ANSWER)	SV-1) 4 = Physically unable to report (Skip to SV-1) 5 = Don't trust / No chance of recovery (Skip to SV-1) 6 = Persuaded by others not to report (Skip to SV-1) 7 = Fear of revenge (Skip to SV-1) 8 = Other(specify) _____(Skip to SV-1) 77 = Don't know (Skip to SV-1) 88 = Refused to answer (Skip to SV-1) 99 = Not applicable (Skip to SV-1)	
PC-10	To whom did you report first? **(DO NOT READ OUT)** **(ONE ANSWER)**	1 = Community Elders 2 = Religious leaders 3 = Non-state police / community based policing 4 = Government Police (Skip to PC-14) 5 = Armed group 6 = NGOs / UN 7 = Other (specify) _____ ___ 77 = Don't know 88 = Refused to answer 99 = Not applicable	
PC-11	Were you satisfied with their response? **(READ OUT)** **(ONE ANSWER)**	1 = Very unsatisfied 2 = Rather unsatisfied 3 = Rather satisfied (Skip to PC-13) 4 = Very satisfied (Skip to PC-13) 77 = Don't know (Skip to PC-13) 88 = Refused to answer (Skip to PC-13) 99 = Not applicable (Skip to PC-13)	
PC-12	Why were you not satisfied? **(DO NOT READ OUT)** **(ONE ANSWER)**	1 = Took time / waited long for first contact 2 = Took time for taking action after reporting 3 = They did not take action 4 = Treatment was not fair 5 = Harassed / Intimidated 6 = Other (specify) _____ 77 = Don't know 88 = Refused to answer	

		99 = Not applicable	
PC-13	Did you also report to the government police? **(DO NOT READ OUT)** **(ONE ANSWER)**	1 = Yes 2 = No (Skip to PC-16) 77 = Don't know (Skip to PC-16) 88 = Refused to answer (Skip to PC-16) 99 = Not applicable (Skip to PC-16)	
PC-14	Were you satisfied with their response? **(READ OUT)** **(ONE ANSWER)**	1 = Very unsatisfied 2 = Rather unsatisfied 3 = Rather satisfied (Skip to PC-16) 4 = Very satisfied (Skip to PC-16) 77 = Don't know (Skip to PC-16) 88 = Refused to answer (Skip to PC-16) 99 = Not applicable (Skip to PC-16)	
PC-15	Why were you not satisfied? **(DO NOT READ OUT)** **(ONE ANSWER)**	1 = Took time / waited long for first contact 2 = Took time for taking action after reporting 3 = They did not take action 4 = Treatment was not fair 5 = Harassed / Intimidated 6 = Other (specify) _____ 77 = Don't know 88 = Refused to answer 99 = Not applicable	
PC-16	Was there any criminal court decision made? **(DO NOT READ OUT)** **(ONE ANSWER)**	1 = Yes 2 = No 77 = Don't know 88 = Refused to answer 99 = Not applicable	

7-3. Sexual Violence

SV-1	Have you or any member of your household experienced sexual violence or rape within the last twelve months? **(DO NOT READ OUT)** **(ONE ANSWER)**	1 = Yes 2 = No (Skip to OV-1) 77 = Don't know (Skip to OV-1) 88 = Refused to answer (Skip to OV-1) 99 = Not applicable (Skip to OV-1)	
SV-2	How many times did it happen within the last twelve months? **(DO NOT READ OUT)** **(ONE ANSWER)**	ROW NUMBER _____ 77 = Don't know 88 = Refused to answer 99 = Not applicable	

	(If respondent have several experiences within last twelve month) Please tell us details of the most recent case.		
SV-3	Was the victim yourself or the other member of household? **(DO NOT READ OUT)** **(ONE ANSWER)**	1 = Myself (Skip to SV-6) 2 = Member of the household 77 = Don't know 88 = Refused to answer 99 = Not applicable	
SV-4	Is the victim; **(READ OUT)** **(ONE ANSWER)**	1 = Male 2 = Female 77 = Don't know 88 = Refused to answer 99 = Not applicable	
SV-5	How old was he or she when the incident happened? **(DO NOT READ OUT)** **(ONE ANSWER)**	ROW NUMBER _____ 77 = Don't know 88 = Refused to answer 99 = Not applicable	
SV-6	Did it happen during; **(READ OUT)** **(ONE ANSWER)**	1 = Morning (between sunrise and midday prayers) 2 = Afternoon (between midday prayers and sunset) 3 = Night (after sunset) 77 = Don't know 88 = Refused to answer 99 = Not applicable	
SV-7	Where did it happen? **(DO NOT READ OUT)** **(ONE ANSWER)**	1 = At home 2 = On the street 3 = At a market / commercial area (shop, store, hotel, bar) 4 = At school 5 = In the work place 6 = In a field / bush / forest 7 = While traveling on public / private transport 8 = Other (specify) _____ 77 = Don't know 88 = Refused to answer 99 = Not applicable	
SV-8	Where did the victim go to receive medication due to the incident? **(DO NOT READ OUT)** **(ONE ANSWER)**	1 = Nowhere 2 = Hospital / Local clinic / Doctor 3 = Traditional healers 4 = Community elders 5 = Religious Leaders 6 = NGOs / UN 7 = Other (specify)	

		77 = Don't know	
		88 = Refused to answer	
		99 = Not applicable	
SV-9	Where did the victim go for psychological assistance? **(DO NOT READ OUT)** **(ONE ANSWER)**	1 = Nowhere 2 = Hospital / Local clinic / Doctor 3 = Traditional healers 4 = Community elders 5 = Religious Leaders 6 = NGOs / UN 7 = Other (specify) ——————————— 77 = Don't know 88 = Refused to answer 99 = Not applicable	
SV-10	Who was / were the perpetrator of the incident? **(DO NOT READ OUT)** **(ONE ANSWER)**	1 = Family / Relative(s) 2 = Friend(s) / Neighbour 3 = Individual criminal 4 = Organised armed group (criminal group, militia group) 5 = Clan group 6 = Government (Including army, police) 7 = Foreigner troops 8 = Other (specify) ——————————— 77 = Don't know 88 = Refused to answer 99 = Not applicable	
SV-11	Did you or your member of household report the incident to public? **(DO NOT READ OUT)** **(ONE ANSWER)**	1 = Yes (Skip to SV-13) 2 = No 77 = Don't know (Skip to SV-13) 88 = Refused to answer (Skip to SV-13) 99 = Not applicable (Skip to SV-13)	
SV-12	Why did you not report? **(DO NOT READ OUT)** **(ONE ANSWER)**	1 = Someone else reported (Skip to SV-19) 2 = Used other means to resolve (Skip to SV-19) 3 = Too embarrassed (Skip to SV-19) 4 = Not available / accessible (Skip to SV-19) 5 = Physically unable to report (Skip to SV-19) 6 = Don't trust (Skip to SV-19) 7 = No chance of recovery / arrest even if reported (Skip to SV-19) 8 = Persuaded by others not to report (Skip to SV-19) 9 = Fear of revenge (Skip to SV-19) 10 = Other(specify)	

		_____(Skip to SV-19) 77 = Don't know (Skip to SV-19) 88 = Refused to answer (Skip to SV-19) 99 = Not applicable (Skip to SV-19)	
SV-13	To whom did you report first? **(DO NOT READ OUT)** **(ONE ANSWER)**	1 = Community Elders 2 = Religious leaders 3 = Non-state police / community based policing 4 = Government Police (Skip to SV-17) 5 = Armed group 6 = NGOs / UN 7 = Other (specify) _____ 77 = Don't know 88 = Refused to answer 99 = Not applicable	
SV-14	Were you satisfied with their response? **(READ OUT)** **(ONE ANSWER)**	1 = Very unsatisfied 2 = Fairly unsatisfied 3 = Fairly satisfied (Skip to SV-16) 4 = Very satisfied (Skip to SV-16) 77 = Don't know (Skip to SV-16) 88 = Refused to answer (Skip to SV-16) 99 = Not applicable (Skip to SV-16)	
SV-15	Why were you not satisfied? **(DO NOT READ OUT)** **(ONE ANSWER)**	1 = Took time / waited long for first contact 2 = Took time for taking action after reporting 3 = They did not take action 4 = Treatment was not fair 5 = Harassed / Intimidated / Stigmatised 6 = Other (specify) _____ 77 = Don't know 88 = Refused to answer 99 = Not applicable	
SV-16	Did you also report to the government police? **(DO NOT READ OUT)** **(ONE ANSWER)**	1 = Yes 2 = No (Skip to SV-19) 77 = Don't know (Skip to SV-19) 88 = Refused to answer (Skip to SV-19) 99 = Not applicable (Skip to SV-19)	
SV-17	Were you satisfied with their response? **(READ OUT)** **(ONE ANSWER)**	1 = Very unsatisfied 2 = Rather unsatisfied 3 = Rather satisfied (Skip to SV-19) 4 = Very satisfied (Skip to SV-19) 77 = Don't know ((Skip to SV-19) 88 = Refused to answer (Skip to SV-19) 99 = Not applicable (Skip to SV-19)	

SV-18	Why were you not satisfied? **(DO NOT READ OUT)** **(ONE ANSWER)**	1 = Took time / waited long for first contact 2 = Took time for taking action after reporting 3 = They did not take action 4 = Treatment was not fair 5 = Harassed / Intimidated 6 = Other (specify) ———————— 77 = Don't know 88 = Refused to answer 99 = Not applicable	
SV-19	Was there any criminal court decision made? **(DO NOT READ OUT)** **(ONE ANSWER)**	1 = Yes 2 = No 77 = Don't know 88 = Refused to answer 99 = Not applicable	

7-4. Other Violence / Crime

[FORCED DETENTION]			
OV-1	Were you or a member of your household forcibly detained within the last twelve months? **(DO NOT READ OUT)** **(ONE ANSWER)**	1 = Yes 2 = No (Skip to OV-4) 77 = Don't know (Skip to OV-4) 88 = Refused to answer (Skip to OV-4) 99 = Not applicable (Skip to OV-4)	
OV-2	How long was the period of detention? **(DO NOT READ OUT)** **(ONE ANSWER)**	1 = Less than one day 2 = One day – 7 days 3 = 8 days – 30 days 4 = One month – 1 year 5 = More than one year 77 = Don't know 88 = Refused to answer 99 = Not applicable	
OV-3	What was the reason of detention / arrest? **(DO NOT READ OUT)** **(ONE ANSWER)**	1 = Crime suspect of physical violence 2 = Crime suspect of property crime 3 = Piracy suspect 4 = Clan / civil dispute 5 = National Security reasons 6 = Discrimination (against IDPs, gender, clan etc) 7 = Other (specify) ———————— 77 = Don't know 88 = Refused to answer 99 = Not applicable	
[KIDNAPPING / ABUDUCTION]			

OV-4	Were you or a member of your household kidnapped / abducted within the last twelve months? **(DO NOT READ OUT) (ONE ANSWER)**	1 = Yes 2 = No 77 = Don't know 88 = Refused to answer 99 = Not applicable	

----------- END OF INTERVIEW -----------

Interview end time (12 hour format):	__ __:__ __

ENUMERATOR DECLARATION

I declare that I have asked this entire Questionnaire as it is laid out and as I have been briefed.

I declare that all the responses and answers recorded by me in this Questionnaire were given to me by the correct respondent. This Questionnaire has been fully checked by myself.

PLEASE PRINT:

Name ....

REFERENCES

Written Sources

Abdullahi, Abdurahman M. 2008. *The Islah Movement: Islamic Moderation in War-torn Somalia.* October 2008. www.islaax.org

ACLED. 2013. Armed Conflict Location and Event Dataset. http://www.acleddata.com/

Adam, Hussein M. 1995. "A Terrible Beauty Being Born," In Zartman, William (ed). *Collapsed States: The Disintergration and Restoration of Legitimate Authority.* Boulder, London: Lynne Rienner Publishers, pp. 69-90.

Afrobarometer. 2002. *Violent Social Conflict and Conflict Resolution in Nigeria.* Afrobarometer Briefing Paper No. 2, August 2002. www.afrobarometer.org

Amir, Yahya Sh. 2009. *Mogadishu Profile.* March 2009. Mogadishu: CRD.

Arednt, Hannah. 1969. "A Special Supplement: Reflections on Violence," *The New York Review of Books* 12(4), pp. 1-33.

Barnes, Cedric. 2006. "U dhashay—Ku dhashay: Genealogical and Territorial Discourse in Somali History," *Social Identities* 12(4), pp. 487- 498.

Besteman, Catherine. 1999. *Unraveling Somalia.* Pennsylvania: University of Pennsylvania Press.

Besteman, Catherine and Cassanelli, Lee V. (eds). 2004. *The Struggle for Land in Southern Somalia: The War Behind the War.* London: HAAN.

Bhavnani, Ravi and Backer, David. 2000. "Localized Ethnic Conflict and Genocide: Accounting for Differences in Rwanda and Burundi," *The Journal of Conflict Resolution* 44(3), pp. 283-306.

Bhavnani, Ravi and Backer, David. 2007. "Social Capital and Political Violence in Sub-Saharan Africa," *Conference on the Micro-Foundations of Mass Politics in Africa.* Michigan State University, 12-13 May 2007.

Bohara, Alok K. et al. 2006. "Opportunity, Democracy, and the Exchange of Political Violence: A Subnational Analysis of Conflict in Nepal," *The Journal of Conflict Resolution* 50(1), pp. 108-128.

Boix, Carles. 2008. "Civil Wars and Guerrilla Warfare in the Contemporary World: Toward a Joint Theory of Motivations and Opportunities," In Kalyvas, Stathis N. (eds). *Order, Conflict, and Violence.* Cambridge, New York: Cambridge University Press, pp. 197-218.

Bradbury, Mark. 2008. *Becoming Somaliland.* London: Progressio.

Bradbury, Mark. 2009. *The Search for Peace: A Synthesis Report of the Peace Mapping Study.* Nairobi: Interpeace.

Bradbury, Mark and Healy, Sally (eds). 2010. *Whose Peace is it Anyway? Connecting Somali and International Peacemaking.* London: Conciliation Resources.

Brons, Maria H. 2001. *Society, Security, Sovereignty and the State in Somalia: From Statelessness to Statelessness?* Utrecht: International Books.

Bryden, Matt. 1999. "New Hope for Somalia? The Building Block Approach," *Review of African Political Economy*, March 1999; 26, 79, pp. 134-140.

Bryden, Matt and Brickhill, Jeremy. 2010. "Disarming Somalia: Lessons in Stabilisation from a Collapsed State," *Conflict, Security, and Development Group* 10(2), pp. 240-262.

Bryden, Matt. 2013. *Somalia Redux? Assessing the New Somali Federal Government.* Lanham: Rowman and Littlefield.

Bryld, Erik and Addow, Abdirahman Moallim. 2011. *Political Economy Analysis in South Galkayo and Abudwaq Final Report June 2011.* Copenhagen: Tana.

Bryld, Erik and Kamau, Christine. 2012. *Political Economy Analysis in Mogadishu. Final draft report May 2012.* Copenhagen: Tana.

Burt, Ronald S. 1992. *Structural Holes: The Social Structure of Competition.* Cambridge, London: Harvard University Press.

Burt, Ronald S. 2005. *Brokerage and Closure: An Introduction to Social Capital.* Oxford: Oxford University Press.

Burt, Ronald S. 2010. *Neighbor Networks: Competitive Advantage Local and Personal.* Oxford: Oxford University Press.

Burt, Ronald S. et al (eds). 2001. *Social Capital: Theory and Research.* New Brunswick: Transaction Publishers.

Carr-Hill, Roy and Ondijo, David. 2011. *Assessment of the Education, Livelihoods, Living Conditions and Welfare of Somali Pastoralists – A Representative, Multi-Sectoral Survey Conducted to Provide a Baseline for Programming.* Nairobi: Horn Relief.

Cassanelli, Lee V. 1982. *The Shaping of Somali Society: Reconstructing the History of a Pastoral People, 1600-1900.* Philadelphia: University of Pennsylvania Press.

Chapman, Terrence L. 2008. "Unraveling the Ties Between Civic Institutions and Attitudes Toward Political Violence," *International Studies Quarterly* 52, pp. 515-532.

Chapman, Terrence L. 2009. "The Pacific Promise of Civic Institutions? Causal Ambiguity in the Study of Social Capital," In Cox, Michaelene (ed). *Social Capital and Peace-Building, Creating and Resolving Conflict with Trust and Social Networks.* Oxon, New York: Routledge, pp. 157-171.

Cohen, Nissim and Arieli, Tamar. 2011. "Field Research in Conflict Environments: Methodological Challenges and Snowball Sampling," *Journal of Peace Research* 48(4), pp. 423-435.

Colletta, Nat J. and Cullen, Michelle L. 2000a. *Violent Conflict and the Transformation of Social Capital: Lessons from Cambodia, Rwanda, Guatemala, and Somalia.* Washington, D.C.: The World Bank.

Colletta, Nat J. and Cullen, Michelle L. 2000b. *The Nexus Between Violent Conflict, Social Capital and Social Cohesion: Case Studies from Cambodia and Rwanda.* Social Capital Initiative Working Paper No. 23. Washington, D.C.: The World Bank.

Collier, Paul and Hoeffler, Anke. 2000. *Greed and Grievance in Civil War.* Policy Research Working Paper 2355, May 2000. Washington, D.C.: The World Bank Development Research Group.

Collier, Paul et al. 2003. *Breaking the Conflict Trap: Civil War and Development Policy.* Washington, D.C.: The World Bank, Oxford University Press.

Communiqué. 2012. *Consultative Meeting of the Somali Signatories of the Process for Ending the Transition – Communiqué.* 26 March 2012, Galkayo.

Cox, Michaelene (ed). 2009. *Social Capital and Peace-Building, Creating and Resolving Conflict with Trust and Social Networks.* Oxon, New York: Routledge.

CRD. 2004. *Somalia: Path to Recovery: Building a Sustainable Peace.* Mogadishu, Nairobi: Centre for Research and Dialogue, War-torn Societies Project.

DDG. 2009. *Community Safety and Small Arms in Somaliland.* Copenhagen, Geneva: Danish Demining Group, Small Arms Survey.

DIAL. 2011. *Training of other Civil Society Actors and Government Actors/Institutions on Conflict Resolution and Peace Building in Gaalkacyo District.* Nairobi: Development Initiative Access Link (DIAL).

Dracopoli, Ignatius Nicolas. 1914. *Through Jubaland to the Lorian Swamp: An Adventurous Journey of Exploration and Sport in the Unknown African Forests and Deserts of Jubaland to the Unexplored Lorian Swamp.* London: Seeley and Service Company.

DRC. 2004. *Advocacy.* Somaliland: Danish Refugee Council.

DSS. 2013a. *Daily Situation Report, DSS Somalia, 1500 hours 16 August 2013 to 1500 hours 19 August 2013.* Nairobi: Department of Safety and Security Somalia.

DSS. 2013b. *Daily Situation Report, DSS Somalia, 1500 hours 20 August 2013 to 1500 hours 21 August 2013.* Nairobi: Department of Safety and Security Somalia.

Durlauf, Steven N. and Fafchamps, Marcel. 2004. *Social Capital.* JEL Classification Codes: E26, O10, O40, L14, Z13. July 13, 2004. Working paper.

EIU. 2012. *Country Report: Somalia August 2012.* London: Economist Intelligence Unit.

Elmi, Afyare. 2010. *Understanding the Somalia Conflagration: Identity, Political Islam and Peacebuilding.* London, New York: Pluto Press.

Farah, Ibrahim et al. 2002. "Deegan, Politics and War in Somalia," In Lind, Jeremy and Sturman, Kathryn (eds). *Scarcity and Surfeit: The Ecology of Africa's Conflicts.* Pretoria: Institute for Security Studies, pp. 321-356.

Field, Andy. 2005. *Discovering Statistics Using SPSS.* 2nd ed. London, Thousand Oaks, New Delhi: Sage.

Fine, Ben. 2010. *Theories of Social Capital: Researchers Behaving Badly.* London, New York: Pluto Press.

Forster, Reiner and Mattner, Mark. 2006. *Civil Society and Peacebuilding: Potential, Limitations and Critical Factors.* Report No. 36445-GLB. Washington, D.C.: The World Bank.

Gambetta, Diego (ed). 1988. *Trust: Making and Breaking Cooperative Relations.* Oxford, Cambridge: Basil Blackwell.

Gellner, Ernest. 1988. "Trust, Cohesion, and the Social Order," In Gambetta, Diego (ed). *Trust: Making and Breaking Cooperative Relations.* Oxford, Cambridge: Basil Blackwell, pp. 142-157.

Gilbert, Leah. 2009. "Analyzing the Dark Side of Social Capital: Organized Crime in Russia," In Cox, Michaelene (ed). *Social Capital and Peace-Building, Creating and Resolving Conflict with Trust and Social Networks.* Oxon, New York: Routledge, pp. 57-74.

Grootaert, Christiaan and Bastelaer, Thierry van (eds). 2002. *The Role of Social Capital in Development: An Empirical Assessment.* Cambridge: Cambridge University Press.

Grosse-Kettler, Sabrina. 2004. *External Actors in Stateless Somalia: A War Economy and its Promoters.* Paper 39. Bonn: Bonn International Center for Conversion.

Gundel, Joakim. 2006. *The Predicament of the 'Oday': The Role of Traditional Structures in Security, Rights, Law and Development in Somalia.* Nairobi: Danish Refugee Council, Novib-Oxfam.

Halpern, David. 2005. *Social Capital.* Cambridge, Malden. Polity Press.

Hansen, Stig Jarle. 2007. *Civil War Economies, the Hunt for Profit and the Incentives for Peace.* AE Working Paper Number 1. London, Oslo, Bath: DFID, NIBR, University of Bath.

Hansen, Stig Jarle. 2013. *Al-Shabaab in Somalia: The History and Ideology of a Militant Islamist Group, 2005-2012.* London: C. Hurst and Company.

Harper, Mary. 2012. *Getting Somalia Wrong? Faith, War and Hope in a Shattered State.* London, New York: Zed Books.

Hoehne, Markus V. 2009. "Mimesis and Mimicry in Dynamics of State and Identity Formation in Northern Somalia," *Africa* 79(2), pp. 252 – 281.

Hoehne, Markus V. 2011a. *No Easy Way Out: Traditional Authorities in Somaliland and the Limits of Hybrid Political Orders.* Working Paper 2011:18. Copenhagen: DIIS.

Hoehne, Markus V. 2011b. "Not Born as a de facto State: Somaliland's Complicated State Formation," In Sharamo, Roba and Mesfin, Berouk (eds). *Regional Security in the Post-Cold War Horn of Africa.*

Pretoria, Dakar, Addis Ababa, Nairobi: Institute for Security Studies, pp. 309-346.

Hoehne, Markus V. and Luling, Virginia (eds). 2010. *Milk and Peace, Drought and War: Somali Culture, Society and Politics*. London: C. Hurst and Company.

Hooghe, Marc and Stolle, Dietlind (eds). 2003. *Generating Social Capital: Civil Society and Institutions in Comparative Perspective*. New York, Hampshire: Palgrave Macmillan.

Interpeace. 2008a. *Peace in Somaliland: An Indigenous Approach to State-Building*. Nairobi: Interpeace.

Interpeace. 2008b. *Peace Initiatives in Puntland 1991-2007*. Nairobi: Interpeace.

Interpeace. 2008c. *Community-based Peace Processes in South-Central Somalia*. Nairobi: Interpeace.

Interpeace. 2009. *A History of Mediation in Somalia since 1988*. Nairobi: Interpeace.

Joint Agreement. 2011. *Somalia: An Agreement Jointly Signed by Puntland and Galmudug*. 17 February 2011. Garowe.

Kalyvas, Stathis N. 2006. *The Logic of Violence in Civil War*. New York: Cambridge University Press.

Kapteijns, Lidwien. 2011. "I.M. Lewis and Somali Clanship: A Critique," *Northeast African Studies* 11(1), pp. 1-24.

Kasaija, Apuuli Phillip. 2010. "The UN-led Djibouti Peace Process for Somalia 2008-2009: Results and Problems," *Journal of Contemporary African Studies* 28(3), pp. 261-282.

Ladan, Affi. 2002. *Somalia: Beyond Tyranny*. Master's Thesis Dissertation, Northeastern Illinois University.

Larsen, Larissa et al. 2004. "Bonding and Bridging: Understanding the Relationship between Social Capital and Civic Action," *Journal of Planning Education and Research* 24, pp. 64-77.

Latin, David D. 1977. *Politics, Language, and Thought: The Somali Experience*. Chicago, London: University of Chicago Press.

Latin, David D. and Samatar, Said S. 1987. *Somalia: Nation in Search of a State*. Boulder: Westview Press.

Le Sage, Andre. 2005. *Stateless Justice in Somalia: Formal and Informal Rule of Law Initiatives*. Geneva: Centre for Humanitarian Dialogue.

Lederman, Daniel et al. 2002. "Violent Crime: Does Social Capital Matter?" *Economic Development and Cultural Change* 50(3), pp. 509-539.

Leonard, David K. and Samantar, Mohamed S. 2011. "What Does the Somali Experience Teach Us about the Social Contract and the State?" *Development and Change* 42(2), pp. 559-584.

Leonard, David K. and Samantar, Mohamed S. 2013. "Reconstructing Political Order Among the Somalis: The Historical Record in the South and Centre," *IDS Bulletin* 44(1), pp. 44-52.

Levy. Andrea L. 2010. *Looking Toward the Future: Citizen Attitudes about Peace, Governance and the Future of Somalia*. Washington, D.C.: National Democratic Institute for International Affairs.

Levy. Andrea L. 2011. *Searching for Peace: Views and Comments from Somalia on the Foundations of a New Government*. Washington, D.C.: National Democratic Institute for International Affairs.

Lewis, Ioan Myrddin. 1998. *Saints and Somalis: Popular Islam in a Clan-Based Society*. Lawrenceville, Asmara: The Red Sea Press.

Lewis, Ioan Myrddin. 1999. *A Pastoral Democracy: A Study of Pastoralism and Politics Among the Northern Somali of the Horn of Africa*. Hamburg, Oxford: LIT, James Currey Publishers.

Lewis, Ioan Myrddin. 2002. *A Modern History of the Somali: Nation and State in the Horn of Africa*. 4th ed. Woodbridge: James Currey.

Lewis, Ioan Myrddin. 2010. *Making and Breaking States in Africa: The Somali Experience*. Trenton, Asmara: The Red Sea Press.

Lin, Nan. 2002. *Social Capital: A Theory of Social Structure and Action*. Cambridge, New York, Melbourne, Madrid, Cape Town: Cambridge University Press.

Lin, Nan et al. 2001. "The Position Generator: Measurement Techniques for Investigations of Social Capital," In Burt, Ronald S. et al (eds). *Social Capital: Theory and Research*. New Brunswick: Transaction Publishers, pp. 57-81.

Little, Peter D. 2003. *Somalia: Economy Without State*. Bloomington: Indiana University Press.

Luling, Virginia. 2002. *Somali Sultanate: The Geledi City-State over 150 years*. London: HAAN.

Luling, Virginia. 2006. "Genealogy as Theory, Genealogy as Tool: Aspects of Somali 'Clanship'," *Social Identities* 12(4), pp. 471-485.

Mahadallah, Hassan Omar. 1998a. *The Origins and Essence of Somali Nationalism*. Ph.D. Thesis, Tulane University. UMI Number 9816775.

Mahadallah, Hassan Omar. 1998b. "The Somali Conflict: Clan Rivalry or the Cabals of a Few?" *Horn of Africa* XVI(1,2,3,4), pp. 163-170.

Marchal, Roland. 2002. *A Survey of Mogadishu's Economy.* Nairobi: European Commission.

Marchal, Roland. 2011. *The Somali Economy as Reflected in Mogadishu in the 2000's.* Paris: CNRS, CERI/Sciences-Po Paris.

Matsukawa, Kiyoshi. 2006. *State of Nature: A Comparison between Theory and Reality for the Case of Somalia.* Master's Thesis Dissertation, Aoyama Gakuin University.

Maystadt, Jean-Francois et al. 2013. *Extreme Weather and Civil War in Somalia: Does Drought Fuel Conflict through Livestock Price Shocks.* Discussion Paper February 2013. Washington, D.C., New Delhi, Addis Ababa, Accra: International Food Policy Research Institute.

Menkhaus, Ken. 1999. "Traditional Conflict Management in Contemporary Somalia," In Zartman, William I. (ed). *Traditional Cures for Modern Conflicts: African Conflict "Medicine".* Boulder, London: Lynne Rienner Publishers, pp. 183-199.

Menkhaus, Ken. 2004. *Somalia: State Collapse and the Threat of Terrorism.* Abingdon, New York: Routledge.

Menkhaus, Ken. 2007. "Local Security Systems in Somali East Africa," In Andersen, Louise et al (eds). *Fragile States and Insecure People?: Violence, Security, and Statehood in the Twenty-First Century.* New York, Hampshire: Palgrave Macmillan, pp. 67-97.

Menkhaus, Ken. 2010. "The Question of Ethnicity in Somali Studies: The Case of Somali Bantu Identity," In Hoehne, Markus and Luling, Virginia (eds). *Milk and Peace, Drought and War: Somali Culture, Society and Politics.* London: C. Hurst and Company, pp. 87-104.

Menkhaus, Ken. 2011. *Conflict Analysis: Somalia.* http://www.scribd.com/doc/78162215/MENKHAUS-Somalia-Conflict-Analysis-UNPOS-Updated-and-Final-December-2011

Menkhaus, Ken et al. 2010. "Somalia: Civil Society in a Collapsed State," In Paffenholz, Thania (ed). *Civil Society and Peacebuilding: A Critical Assessment.* Colorado, London: Lynne Rienner, pp. 321-349.

Ministry of Justice. 2013. *Revival of the Somali Traditional and Religious Justice System. Official Document of the Government of Somalia (Annex B) May 2013.* Mogadishu: Ministry of Justice, Religious Affairs, Constitution, Federal and Reconciliation.

Mohamed, Jama. 2007. "Kinship and Contract in Somali Politics," *Africa* 77(2), pp. 226-249.

Mubarak, Jamil Abdalla. 1996. *From Bad Policy to Chaos in Somalia: How an Economy Fell Apart.* Westport: Praeger Publishers.

Mubarak, Jamil Abdalla. 1997. "The 'Hidden Hand' Behind the Resilience of the Stateless Economy of Somalia," *World Development* 25(12), pp. 2027-2041.

Nan, Susan Allen. 2009. "Social Capital in Exclusive and Inclusive Networks: Satisfying Human Needs through Conflict and Conflict Resolution," In Cox, Michaelene (ed). *Social Capital and Peace-Building, Creating and Resolving Conflict with Trust and Social Networks.* Oxon, New York: Routledge, pp. 172-185.

Norton, Gregory. 2008. *Land, Property, and Housing in Somalia.* Oslo, Nairobi, Geneva: UNHABITAT, Norwegian Refugee Council, UNHCR.

OCVP. 2013. *District Conflict and Security Assessment Report – Galkayo District July 2013.* Hargeisa: Observatory of Conflict and Violence Prevention.

Osman, Abdulahi A. and Souaré, Issaka K. (eds). 2007. *Somalia at the Crossroads: Challenges and Perspectives in Reconstituting a Failed State.* London: Adonis and Abbey.

Paffenholz, Thania and Spurk, Christoph. 2006. *Civil Society, Civic Engagement, and Peacebuilding.* Social Development Papers, Conflict Prevention and Reconstruction, Paper No. 36, October 2006. Washington, D.C.: The World Bank.

Paffenholz, Thania. 2006. *Community-based Bottom-up Peacebuilding, The Development of the Life and Peace Institute's Approach to Peacebuilding and Lessons Learned from the Somalia Experience (1990-2000).* 2nd ed. Uppsala: Life and Peace Institute.

Paffenholz, Thania. 2009. "Exploring Opportunities and Obstacles for a Constructive Role of Social Capital in Peacebuilding: A Framework for Analysis," In Cox, Michaelene (ed). *Social Capital and Peace-Building, Creating and Resolving Conflict with Trust and Social Networks.* Oxon, New York: Routledge, pp. 186-201.

Paffenholz, Thania. 2010. "Conclusion," In Paffenholz, Thania (ed). *Civil Society and Peacebuilding: A Critical Assessment*. Colorado, London: Lynne Rienner, pp. 425-430.

Paffenholz, Thania et al. 2010. "Enabling and Disenabling Factors for Civil Society Peacebuilding," In Paffenholz, Thania (ed). *Civil Society and Peacebuilding: A Critical Assessment*. Colorado, London: Lynne Rienner, pp. 405-424.

Paul, Jacqueline. 2012. *Violence in the Lives of Girls and Women in the Somali Republic*. Nairobi: United Nations Development Programme, United Nations Political Office for Somalia, UN Women.

Peterson, Scott. 2001. *Me Against My Brother: At War in Somalia, Sudan, and Rwanda*. New York, London: Routledge.

Posner, Daniel N. 2004. "Civil Society and the Reconstruction of Failed States," In Rotberg, Robert I. (ed). *When States Fail: Causes and Consequences*. Princeton, Oxfordshire: Princeton University Press, pp. 237-255.

Posner, Daniel N. 2005. *Institutions and Ethnic Politics in Africa*. Cambridge, New York, Melbourne, Madrid, Cape Town, Singapore, Sao Paulo: Cambridge University Press.

Puntland Ministry of Security. 2013. *Press Release*, 22 April 2013. Garowe: Ministry of Security and DDR Puntland State of Somalia.

Putnam, Robert D. 1994. *Making Democracy Work: Civic Traditions in Modern Italy*. Princeton: Princeton University Press.

Putnam, Robert D. 2000. *Bowling Alone: The Collapse and Revival of American Community*. New York: Simon and Schuster.

Putnam, Robert D. (ed). 2002. *Democracies in Flux: The Evolution of Social Capital in Contemporary Society*. Oxford, New York: Oxford University Press.

Quero, Yann-Cédric et al. 2011a. *Safety and Security District Baseline Report: Burao*. Hargeisa: Observatory of Conflict and Violence Prevention.

Quero, Yann-Cédric et al. 2011b. *Safety and Security District Baseline Report: Galkayo*. Hargeisa: Observatory of Conflict and Violence Prevention.

Ramadhan, Shamsia and Rynn, Simon. 2010. *Conflict Analysis of Burco District, Version 2, 06/09/2010*. Nairobi: Saferworld.

Renders, Marleen. 2007. "Appropriate 'governance-technology'? – Somali Clan Elders and Institutions in the Making of the 'Republic of Somaliland'," *Afrika Spectrum* 42(3), pp. 439-459.

Renders, Marleen. 2012. *Consider Somaliland: State-Building with Traditional Leaders and Institutions.* Leiden, Boston: Brill.

Rosenfeld, Richard et al. 2001. "Social Capital and Homicide," *Social Forces* 80(1), pp. 283-310.

Sacks, Harvey. 1992. *Lectures on Conversation.* Malden, Oxford, Victoria: Blackwell.

Saferworld. 2010. *Focus Group Discussion – Galkayo, Version 20/04/2010.* Nairobi: Saferworld.

Saferworld. 2011. *Community Security: An Approach to Grassroots Peacebuilding – Community Safety and Security Analysis Galkayo District, Somali Community Safety Framework, January 2011 – Version 4.* Nairobi: Saferworld.

Saferworld. 2012. *Mogadishu Rising? Conflict and Governance Dynamics in the Somali capital.* Nairobi: Saferworld.

Samatar, Abdi Ismail. 1997. "Leadership and Ethnicity in the making of African State Models: Botswana versus Somalia," *Third World Quarterly* 18(4), pp. 687-707.

Sen, Amartya. 1999. *Reason before Identity.* 1st ed. Oxford, New York: Oxford University Press.

Silverman, David. 1998. *Harvey Sacks: Social Science and Conversation Analysis.* Oxford, New York: Oxford University Press.

SOYDEN. 2010a. *Report on Focus Group Discussion on Conflict and Violence in Four Districts of Banadir Region: Wadajir, Dharkeynley, Waberi and Hodon.* Mogadishu: Somali Youth Development Network (SOYDEN).

SOYDEN. 2010b. *Community Security: An Approach to Grassroots Peacebuilding – Community Safety and Security Analysis for Mogadishu, Somali Community Safety Framework – November 2010 – Version 1.* Mogadishu: Somali Youth Development Network (SOYDEN).

Spurk, Christoph. 2010. "Understanding Civil Society," In Paffenholz, Thania (ed). *Civil Society and Peacebuilding: A Critical Assessment.* Colorado, London: Lynne Rienner, pp. 3-28.

Stewart, Frances. 2008. "Horizontal Inequalities and Conflict: An Introduction and some Hypotheses," In Stewart, Francis (ed). *Horizontal Inequalities and Conflict – Understanding Group Violence in*

Multiethnic Societies. Hampshire, New York: Palgrave Macmillan, pp. 3-24.

UNDP. 1998. *Human Development Report Somalia 1998*. Nairobi: United Nations Development Programme.

UNDP. 2001. *Human Development Report Somalia 2001*. Nairobi: United Nations Development Programme.

UNDP. 2010. *A Community Safety and Security Approach to Grass Roots Peacebuilding: Monitoring and Assessment Toolkit, Version 16 – September 15*. Nairobi: United Nations Development Programme.

UNDP. 2012. Somalia *Human Development Report 2012: Empowering Youth for Peace and Development*. Nairobi: United Nations Development Programme.

UNFPA. 2012. *The United Nations Population Estimation Survey, Draft Project Document*. Nairobi: United Nations Population Fund.

UNHCR. 2011. *Mogadishu IDP Settlement Assessment October 2011*. Nairobi: United Nations High Commissioner for Refugees.

UNHCR. 2013a. *Somali Refugees in the Region as of 10 September 2013*. Nairobi: United Nations High Commissioner for Refugees.

UNHCR. 2013b. *Total IDPs by Region – September 2013*. Nairobi: United Nations High Commissioner for Refugees.

UNICEF. 2006. *Somalia: Monitoring the Situation of Children and Women 2006 – Multiple Indicator Cluster Survey*. Nairobi: United Nations Children's Fund.

UNPOS. 2012. *Mapping of Key Stakeholders in the Benadir Region*. Nairobi: United Nations Political Office for Somalia.

Varshney, Ashutosh. 2001. "Ethnic Conflict and Civil Society: India and Beyond," *World Politics* 53(3), pp. 362-398.

Varshney, Ashutosh. 2002. *Ethnic Conflict and Civic Life: Hindus and Muslims in India*. 2nd ed. New Haven, London: Yale University.

Warren, Mark R. et al. 2001. "The Role of Social Capital in Combating Poverty," In Saegert, Susan et al (eds). *Social Capital and Poor Communities*. New York: Russell Sage Foundation, pp. 1-28.

Webersik, Christian. 2004. "Differences that Matter: The Struggle of the Marginalized in Somalia," *Africa* 74(4), pp. 516-533.

Webersik, Christian. 2005. "Fighting for the Plenty: The Banana Trade in Southern Somalia," *Oxford Development Studies* 33(1), pp. 81-97.

Webersik, Christian. 2006. "Mogadishu: An Economy without a State," *Third World Quarterly*, 27(8), pp. 1463-1480.

Webersik, Christian. 2008. "Wars Over Resources? Evidence from Somalia," *Environment* 50(3), pp. 46-58.

Widner, Jennifer. 2004. "Building Effective Trust in the Aftermath of Severe Conflict," In Rotberg, Robert I. (ed). *When States Fail: Causes and Consequences.* Princeton, Oxfordshire: Princeton University Press, pp. 222-236.

Widner, Jennifer and Mundt, Alexander. 1998. "Researching Social Capital in Africa," *Africa* 68(1), pp. 1-24.

Woolcock, Michael and Narayan, Deepa. 2000. "Social Capital: Implications for Development Theory, Research, and Policy," *World Bank Research Observer* 15(2), pp. 225-249.

Woolcock, Michael et al. 2004. *Measuring Social Capital: An Integrated Questionnaire.* Washington, D.C.: The World Bank.

World Bank, The. 2011. *World Development Report 2011: Conflict, Security, and Development.* Washington, D.C.: The World Bank.

Interviews

This list includes interviews that are cited in the research inquiry and also includes interviews that are not cited in the thesis. The non-cited interviews attempt to provide a backdrop of the key informants and interlocutors interviewed. The references listed are not an exhaustive list of all the interviews and discussions I conducted over the years. Interviews not listed here were used mainly to provide a cross-reference check for the key interviews and discussions. Interviewees that are referred as anonymous have been quoted at the request of the interviewee or for security reasons. Details of transcriptions are available upon request on a case-by-case basis.[1]

Academics based in Mogadishu. 2011. 5 August, Mogadishu, Somalia.

Akhtar, Saeed. 2011. 11 December, Dubai, UAE.

Ali, Iman Mohamed. 2011. Chamber of commerce representative. 3 August, Mogadishu, Somalia.

Ali, Mohamed Osman. 2011. Ex-mayor of Mogadishu. 22 May, Mogadishu, Somalia.

AMISOM Force Commander. 2011. 20 May, Mogadishu, Somalia.

Benadir Regional Administration representatives. 2011. 9 July, Mogadishu, Somalia.

Bryden, Matt. 2011. 27 October, Nairobi, Kenya.

Businessman. 2013. Businessman based in north Galkayo. 8 April, north Galkayo, Somalia.

Chamber of commerce "president". 2011. 20 May, Mogadishu, Somalia.

Chamber of commerce representatives. 2012. 22 November, Mogadishu, Somalia.

CSOs. 2011. A group of ten civil society organizations. 5 July, Mogadishu, Somalia.

CSOs representatives in Baidoa. 2012. 21 November, Baidoa, Somalia.

District Commissioners of Beletweyne. 2013. 23 March, Beletweyne, Somalia.

District Commissioners of Jowhar. 2013. 20 March, Jowhar, Somalia.

District Commissioners of the Benadir Regional Administration. 2012. 24 November, Mogadishu, Somalia.

Djibouti based Somali business community. 2011. 20 October, 22 November, Djibouti.

"Egal". 2011. Businessman from Puntland. 23 May, Mogadishu, Somalia.

FAO consultant. 2013. 5 April, Bosaso, Somalia.

Focus group discussion in Burao. 2013. 2 April, Burao, Somalia.

Focus group discussion in north Galkayo. 2013. 9 April, north Galkayo, Somalia.

Focus group discussion in south Galkayo. 2013. 8 April, south Galkayo, Somalia.

Focus group discussions in Mogadishu. 2013. 29, 30 January and 2, 5 February, Mogadishu, Somalia.

Haber Gedir business community representatives. 2012. 2 February, Mogadishu, Somalia.

Haji, Abdirizak Mohamed. 2013. 7 April, north Galkayo, Somalia.

Hansen, Stig. 2012. Researcher. 6 July, Nairobi, Kenya.

Health worker. 2013. 8 April, north Galkayo, Somalia.

Human rights activist. 2012. 4 February, Mogadishu, Somalia.

Jama, Abdigani. 2011. Somali telecoms expert. 9 November, Nairobi, Kenya.

Jamalle, Hussein. 2011. CRD. 20 May, Mogadishu, Somalia.

Jilao, Muhiadin Ali. 2012. Mogadishu Ports Authority. 28 January, Mogadishu, Somalia.

Kimiko, Ahmed Mahamed Ali. 2004. Chairman of Sohriden. 17 September, Mogadishu, Somalia.

Mahdi, Abdile Abdi. 2012. 25 June, Nairobi, Kenya.

Marchal, Roland. 2012. Researcher. 26 June, Nairobi, Kenya.

McAuslan, Patrick. 2012. UNDP Somalia consultant. 16 August, email correspondence.

Ministry of Finance representatives. 2012. 3 February, Mogadishu, Somalia.

Ministry of Fisheries representatives. 2011. 19 May, Mogadishu, Somalia.

Ministry of Information and Telecommunications representative. 2011. 19 May, Mogadishu, Somalia.

Ministry of Public Works and Reconstruction representatives. 2011. 7 July, 3 September, Mogadishu, Somalia.

Ministry of Transportation representatives. 2011. 4 August, 7 September, 1 September, Mogadishu, Somalia.

Mogadishu focus group respondent number "thirteen". 2011. Anonymous participant in the focus group discussion. 30 January, Mogadishu, Somalia.

Mohamed, Ahmed Jama. 2011. Restaurant owner of "the Village". 22 May, Mogadishu, Somalia.

Mohamed, Haji. 2013. Galmudug administration representative. 26 January, Nairobi, Kenya.

NGO. 2013. Non-governmental organization based in north Galkayo. 9 April, north Galkayo, Somalia.

President of Somali Appeals Court. 2011. 17 May, Mogadishu, Somalia.

PSU. 2013. Focus group discussion with Puntland State University officials. 8 April, north Galkayo, Somalia.

Randall, Tim. 2012. United Nations employee. 24 November, Mogadishu, Somalia.

Randall, Tim. 2013a. United Nations employee. 28 August, email correspondence.

Randall, Tim. 2013b. United Nations employee. 16 September, email correspondence.

Renders, Marleen. 2013. Researcher. 28 January, Nairobi, Mogadishu.

Saferworld. 2013. 26 February, Nairobi, Kenya.

SAHDO. 2012. 3 February, Mogadishu, Somalia.

SCODA. 2011. 12 July, Mogadishu, Somalia.

Sheikh, Abdinasir Mohamud. 2013. DIAL Executive Director. 20 August, email correspondence.

SKA representatives. 2011. 3, 4 August, Mogadishu, Somalia.

Somali Ports Authority representatives. 2011. 10 July, 29 November, Mogadishu, Somalia.

SOYDAVO. 2013. Civil society organization based in Burao. 2 April, Burao, Somalia.

SOYDEN. 2011. 12 July, Mogadishu, Somalia.

SWDC. 2011. 9 July, Mogadishu, Somalia.

United Nations employee. 2011. 8 September, Mogadishu, Somalia.

United Nations staff member. 2013. 16 August, email correspondence.

Warsame, Jamal Mohamed. 2013. Member of District Safety Committee. 3 April, Burao. Somalia.

Yusuf, Muhyadin Ali. 2011. 4 August, Mogadishu, Somalia.

Personal Communication

AMISOM troop commander. 2011. 24 May, Mogadishu, Somalia.

Bancroft mentors. 2011. 23 May, Mogadishu, Somalia.

Nakamaura, Yusuke. 2013. Associate Professor at the University of Tokyo. 10 July, Tokyo, Japan.

Nakanishi, Toru. 2013. Professor at the University of Tokyo. 24 July, Tokyo, Japan.

Schumicky, Lilla. 2013. UNDP Somalia. 10 April, Garowe, Somalia.

Shimizu, Takashi. 2013. Professor at the University of Tokyo. 27 July, Tokyo, Japan.

Thesis Committee. 2013. Endo, Mitsugi; Nakanishi, Toru; Nakamura, Yusuke; Ishida Atsushi. 13 December, Tokyo, Japan.

Notes

1   This caveat is based on Renders (2012:279).

INDEX